COMING
TO MY
SENSES

COMING
TO MY
SENSES

A Story of Perfume, Pleasure,

and an Unlikely Bride

ALYSSA HARAD

VIKING

VIKING
Published by the Penguin Group
Penguin Group (USA) Inc., 375 Hudson Street,
New York, New York 10014, U.S.A.
Penguin Group (Canada), 90 Eglinton Avenue East, Suite 700, Toronto,
Ontario, Canada M4P 2Y3 (a division of Pearson Penguin Canada Inc.)
Penguin Books Ltd, 80 Strand, London WC2R 0RL, England
Penguin Ireland, 25 St. Stephen's Green, Dublin 2, Ireland
(a division of Penguin Books Ltd)
Penguin Books Australia Ltd, 250 Camberwell Road, Camberwell,
Victoria 3124, Australia (a division of Pearson Australia Group Pty Ltd)
Penguin Books India Pvt Ltd, 11 Community Centre,
Panchsheel Park, New Delhi–110 017, India
Penguin Group (NZ), 67 Apollo Drive, Rosedale, Auckland 0632,
New Zealand (a division of Pearson New Zealand Ltd)
Penguin Books (South Africa) (Pty) Ltd, 24 Sturdee Avenue,
Rosebank, Johannesburg 2196, South Africa

Penguin Books Ltd, Registered Offices: 80 Strand, London WC2R 0RL, England

First published in 2012 by Viking Penguin, a member of Penguin Group (USA) Inc.

1 3 5 7 9 10 8 6 4 2

LIBRARY OF CONGRESS CATALOGING-IN-PUBLICATION DATA
Harad, Alyssa.
Coming to my senses : a story of perfume, pleasure, and an unlikely bride / Alyssa Harad.
p. cm.
ISBN 978-0-670-02361-5 (hardback)
1. Feminists—United States—Biography. 2. Perfumes industry—United States. 3. Perfume—
United States. 4. Femininity—United States. 5. Feminism—United States. I. Title.
HQ1413.H37A3 2012
305.42092—dc23
[B]   2011046010

Printed in the United States of America
Set in Garamond Premier Pro   Designed by Francesca Belanger

*Penguin is committed to publishing works of quality and integrity.
In that spirit, we are proud to offer this book to our readers;
however, the story, the experiences, and the words
are the author's alone.*

To my mother, who was the beginning of it all.
And to my father, for loving both of us.

CONTENTS

AUTHOR'S NOTE

In most cases, I have changed the names and identifying details of the people I describe to protect their privacy. Occasionally, I have compressed or combined events.

I have provided the names of the perfumes featured when I felt it was crucial to the telling of this story. However, in some cases I preferred to leave the names out and keep the emphasis on the description of their scents and the emotions they evoked at the moment. Doing so allowed me to avoid recommending perfumes that may be discontinued or reformulated by the time this book is published. I invite all curious readers to visit www.alyssaharad.com where I can give you the latest, updated scoop.

PART I

LEARNING
HOW TO SMELL

1: THE BEAUTIFUL SURPRISE

Perfume tells a story on the skin. It has a beginning, a middle, and—if it's good—a long, lingering end. To try a new perfume is to give yourself over to this story for at least an hour or two, sometimes much longer. It's a risky endeavor. Not because there is so much bad perfume crowding the counters today. (You can always wash it off.) And not because others will accuse you of stinking up the joint. (You can always wear less, and what do they know, anyway?)

The story a new perfume tells is dangerous—and exciting—because it is unabashedly intimate. It depends on the heat of your body to give it life, and on your memories and fantasies to give it depth. To smell it, you must breathe it in, and when you move close to others, they breathe it in, too, along with your warmth and your presence. Like all scents, perfume seeps into your memories whether you want it to or not, preserving and enriching them. But it can do something far stranger: It can turn your moods and desires into a living presence, surprising you with something, or someone, you didn't know you knew. When we approach the perfume counter we are always a little bit vulnerable. We think we're looking for a pleasant smell, or something sexy, maybe a bit of art or romance to grace a special day, but our dreams get into the mix. They tug us down toward the questions lurking underneath all such small decisions: Who am I? What do I want?

My affair with perfume began as a slow, secret flirtation, carried on late at night by the glow of my computer screen. Lurking in the electronic shadows, I left no comments, and I told no one in my waking life that what had begun as an occasional dalliance was growing into a daily ritual. I was a serious, Birkenstock-wearing feminist in my mid-thirties, and my sudden passion for reading about perfume left me baffled and not a little embarrassed.

But then, I was embarrassed about a lot of things in those days. My life had come to a kind of pause. When I ran into old friends or was introduced to strangers, I no longer knew how to explain myself. I'd moved to Austin to get my doctorate, but there wasn't much demand for English PhDs when I began my studies, and there was even less eight years later, when I emerged, degree in hand. The most sensible of my fellow students dropped out after a few years. Those of us more adept at denial or faith kept going, hoping we'd be the exception.

I told myself I was keeping my options open, and I always had a side project or two going. But I stayed too long. I grew deeply attached to my work and to teaching, and poured my heart into both. This turned out to be a mistake—a serious, passionate, complicated mistake, like marrying the wrong person or moving to the wrong country. It took me several years to fully extricate myself. And during that time I wandered around like an exiled divorcée—stunned, brokenhearted, a stranger to the world and to myself.

Only the man who had loved me and lived with me all through graduate school and its aftermath saw me that way, though. (If he had a choice, I wouldn't be talking about him at all, so let's call him V.) Outside our home, I was always busy—very, very busy—first, trying to create a job for myself, and then working for a small nonprofit. But the spring I turned thirty-six, something in me rebelled against all that busyness, and I quit my job. I had an idea—really, no more than a secretive wish encouraged by V.,—that I wanted to write, but I had no idea how or what. For the first time in my much-scheduled life, I had no project and no plans.

I stitched together some freelance work—book reviews, copy for Web sites, standardized-test questions, and whatever else I could scare up and settled into the typical freelancer's schedule of concentrated bursts of activity followed by long stretches of open space and time. By August my life had grown very slow. It was summer—high Texas summer, with cicadas and thunderstorms and day after day after day of syrupy, bone-melting heat that makes it impossible to take anything very seriously.

It was then, late at night, in the middle of a deadline for another not very interesting freelance job, that I went clicking across the Internet and stumbled across my first perfume blog. I didn't think of myself as someone who liked perfume. But startled by the vivid prose I found there, impressed that it was written simply for the joy of it, I found myself sneaking over to read a few more reviews every few days or so. Soon enough, I was following links to other writers and reading the comments on their posts, and a lovely dreamworld populated by gentle, scent-mad sophisticates unfurled before me.

My reading had no practical value. I wasn't looking for a signature scent or trying to replace an old favorite. I was hooked on the stories. Even the most matter-of-fact perfume reviews had a hint of suspense and romance. Would there be dramatic plot reversals? (Sometimes.) Grand resolutions? (Rarely.) Or would the whole thing simply crash and burn? (Far too often.) And, most important: Would the reviewer fall in love? Could I?

I carried on that way for months—confused, shy, smelling the scents only in my mind. Then, one evening, I read a favorite blogger's tribute to the fierce chic of designer Paloma Picasso's Mon Parfum. She described not only the perfume's scent, but the way it helped her recapture an earlier, more glamorous, high-heeled version of herself. Without quite knowing what I was doing, I turned off my computer, got in my car, and drove to the decaying mall near my house.

The beauty floor of the largest department store was empty, the tinny background music playing on for no one. The only visible sales assistant leaned her elbows on the counter farthest from the entrance. I fought back my usual urge to turn around and leave—I am terminally shopping-averse—and made my way to her through the maze of glass and mirrors. When I arrived, she brightened, and launched into a pitch for a series of things as new and pink as she was. I listened while she spritzed the test cards and clouds of powdered strawberry candy, high-grade fabric softener, and preadolescent longing filled the air. Then I asked, firmly, for the Paloma. She was startled ("That's an old one!") but found it, and sprayed it on my outstretched arm.

The scent that wafted up to me then was deep-throated, unapologetic, and a little shocking. I didn't know yet how to separate the sharp prickle of coriander from the lush sweetness of ylang-ylang and rose, the leathery growl of civet and vetiver. But I understood the writer's story, and a few things about myself that I wouldn't be able to talk about until much later. I left the mall empty-handed, my heart thumping as though I had stolen the bottle. I went home and lay on the bed, nose pressed to the soft skin just below my wrist. I breathed in. I waited to see what would happen next.

One version of my perfume story is a tale of pure, giddy delight. I dove into the world of perfume headlong, inhaling history, gossip, science, and scent. For the first year or so, I felt like I was living in a state of grace. Everything I wished for—perfume, a reason to go to New York, a chance to smell rare and precious materials, a friend, a community— came to me without effort.

But that's not the whole story. I was unaccustomed to so much luck and kindness, and it made me suspicious. Part of my giddiness came from the dizzy feeling of floating above my own dark murmurings about decadence, corruption, and escapism. I thought of my passion for perfume as a kind of fever and kept expecting—hoping, fearing—it would break. Each night I went to bed, after another evening of reading and sniffing, with a different perfume on each wrist and a third on the back of my hand, and each night I thought I would wake up the next morning with a clear head and cool, damp skin, filled with relief and just a touch of regret to be back in the real, relatively unscented world.

Luckily, I was old enough to find my predicament funny. After all, in the annals of seduction stories, mine was an old chestnut: the well-behaved schoolgirl who finds herself making out with some deliciously wrong person and runs off crying, savoring the thrilling taste of liquor and cigarettes in her mouth while she figures out exactly when and how to make it happen again.

I was headed across the tracks. It just so happened that Bergdorf's was on the other side.

I keep my perfumes in a closet. This is not a metaphor. The natural enemies of perfume are heat, light, and humidity, and my closet is cool, dark, and dry. The conversations of perfume people are sprinkled with references to "my perfume closet," as in, "Oh, I think I have a bottle of that. I'll have to dig it out from the back of my perfume closet." Often, the people saying such things have been collecting for decades, and they really do have a whole closet full of perfume—shelf after shelf of bottles, and more in boxes on the floor—that they take out and rotate through as the weather changes or the mood strikes.

My perfumes take up three short shelves of an old nightstand bookcase that is part of the jerry-rigged system of my office storage. They share space with printing paper and ink, packing tape, art supplies, tax records, fabric saved for an indeterminate purpose, bubble wrap, a huge basket of old purses, a storage container still in its original package, and several boxes of files that I should have thrown away the last time we moved. Nevertheless, I too refer to my perfume closet.

Though my perfume closet is not a metaphor, it is, like so many things about perfume, always on the edge of dissolving into one. There is something about a collection of any kind that suggests both a hoarding instinct and a special brand of geekery. Perfume is decidedly not among the rarefied objects of desire—wine, music, art, and so on—whose collectors have celebrity advocates and a widely read literature of their own. The online forums for perfume lovers are full of joyous declarations of relief from recent arrivals: *I am so happy to have found you. I thought I was the only one. No one understands how I feel.* To which we all chorus in reply: *We know exactly what you mean. Welcome.*

My own worries over perfume went beyond being misunderstood. To explain them I have to tell you a little bit about who I am and where I came from. I grew up in Boise, Idaho. My first and abiding passion in life was reading, followed closely by talking about what I had read. Writing was what I did when I couldn't find anyone as interested as I was in the books or the talking, which was often. The only place outside my childhood home where I was encouraged to read, write, and talk was school, and so, for many years, many more than most people, I was a good schoolgirl, working and worrying, testing well and pleasing my teachers. These are habits that last a lifetime. I often find myself thinking, all evidence to the contrary, that everything would be just fine if only I could get my homework, my endless, ever-present homework, finally and truly done.

Like many people who do well in school, I followed the rules as a matter of course. When I learned, as most of us eventually do, that the rules were unfair, that the world itself is an unfair and broken place, it no longer seemed like enough to read books and talk about them. I felt, vaguely but passionately, that Something Must Be Done and that I, personally, was responsible for Doing Something, though I was never quite sure what. While other friends joined the Peace Corps or went to teach in inner-city schools, I went home to Boise, began writing for the weekly paper, and took a job teaching creative writing and a few other things to adolescents at the local psychiatric hospital. Two years later the paper ran out of money for freelancers and the hospital decided to replace the creative arts classes with courses in socialization, but by then both jobs had restored my faith in the importance of reading and writing, and I ended up back in school.

For nearly a decade, while the stock market roared, my fellow students dropped out to take tech jobs, and all the talk was of expansion, invention, gleeful consumption, and bright futures, I wrote about authors who bore witness to poverty, violence, the hard work of survival, and the impossibility of escaping the past. I was teaching undergraduates, and I never stopped trying to Do Something. Mostly, I collaborated with therapists and artists. I spent a lot of time in poorly lit borrowed spaces—reclaimed warehouses, after-hours conference rooms, weekend classrooms—listening to women and girls tell their own stories about violence and survival.

I was a slow, soft kind of activist, too interested in complexity to get much done, but my work gave me a certain point of view. Paging through a waiting-room fashion magazine, I was more likely to grieve over the youth and frailty of the models than I was to lust after their shoes. And there were moments—electric, insistent, more frequent than you might think—when I felt sure I was part of something urgent and important, something much larger than myself. I had little time or patience for anything else.

So when—just as everything began to slow and fail, and the talk turned to cutting back and working together—I became passionately interested in the useless beauty of perfume, it was not as though I had simply taken up a new and unexpected hobby: long-distance motorcycle riding, say, or pole vaulting. It was more along the lines of announcing, after a lifetime of being allergic to mosquitoes, deathly afraid of snakes, and inclined to narcolepsy in heat and humidity, that my life's true calling was to gather small poisonous frogs in the Amazon jungle. My friends looked at me with the gentle concern we reserve for the harmlessly insane. My mother said, "Really?" And then there was silence.

I suppose that, knowing all this, I should have kept the whole thing under wraps. But I am very bad at keeping quiet, even when I ought to know better. So after my obsession reached a certain point, I began to have the same conversation at a lot of different parties:

I am standing in the corner with my drink when a scholar or social worker or therapist or nonprofit director or performance artist—these are the kinds of people I know—comes over to chat. So, they ask, what are you writing about these days?

There is a pause while I decide whether or not to tell the truth. Most evenings, I take a sip of my drink and a deep breath, and with the feeling of beginning to run toward the edge of a cliff I say, Well, I've gotten really interested in perfume.

Another silence falls while my acquaintances look at me—hostile, bored, or slightly interested, but always very puzzled—and then they say: Perfume? You mean like essential oils?

This is an act of translation. In Austin, essential oils are available at the farmers' market, the health-food co-op, and the women's bookstore. They scent the air at yoga classes and the massage therapist's office and the acupuncturist's, too. The cheerful, blue-haired girl serving your latte (in Austin all our rebels are cheerful) may reek of patchouli oil, but she doesn't wear perfume. Perfume is for her mother, who lives in Dallas. My acquaintances know I'm not a Dallas kind of girl, so they give me an out, a chance to redeem myself. *You didn't really mean to say perfume, did you?*

But I did mean to say perfume, so I have to tell them: No. Not oils. Perfume. And then they say, You mean you *like* perfume? (Because surely there is some other reason I'm writing about it.) And I keep right on going, off the cliff and into the air, and I say, Yes. Yes, I like perfume. Then all communication breaks down and they say, I don't understand. What exactly are we talking about here?

So while I'm falling through the air, I do my best to explain. I speak of history. (But never science. There are wonderful science stories to be told, but even I know better than to try to sell chemistry to this crowd.) I trot out perfume's pedigrees, both sacred and profane, the long and winding road from the holy incense of the East to the precious oils that cost Marie Antoinette her head. (The rebels who captured her carriage had never seen her, but they knew only a royal could smell like that.) I talk about the modern classics, rising up out of war, glamour, magic, and mistakes. I tell a few of the secret stories of the perfume world, tales of its shadowy geniuses and generous madnesses, the perfumer on his knees in the garden trying to re-create the scent of a tiny white flower, the great fields of roses and jasmine reserved for a single scent. If I sense genuine curiosity hidden behind the puzzlement, I tell stories about memory and love, the worlds conjured up by the scents of our childhood, and the way perfumers use these to weave new, more adult memories, the way Jacques Guerlain turned lemon ice and vanilla into the feral darkness of Shalimar, leaving several generations of men to trail after disturbingly edible women. Sometimes, with the wind whistling past my ears and the ground coming up fast below my feet, I face off hostility with brazen effrontery and I say I like the way perfume forces me to think about art and money, how it is so obviously and unashamedly commercial I can't pretend, the way I sometimes do with other kinds of art, that it's all for some high, pure, romantic purpose, and how, far from tainting its beauty, the sideshow of money makes the best perfume—and art—seem wilder, more real and insistent, and that thinking about these things makes me feel like a citizen of the world.

All these stories are true, and I love telling them. But they are not the plain and delicate thing, the thing I never say (while I am falling, still falling), which is that perfume makes me happy, and that what we are talking about here is pleasure.

The scent of dry summer heat shimmering above asphalt, dusty earth, and the blond grass of the foothills that surround the city of my childhood. The scent of sun-warmed wood, smooth under your wet cheek when you sprawl on the dock in the middle of the lake, the surrounding water brackish and tea-sweet. The cool blood scent of wet iron, rain on cobblestones, and a lilac bush one block away. The high, singing scent of lemons fading to the spring green of honeysuckle growing along a creek, and a bit of the muddy banks, too. The scent of night-blooming jasmine, heady and heavy with fruit and a touch of ashtray—the lovers were smoking before they disappeared into the brush. The soft smoke blanket of incense pierced by a fretwork of spice—mace, nutmeg, clove. The lush rot of overblown roses wrapped in old velvet. The jewel-bright scent of mandarins deepened by bitter chocolate and smoothed by worn leather. The scent of peaches ripe to the point of decay, which is also the scent of soft flesh, the most luscious kiss. The thick wine scent of honey, viscous at the back of the throat, lit from within by the flowers it came from and the golden sunlight of late summer. The sweet grass scent of new hay, the horses somewhere nearby. The scent of salt, of seawater dried on skin. The acrid tang of chlorine—seawater abstracted, metallicized—and the scent of clean sweat, and, underneath it, the close musk of warm, sleeping bodies, of tangled sheets, of the still-warm pillow. The waxy animal-fur scent of human hair breathed in at the nape of another's neck.

These are a few of my perfumes.

I fell for perfume in a time of war and disaster, and I am writing this in the middle of more of the same. It would be the easy thing to say that perfume is an escape for me, a sensual distraction from more important things, a kind of giving up and selling out. I have said it myself more than once, sometimes in a stern, moral tone and sometimes in a more forgiving one. In my circles, where so many people are engaged in serious and permanent combat with equally serious and permanent crises, the deliberate pursuit of pleasure is always suspect, but in times like these it is something close to a scandal.

And it's true—perfume is distracting. When I try to think about the scandal of extravagance in hard times, I end up thinking instead about Lanvin's Scandal, released in 1933, in the depths of the Great Depression. Discontinued in 1972 but still widely revered and avidly pursued by perfume people, Scandal is one of the few perfumes I know that thoroughly lives up to its name. In its original incarnation it was flowers, spice, leather, and sex—armor for hard times present, protection against threats looming on the horizon, and an invitation to defy both. The flowers have faded with time. The leather and sex have not. The first time I put on a few drops from my precious vintage supply, I immediately left my office to find V. When I did, held my arm up wordlessly for him to sniff. His eyes widened and his eyebrows shot up. "It's not pretty," he said. "It's not pretty at all. But . . ." He breathed in sharply, and held that breath. "Yes," I said. "I think so, too."

Before Scandal, there was Joy. In 1929, Jean Patou looked across the Atlantic at Wall Street in ruins (or so the oft-repeated story goes) and ordered perfumer Henri Alméras to make the most luxurious, most expensive perfume he could imagine. If Scandal was defiance, Joy was transcendence, an aria of pure flowers—roses and jasmine, thousands of them in every bottle—soaring above the anchor of an animalic base. It was radiance over darkness, distilled. It still is. Scandal may have disappeared from the perfume counters, but Joy remains.

When I was a deadly earnest graduate student, living the cramped, slightly miserable life that all graduate students live, I thought of this kind of romantic distraction as a great evil. I would have been the first to point out that the only reason Lanvin and Patou were releasing perfumes in the middle of a depression was to bolster the sagging profits of their couture businesses. Perfume was, and still is, a cheap way to extend the value of a brand—a whiff of fashion's glamour for the hoi polloi. And I would have added, for good measure, that some of my perfume books say Joy was created and made available to couture customers before the Crash, and that others claim it was an exasperated Alméras who, finding it impossible to please Patou and his publicist— that expert in self-invention, Elsa Maxwell—finally proffered the formula for Joy with the wily caveat that there was no use trying it, since it was far too expensive to produce. In this version of the story, Maxwell pounces on the idea of outrageous luxury and immediately pens the famous tagline still used today (though it is no longer true, if it ever was): *Joy. The costliest perfume in the world.* I would have seen myself as doing a service, presenting the hard-nosed facts so we can face the world with clear heads. *See?* I would have said. *This is the truth.*

Now, I am not so sure. Now I pause to consider the tangible beauty of the scent itself, which is surely as much of a truth as any other. These French fairy tales, these names that keep meaning more than they ought to, may begin as marketing strategies, but if they end in the pleasure of perfume on the skin, does it matter?

Because I can't help thinking of the women who might have worn these perfumes. Joy and Scandal sold well—too well to be solely the property of the rich. I think about what it might have meant to be clothed in crystalline beauty or tough eroticism while walking through the streets in worn shoes and a carefully mended dress. I think about what it might have meant simply to know the bottle was there, displayed proudly on a dresser or secretly tucked away in a drawer, a token of hope for better times to come, a covenant kept with the notion that life should be about more than the bare necessities.

I think of my father's mother, who was raised to expect a life of glamour and ease that disappeared in 1929, when she was in her early twenties. She spent most of her life working the floors of the large, fancy stores where she once shopped, but never stopped loving the clothes and perfumes she sold there. My own mother's hard times came in the midst of the postwar boom. She received the first bottle of her signature scent, the design house Rochas' opulent classic, Femme as a tip from a Texas heiress staying at the mountain resort where she was a waitress.

I think of what I know about largesse. More than half of my own perfume has come to me as a gift. The generosity of perfume enthusiasts is matched only by that of gardeners in zucchini season. More times than I can count, near strangers have said to me, *You really must try this. Let me send you some, I have plenty.* My tiny sample vial of Joy arrived in one such package, and for more than a year it's been all the Joy I need.

When I give my long-winded defense of perfume, there is always someone whose eyes light up, someone who leans in closer, and it is almost always a woman. Almost always, someone blushes and stays silent, trying not to smile. And often, someone gets my phone number so that we can sneak off by ourselves later and meet up at my house, for wine and more talk, and to smell the perfumes themselves and see if we can find something, or many things, for her to love.

When we are finally sitting down together, these women tell me stories. What they tell me is not always about perfume, but it is always about pleasure. They aren't always easy stories to tell—pleasure remembered is so often pleasure lost or denied—but they tell them anyway, in between sips of wine and exclamations over one scent or another.

The documentary filmmaker, all nerves and bones, inhales the boozy amber I've found for her, a rare, perfect first guess, and tells me about the breakdown she had when she went to France in her early twenties and how her Parisian aunt cured her by taking her to buy silk stockings, makeup, a corset, and perfume. "She told me I had to learn how to accept myself as a woman. That's so wrong, isn't it? But they were lovely things. And oh, how I loved that perfume!" The counselor who works the emergency phone line at the battered women's shelter tries on a series of scents, looking each time for something still deeper, richer, *more*, and she talks about how for years she kept her blond hair short and her face scrubbed clean, because her lipstick and tresses made her an object of suspicion among her peers. The director of an after-school program for kids from low-income families, herself a survivor of poverty and worse, flushes at her own audacity when she tells me how much she likes the scent of whiskey and leather. Closing her eyes over a memory, she sighs. "And sweat. Is there one with whiskey, leather, and sweat?" (There is—more than one.) They tell me, these women, a little bit about who they are, and what they want.

While we talk, the world, with all of its terrible troubles, rolls on. There will never be enough money. There will never be enough time. There will always be more work to do. But every now and then we find a small extra thing, a necessary sweetness, that keeps us from believing we know everything and all the news is bad. The wild card that leads to one of those hairpin turns in a life story when the grim facts shake themselves loose and we find ourselves in a new and unexpected place. The utterly unlikely thing. The beautiful surprise.

And that, more than anything else, is what perfume has been for me. For many years, I thought the answer to my troubles—and maybe the troubles of the world, too—was vigilance and hard work. I thought I understood frivolous, treacherous things like perfume and the kind of people who loved them. I thought I knew who I was, what I had to do, and what was coming next. But I was wrong about all of it— wonderfully, gloriously wrong.

2: THE LIBRARIAN, THE RUSSIANS, AND THE SCENT OF HONEY

We're born with curious noses, and we grow up sniffing actively, instinctively. Children love smells—even bad smells (they find them funny)—and I suspect that many perfume people were the sort of children who loved them to excess and never got over it. We grew up bee-stung and sticky, our fingers constantly reaching out to crush a fragrant leaf or press into the sparkle of oozing tree sap. We ranked our favorite relatives by their respective auras. (My mother's mother smelled of Aqua Net hair spray and Doublemint gum.) We hung our heads out of the car window to breathe in the sweet mint of passing alfalfa fields or the salt promise of the approaching sea until our wind-blown families pleaded for mercy. Like everyone else, we marked the start of a new school year by the glue-and-paper scent of textbooks and the cedar dust of freshly sharpened pencils. Unlike everyone else, we grew up to be people who nip into bookstores for a quick whiff of the new hardbacks, and who can't leave a hardware store without a detour through the lumber section.

But we're furtive about it. We know it makes us strange. The fact is, we all look a little odd when we sniff at things. It's an intimate gesture, bringing one's face close to something and breathing it in. It feels as though it ought to be done in private. Vision rules our world; every time we close our eyes to smell something, we upend that hierarchy. There are a few things we are culturally sanctioned to sniff—flowers, fruit, a pot of stew bubbling on the stove—but beyond those boundaries we're sticking our noses where they don't belong, and we know it.

Smell is our most ancient sense. It is preverbal, precognitive. We react to smells physically and emotionally before we can begin to name and analyze them—a possible evolutionary advantage when it comes to danger, sex, and food. The reasons why we privilege vision over smell are difficult to tease out from their complex weave of culture and biology, but I sometimes wonder whether we find it disturbing to know that our animal selves are still so present. Compared to a dog's sense of smell, everyone seems fond of pointing out, a human's sense of smell is paltry, one might even say (though no one ever goes this far) vestigial, like the tiny tail at the end of our spines.

And yet we use our sense of smell for far more than sex and food. The word *perfume* comes from *per fumar*, Latin for "through the smoke." It's a reference to burning incense, a ritual that is about spirit and connection. The fragrant smoke of incense is prayer made tangible—a link from this world to the next. Scent links us across time, back to places and people we thought we had lost or forgotten. It links us to the changing world: We smell snow before it falls, and the warming mud of spring before a single flower blooms. And it links us to one another: Parents know the scent of their children, lovers the scent of their beloved. The scent of a passing stranger can catch our attention like a fragment of overheard conversation. Some studies suggest that when people are depressed their sense of smell is less acute. People who lose their sense of smell often feel sad and isolated and find it difficult to eat. Some become suicidal. They have fallen out of the invisible web of scents that tell us, over and over again: *You are alive.*

I had fallen out of another kind of web. So perhaps it's not surprising that, floating through the drowsy heart of my first Texas summer with no colleagues, no expectations, and no idea where I might land, the link that caught my eye was to something called Now Smell This. It was a quiet joke, but also a command, straight out of *Alice in Wonderland*: *Eat me. Drink me. Now smell this. Okay*, I thought with a giggle, *why not?*

What I found on the other end of the rabbit hole looked less like a magical underworld than a busy modern library, streaming with people and sunlight. In theory, Now Smell This is a blog about perfume. In practice, it is a clearinghouse, a daily newsletter, a discussion forum, and a reference room for all matters relating to perfume, scent, and the sense of smell. Its sprawling archives are cross-referenced, searchable, and augmented by background articles on where to shop, thumbnail histories of all the houses whose perfumes have been reviewed, a handy FAQ, and an alphabetized list of perfumers, each with his or her biography and updated list of credited perfumes. (This feature alone constitutes a small triumph of accumulated data—until recently, most perfumers were deliberately kept anonymous.) It is thanks to NST that I can tell you how many design houses will be joining the high-end niche bandwagon, which celebrities will be piling onto the low end, the name of the island where archaeologists discovered five-thousand-year-old perfume bottles (Cyprus), which museum recently hosted a scent opera played in the dark with puffs of scent for characters (the Guggenheim), and the latest developments in the race to build a better electronic nose (to sniff out everything from cancer to pollutants on spacecraft).

But that first day, and for many days and weeks afterward, I ignored all these riches, just as I ignored all the names of materials I didn't know, the thickets of acronyms, the straight-faced quotes from the ludicrous PR materials, and the intricate discussions of perfume rituals. I was interested only in the thing that drew me in again and again until I started to notice and love all the rest of it: the lucid, step-by-step descriptions of the way the perfume smelled as it unfolded over time.

I read about vague flowers fading in seconds to vanilla and rice steam, how pink pepper fizzed and sparked, then gentled into soft jasmine and dark woods, and how lemon sharpened, flattened, and then turned into floor polish. The pileup of fragrant words alone delighted me—coriander and wet cardboard, black rubber and roses, toasted almonds and Play-Doh. But what really caught my attention was the idea that a perfume's smell could be traced and teased apart. I'd never read anything like it before. Food and wine writing came close, but you can see and swallow food and wine. Once you apply it, perfume is invisible. It rises up into the air, and then it simply isn't there anymore. To describe something so ephemeral in such concrete prose seemed like a magic trick. It made me want to clap my hands and say, *Again!*

Now Smell This has half a dozen contributing writers, and I grew to enjoy them all, but it was Robin Krug's reviews I looked for every time I snuck back onto the site. On the blogs, where it is all first names, she was known simply as Robin, but when I talked about her to V., I called her the Librarian. Not because she was pinched or tweedy—quite the opposite—but because NST is her blog, and every meticulously updated link, carefully moderated comment section, and double-checked fact is the work of her hand. And because her prose has a strictness and a dry, flashing wit that made me imagine her as a character in an English novel I'd never read—Elizabeth Bennet's perfume-loving Pennsylvanian cousin.

Robin's reviews were restrained, diplomatic, clear as water, and nearly as subtle. I am none of these things, and it took me a while to tune in. I would finish reading, sigh happily, realize I had no idea whether the perfume had been praised or panned, and then—just as happily—read it a second time to find out. *I'm sure it will sell very well,* she would say after a devastatingly even-handed description of the latest celebrity dreck—a line not so different from some of her highest praise: *It is very well done.* Her wry, slightly jaded modesty was partly temperament and partly the result of years spent watching the perfume industry hurtle itself forward along a trajectory that, from a fan's point of view, looks plainly suicidal—reformulating or discontinuing beloved classics, launching hundreds of new perfumes a year into an already confused and overcrowded marketplace, continually cheapening their product, and plying consumers with lies and misdirection. *If they asked me*—she would write, in preface to one good-humored critique or another—*but they never do, do they?*

All in all, she made an unlikely temptress. And yet for someone like me, still recovering from my years in academia, tetchy and suspicious and inclined to check sources, she was perfect. Robin made perfume something that could be studied and understood, and she made loving it seem perfectly reasonable. So reasonable that I missed the patently obvious fact that Now Smell This was the work of a woman obsessed—and that soon enough, I would be one, too.

The step-by-step descriptions in Robin's reviews depended on her ability to identify a perfume's notes, the individual smells that combine to make up the perfume—and to describe its development, the way those notes play out as the perfume disperses into the air, or "dries down." Notes are not ingredients; they are miniature portraits of smells, limited only by the bounds of chemistry, the perfumer's art, and the marketing director's imagination. They can smell of almost anything, from violets and vinyl to sweat, snow, and outer space. A good rose note, for example, is a work of art unto itself, and may or may not include rose oil. It can smell dewy and pink, or round and plummy, or dark and resinous, or any of a thousand other things, depending on the facets of the flower the perfumer wants to emphasize.

Perfumes can develop in many different ways. The most well-known version is the classical French one, in which the perfume not only has a beginning, middle, and end, but a head (or top), a heart, and a base (or bottom). The head notes are the light, volatile molecules, bright, fleeting scents like citrus and herbs that fly up off the skin like bubbles from champagne—or the burst of scent from a peeled tangerine—immediately after the perfume is applied. Next come the heart notes, heavier molecules that make their presence known early on but grow and change over time as they warm on your skin. These include not only roses and jasmine (known respectively as the queen and king of perfume essences) but also tuberose, ylang-ylang, plums, peaches, and all the other tender fruits and flowers of the world—lush, round smells that bind and smooth, bringing the perfume together into a cohesive whole. Grounding the head and heart notes are the slow-moving base notes. Their large, heavy molecules cling to the skin and linger the next morning on a scarf or a pillow, revealing their full glory after the rest of the perfume has faded. Basenotes are, quite often, scents we associate with food, like vanilla, or with sex, like the animal-skin smells of leather and musk, or—traveling still lower—with the earth beneath our feet, as in the rooted warmth of woods and resins and the loamy dirt of patchouli and moss.

But all of this is only the beginning. There are perfumes that shuffle the smells above into different places, and there are perfumes that don't use any of them. There are perfumes that are all sparkling top, like colognes, or all heart, like the portraits of a single flower known as soliflores, and some that are one long, rootsy, resonant base solo. Many modern perfumes are panoramic: They strike a single, expansive chord in which every note is present from the opening and stays until the end. Others have notes that disappear and then reappear, weaving their way in and out of the composition, or that arrive with a firework's burst and then scatter like falling sparks. No doubt a perfumer somewhere is experimenting with a new structure right now. In perfume, as in all arts, the rules exist to be bent, broken, and reinvented.

Because of all the possible variations on notes and development, a simple list of notes as they appear in the perfume provides only the barest notion of what it will smell like. The magic of Robin's reviews lay in the precise way she made the notes and their progression comes alive on the page.

It has often been pointed out that we have no separate vocabulary for smells—to describe scent we must rely on simile and metaphor, borrowing from the descriptors we use for vision, touch, taste, and hearing. That is more or less true, but it is also true that we all have a private internal vocabulary of smell, a collection of memories that we can conjure up at will. Robin's reviews taught me to conjure up those remembered scents and bring them together in new combinations. She asked me to imagine not just apricots, but apricot preserves with a touch of brandy; not just figs, but the whole fig tree, from the roots resting in cool dirt right to the tips of the green leaves; or, memorably, not just cinnamon, but Red Hots melting into orange juice.

From there it was only a small leap to begin imagining smells that were really flavors (like the scent of a salty orange or sweet leather) or textures (like the difference between a velvety vanilla and a scratchy, woolly one) or colors and sounds (like the loud, neon-pink fruit of the latest mess designed for tweens). She led me through the story of the development, too, explaining the way some scents were grace notes and others were sustained melodies, and the way one could conjure up another—pine needles and winter air ceding to incense. I followed along, reading, imagining all of this, and, without my realizing it, I let Robin teach me how to smell.

To say that I learned to smell by reading sounds strange, even to a bookworm like me. But without language, without a name and a context, even the most familiar smells can be fugitive, teasing things. Time and again, I've seen friends walk into my kitchen and sniff at the air, brows creased with the frustration we feel when the word we want is just at the tip of our tongues: "What *is* that smell?" they say. And when I say, "Clove" (or "Saffron," or "Basil," or . . .), they smile broadly with relief. "Of course! How could I not have known that?"

When we learn a new word, we begin to hear it everywhere: I was suddenly surrounded by smells. What had once been blurry, vague, and indistinct took on a vivid clarity and presence. It started in the kitchen, where I had always depended on my nose to separate fresh from spoiled, to know when the raw was cooked, or to make an educated guess about the effect of an herb or spice on the final flavor of a dish. Now I found myself conducting little science experiments, comparing the scent of the coffee grounds before (rich, woody, slightly sweet) and after (paler, and with a damp, earthy bitterness) they gave up their flavor to the hot water, or trying to describe how the scent of the oil from a lemon peel on my hands (cheerful but suave, almost flowery) was different from the scent that burst forth when I sliced into the fruit (bright, tangy, with a soapy edge).

At the grocery store, I sought out Robin's reference points, sniffing surreptitiously at ripe melons and mangoes, lingering over the bins of loose tea to learn the differences between oolong, Yunnan, and Lapsang souchong, cruising the aisle stocked with fancy soaps and bath salts to look for frankincense and myrrh, vetiver and verbena. On my morning walks, my dog sniffed along the ground as I sniffed at the air, thinking, *musty . . . woody . . . honeyed . . . floral,* parsing out the waves of magnolia, mimosa, and honeysuckle from the fresh-cut grass, the swampy creek, the pile of pruned branches drying in the sun, the simple wet green of the humid late-summer air.

I was enchanted, enraptured, and—as always when I discover something fabulous that's been there all along—indignant. Why had no one told me about this before? Where was the literature of smell on my shelves of books about food and music and art? How could I not have known?

By the time I was sniffing my way through the produce section, reading Now Smell This had become a daily habit. Soon enough, I began clicking through the list of links on the blogroll, looking for another fix, which is how I began reading the Russians—Victoria Frolova, of Bois de Jasmin, and Marina Geigert, of Perfume-Smellin' Things.

I found them at the same time, and though they have distinctly different personalities and tastes, they share a similar lyricism, so I always think of them together: a matched set. Eventually I picked up enough details to realize that Victoria's Soviet childhood had been redolent with the lilacs and chestnut blossoms of springtime in Kiev— which is to say, she was actually Ukrainian. But by then it was too late. For months on end all I'd had to go on were references to Russian books, Russian holidays and summer dachas, exotic bursts of Cyrillic type, and the Russian diminutives they made of each other's names in their affectionate comments on each other's posts—*Dearest Vika, Dear Marinochka.* I had never met a single soul from Russia, but since I already felt vaguely as though bloggers were characters from my favorite novels living surprising but delightful alternative lives, it seemed entirely natural to me that Victoria and Marina should call each other by three or four different names, speak French, and quote poetry and philosophy in the manner of the Russians I knew and loved from Tolstoy and Dostoevsky. That Victoria was a former ballerina with a degree in chemistry and Marina had met her American husband while studying abroad at Oxford did not help to disabuse me of this notion.

Victoria was the more formal of the two. She was always reading something important or cooking something exquisite, always learning yet another language, always on her way to or from some faraway place. Under the spell of her resonant, assured prose, I imagined her holding court in a richly appointed salon—mahogany floors, oriental rugs, armchairs covered in damask and velvet, and the mistress herself sitting gracefully upright in the best chair by the fire, in a rustling gown of dove gray silk, the light glinting off her dangling ruby earrings when she turns her head toward the speaker lucky enough to say something worthy of her attention. I never could shake this overheated impression, not even when further reading revealed that Victoria was a graduate student in economics living in a small apartment that doubled as the makeshift lab for her perfumery experiments. Bois de Jasmin was her salon, and when we came to visit, she welcomed us in and lent us a little of her glamour.

Robin had given me language. Victoria gave me context. Her reviews were works of passionate scholarship—intimate, evocative descriptions layered over technical explanations of materials and construction and festooned with a dazzling number of casual but learned references to history, art, music, and literature. In fact, in the beginning, there were times when the thicket of references to perfumes I'd never heard of, aromachemicals I couldn't pronounce, and books I hadn't read threatened to obscure my view of the perfume itself.

It didn't matter. Because what I understood, immediately and with excitement, was that Victoria wasn't just evaluating and describing perfume; she was *reading* it—using it to think and imagine with, the way I did with books. In her hands, perfume became a way to consider questions of art and difficulty, to conjure up the dreams and yearnings of another era, or to remember and clarify her own.

On Bois de Jasmin, the question "Will I like it?" often seemed beside the point. Whether or not I ever want to wear Guerlain's Après L'Ondée (and so far, heretically, I do not), I will always think of it as a wistful, melancholy perfume of great, tender beauty, because when I hear its beautiful French name—*after the rain shower*—I remember Victoria's story. I see her, a fifteen-year-old ballet student, "shy and serious," homesick for the country she just left behind, coming through the doors of a Chicago department store to take refuge from the unfamiliar streets at the Guerlain counter. And when I think of what Après L'Ondée smells like, I think not of the scent on my own skin, but of the sun-through-the-rain violets and iris that girl smelled, the perfume she grew up to describe as "a garden in the first flush of bloom, yet to reveal all of its secrets."

But that's not all. Thanks to Victoria, I also think of Après L'Ondée as a technological and artistic breakthrough. To create his 1906 masterpiece, perfumer Jacques Guerlain employed a new synthetic aroma material called heliotropin. In its raw form it smelled of almonds and heliotropes, but in his hands it became the scent of soft melancholy, the scent of rain clouds. The result was a perfume still revered by perfumers today.

Spurred on by Victoria's history lessons, I combed the Internet for books on perfume. As I read, the outlines of a century-long French soap opera emerged, populated by a motley crew of con men, geniuses, provocateurs, and magnates. Perfumer François Coty, the scrappy outsider from Corsica—Napoleon's homeland—was all four. When he arrived in Paris, perfumery was a closed society of small, carefully guarded family businesses. In 1904, when he brought his first perfume to the city's grandest department store, the head buyer refused him. Coty turned away in apparent defeat. Then, just before he reached the front door, he let a bottle slip from his fingers and smash into pieces on the floor. A delicious wave of scent swept over the fine ladies at the perfume counter, who turned, sniffed, and demanded that the now-harried buyer bring them some immediately. (Some say these ladies included Coty's wife and her friends, but what of it?) Coty went on to create a series of bold new perfumes that set the templates for the next century, invented perfume branding by hiring his neighbor, the great glass artist René Lalique, to make special bottles for his perfumes, and built the first mass-market perfume empire.

I began to get a feeling for the push and pull of creation and how, occasionally, a savvy perfumer tuned in to the zeitgeist could influence a whole generation of women. It is often said that the most famous perfume of all, Chanel No. 5, was created by mistake, when Ernest Beaux accidentally added a massive overdose of aldehydes to his formula. But he knew what he was looking for: His temperamental boss had demanded a perfume to match her vision of a modern woman freed from Victorian corsets, Victorian mores, and the pale violet, rose, and orange blossom waters that were the only fragrances a proper Victorian lady could wear. "A woman should not smell like a flower," Coco declared, and Beaux gave her the wholly abstract No. 5, a perfume that always makes me think of white marble—cool, polished, powerful, and expensive.

I discovered perfume's Shakespeare, Edmond Roudnitska, whose brilliant ghost still hovers over perfumers today, encouraging and rebuking them. His perfumes were earthy, refined, complex, and utterly human, and he worked in all olfactory registers and under all conditions, reinventing himself as he went. He was the creator of my mother's signature scent, the great Femme, made out of whatever he could scrounge up, working in 1943, as he told an interviewer, "in Paris, during the worst days of the war in a building that had a rubbish dump on one side and a paint factory on the other."

But none of the perfumers I read about intrigued me quite as much as the mysterious Germaine Cellier. Tall, blond, beautiful, and notoriously foul-mouthed, she was one of the first women to be recognized as a master perfumer, and she bowed to no one. Her amazing run of classics from 1944 to 1948—three stunning releases in four years—reads like a series of object lessons on women and power. First, in 1944, came Bandit, a fierce, smoky leather whose modicum of flowers did nothing to soften the fact that it goes straight to the whip, taking no prisoners along the way. Next came Vent Vert, in 1947, a green slap of galbanum that stayed true to itself, sharp and dry, until anyone who did not enjoy that sort of thing had long ago left the room, at which point a tender rose opened in its heart. And then the grand finale (though by no means Cellier's last masterpiece), in 1948: Fracas, a wondrous grand diva of tuberose and orange blossom so outrageously, excessively female that it is very nearly the perfect perfume for drag queens. I could almost hear Cellier muttering in her lab: *You want feminine? I'll give you f**cking feminine.*

Which brings us back, at last, to Marina. While Victoria reigned over her salon on Bois de Jasmin, Marina carried on a similar conversation over at Perfume-Smellin' Things. It was just as erudite, and just as glamorous, but it took place in a slightly sexier, more intimate room. Not the bedroom, exactly, but the room adjoining it—the lady's boudoir. The room, so useful to the screenwriters of black-and-white Hollywood movies, where a heroine might sit at a vanity table in a long satin robe and a filmy peignoir trimmed in a feathered froth of marabou, or undress behind Chinese screens with discarded silk stockings draped over the edge, while Gary Cooper or Henry Fonda fidgets on her fainting couch. Marina was perfectly capable of deconstructing a perfume by notes, considering its chemistry and history lessons, or quoting the perfect stanza of Baudelaire (in French) or Neruda (in Spanish) to explain its presence and importance, and she did so with style, but it was clear that it was all for fun, and that perfume itself was a game of dress-up. After visiting Robin's library and Victoria's salon, it was a joy to loll around on the floor at Perfume-Smellin' Things, eating chocolates and paging through a collection of vintage fashion magazines.

Marina wrote about perfumes as though they were people—mostly women—with moods, quirks, and histories. Her perfumes teased and flirted. They were haughty and cruel, or dreamy and languorous. They were cheerfully outré. They refused to behave.

Her reviews were full of glimpses into her own life, many of them moving—it was Marina who had written the review of Paloma's Mon Parfum that sent me to the mall. But other mysterious perfume-wearing women strolled through her reviews—in the illustrations she chose for her posts, and in the little fictions she invented, fragrant scenes from a perfumed life. They went to the opera in fur coats, these women, and got bored with their lovers. They posed for pinup photos in high heels and push-up bras, smelling of lipstick and powder. They lay alone, undressed, on rumpled sheets in beautiful hotel rooms, or clothed themselves in the armor of good tailoring and cool reserve. They were never at a loss for something to say.

Diplomacy and gentleness still reigned on PST, but clear opinions were easier to come by. In fact, it was often possible to find two or three opinions about the same perfume. Both Robin and Victoria revisited perfumes. Robin, especially, was so scrupulously fair in her testing that she often came around to things that had originally left her cold. But Marina declared her passionate love for a perfume, sometimes an entire genre of perfumes, only to break up with it—to her own mock despair—a few weeks or months later. Then she would find herself falling for something, or a whole category of somethings, that she had previously dismissed as having nothing to do with her. Her taste was constantly unfolding, taking her in revelatory new directions. To our delight, and her own, she surprised herself. It made for great reading.

It didn't make such a bad model for exploration, either. *It's a woman's prerogative to change her mind.* The retrograde old saying kept flitting through my head as I read about Marina's adventures. It had a strange, subversive new sound. Why declare that you know who you are and what you like, like a fussy child at a banquet who refuses to eat anything but toast? Why not cultivate a restless appetite—allow yourself to be seduced, not just once but again and again, come what may? After all, it's just perfume we're talking about here. Isn't it?

I stood at the mailbox, embarrassed by the butterflies fluttering in my stomach, glad that I was the only one home. There, among the junk mail and the bills, was a small white padded envelope with a Los Angeles postmark. I knew what was inside. I had placed the order, paid for it, and waited for it to arrive. In spite of all that, I couldn't quite believe it was there—a little piece of my secret online life, plain and solid in the afternoon light.

A short time after that first trip to the mall, I figured out that I could buy perfume samples online. There were, and are, only a few boutiques that offer this service. In my early sampling days, I ordered from three: LuckyScent and Beautyhabit, in California, and Aedes de Venustas in New York. I don't know why sample programs aren't more common—perhaps the time and materials involved makes them prohibitive. What I do know is that they were my final undoing.

Sample programs meant that I could go directly from the blogs to the boutiques. It meant I could browse the descriptions of perfumes on their sites, comparing them with reviews I had read, and the imagined perfumes I had in my head, putting things in and out of my electronic shopping cart, in between rounds of work on my latest freelance assignment. Then, for around twelve or fifteen dollars, I could buy a small but significant amount of four or five or seven or eight expensive perfumes, without ever leaving my computer or waking up from the light trance of my perfume reading. Most of all, sample programs meant I could keep on avoiding the malls, especially the terrifying upscale malls that were, in any case, so far away from my part of Austin—geographically, culturally, and psychologically—that as far as I was concerned they might as well have been in Dallas.

And in many cases, I would have had to go to Dallas or Houston, or New York or L.A., to find the perfumes I was ordering. The boutiques, like the blogs, focused on hard-to-find perfumes from the smaller, quirkier houses that have found a place for themselves in the shadow of the slow-moving behemoths that make up the commercial mainstream. With their small—or nonexistent—advertising budgets and their limited distribution, the niche houses can afford to spend more time and money on the "juice." (Often, the actual cost of the perfume in a fifty-dollar bottle of commercial stuff is pennies. The entire budget goes to packaging and promotion.) And they can take risks. Free from focus groups and marketing strategists, they can wander away from current trends to reinterpret the complex old styles that have fallen out of fashion, turn their eyes toward the non-Western perfume histories of the Middle East and India, or look for weird new postmodern beauties. Not all of them do, of course—and some try and fail. But when I took that first, magical packet into the house, opened it, and tipped the little vials inside onto my desk, there wasn't a single whiff of the familiar miasma that hangs over most department store counters.

That didn't mean I liked them all. Far from it. Charmed by the idea of violets, I had ordered two samples of perfumes I'd never read about on the blogs, imagining shy, woodland scents, the smell of purple shadows under the trees. What I got, when I put a cautious amount of each onto the backs of my hands, was a choking faceful of powder on my left and a toothachingly sweet pastille on my right. I hung on for the ride, hoping they would change after a while. They did. The powder collapsed into treacle, and the pastille turned into something close enough to melting plastic to send me running to the kitchen sink, where I squirted on some dish soap and rubbed my hands together vigorously under the running water until the familiar smell of chemical lemons took over. *Hey,* I thought, watching the soap bubbles swirl down the drain, *this must be what people mean on the blogs when they talk about scrubbers!*

The next one was pleasant enough, a cheerful citrus-and-herbs concoction that I enjoyed wearing for a few days. When I looked it up again I saw, to my puzzlement, that it was supposed to be a men's cologne—my first lesson in the nonsense of dividing up perfumes by gender. The next opened with a blast of creosote that made me recoil from the vial before I could put it on—and then come back for another sniff. Then came a couple that conjured up places: the cool stone interior of a church I'd never actually been to, and a scent so close to the hot summer dust I knew from my childhood that it made me gasp.

The next one I tried was something that the blogs and the boutique had described as the perfume version of chai. It delivered handily on that promise, sweetly dark and spicy, with a base of smoky tea, and I liked it very much. It was all the things I thought I would like, and it smelled the way I thought I should smell. It had a bookish, coffeehouse kind of glamour, and it made me feel like a hip, black-clad version of myself—thinner and longer-legged, with one of those rumpled haircuts and the black-framed glasses all the people who intimidated me in college used to wear.

And so it went—slowly, cautiously, a tiny dab at a time. In spite of my admiration for Marina, I was a nervous sampler, always afraid of being overwhelmed or repelled. When I liked something, I meted it out, making it last. Buying a whole bottle of anything seemed like an impossible extravagance and, for a long time, an unnecessary one. Given a choice, I prefer many small tastes—tapas, appetizers, antipasti, those little dishes that come along, unordered, with Korean entrées—to a whole meal of anything. For the price of a single bottle of high-end perfume I could acquire an archive, a library, a gallery of scents. I kept my growing collection hidden away in a wooden cigar box, like the eccentric, private treasures that they were, and I liked that, too.

In the very beginning I would hold an arm out to V., who sniffed obligingly and gave me one-word responses: *vanilla* if he liked it, *powdery* if he didn't. But after a while, I wore my perfumes only when I was alone—at home in the middle of the day, while I was working, or late at night, if I was up trying to meet a deadline. I would take a sample vial out of the box, put on a dab of scent, and then look up all the reviews I could find, sniffing along as I read. I worked awhile, then paused to sniff again and see if I could detect the next phase the writers had described.

Gradually, without really trying, I began to recognize notes, like a traveler in a foreign country picking up a few familiar words. I splurged on a couple of the glossy coffee-table tomes that dominated the short

list of available books on perfume, and a smaller one on natural perfumery, full of useful information about plants and resins and wonderfully mysterious engravings taken from old alchemical texts. Often, my
reading led me back to the blogs to look up the perfumes mentioned,
and then onward to order more samples or, when they weren't available,
to simply sit and dream up the perfumes in my head.

I was very happy in this secretive, studious, closed circle and probably would have remained so forever if trouble hadn't come along, as it
inevitably does, in the form of undeniable gorgeousness. I could smell
it as soon as I opened the latest envelope. I rifled through the other
little packets inside, looking for the source, but it took me a while to
find it because I kept pausing to take another hit from the inside of the
envelope. When I did, I popped the top of the vial open and applied
the contents generously to my wrists and throat. The scent rose up all
around me, and I closed my eyes and leaned against my desk as my
knees went weak, clichés be damned. I may have moaned a little.

When the initial burst subsided, I recovered enough to lean my
head over my wrist and breathe in more slowly. There it was, the raw
sweetness of wine and wild honey, with the tang of muscat grapes and
falling leaves running through it, giving it life and movement—a scent
of October light and blue autumn skies. It had melted into my skin
instantly, and now it was radiating out from it, surrounding me in a
glowing golden haze.

I didn't get many test questions written that afternoon. It's hard to
type with your nose two inches from your wrist. But it was more than
that. I felt strangely agitated. My heart was beating faster than usual. I
kept getting up, walking down the hall to the bedroom, then into the
kitchen, then back to the office, only to repeat the process half an hour
later. On the third round, I stopped in front of the bedroom mirror and
recognized, in my bright eyes and flushed cheeks, the fluttery begin-

nings of an enormous, adolescent crush. I looked, and felt, like a fifteen-year-old girl waiting for the phone to ring. I wanted someone to smell what I had smelled, and I wanted that person to smell it on my skin. I wanted V. to come home.

Usually when I thought of V., I was thinking of something he'd said or done—laughing to myself over the morning's latest nonsense song, or grumbling under my breath as I searched the kitchen for a pot put away in yet another new and inventive place. But now I thought, for a moment, about V. himself. His square shoulders, broad for a man only a few inches taller than me. The fine bones of his face and his smooth brown skin, still unlined in spite of the silver glinting in his black hair. His dark eyes, large and shadowed in a way that made him look worried when he wasn't smiling. The warm curve of his generous mouth. His hands.

Then I looked in the mirror again. As is usually the case when I'm working, I was dressed like an unmade bed. Suddenly my rumpled, faded clothes were all wrong. Before I could ask myself what I was do-ing, I began dressing up for my perfume. It had been a long time since I'd thought about dressing up for anything but a job interview, and my options were limited, but I did the best I could: flowing black pants, a loose honey-colored sweater, my thick tangle of curls set free and then pulled gently back into a low ponytail, a few escaping tendrils around my face. I put on a pair of small gray pearls, then took them off again. I wanted swing, sparkle, something red. Fifteen minutes of fishing through various boxes produced a pair of garnet drops. I looked in the mirror again and sighed with relief, as though I'd just straightened up a distressingly messy room. Probably no one but me could tell much difference, but it was enough. *Now,* I thought, *maybe some makeup.*

I was putting on a second coat of mascara when I heard V. come in the front door. I waited, listening to him greet the dog, put his bag down, get a glass of water, set the glass down on the counter, and call out to me. I was nervous without having any idea why. *Oh, this is just ridiculous,* I scolded myself. I gave a last glance at the mirror and walked out into the living room to say hello to the same man I'd said hello to every day for the past ten years. He watched me walk into the room, took everything in at a glance, and then casually, as though it were nothing, showed me exactly why I loved him.

"Hello, beautiful woman," he said.

Blushing, I crossed the room, kissed him, and then held out my wrist.

"Smell," I said.

He bent his head as I had bent mine and sniffed once, to oblige me. And then again, longer, more thoughtfully.

"Mmmm. I like this one. It smells like . . ."

I waited. He sniffed. And said:

"It smells like you."

Did I walk back to my office and sit down to order a bottle—overnight shipping, please—and wear it day in and day out forever after? Alas, I did not.

To begin with, it was expensive. The feast-or-famine income of freelancing, plus a hereditary reluctance to buy anything at full retail, meant my rare impulse buys were strictly in the under-twenty-dollar range—usually edible. I was not yet proficient in Perfume Math, the fuzzy logic whereby a one-hundred-dollar bottle becomes a bargain after it is divided by the number of months or, more likely, years it will take to use it up. *Let's see, three spritzes last about six hours, so that's six hours of beauty and entertainment for about ten cents, versus a two-hour dinner with drinks for fifty bucks. Look at that: I can order an extra bottle!*

I was, however, already expert in greedy curiosity. So what might have been the end of the story became the beginning, the tipping point that perfume lovers talk about, when excitement starts to look a lot more like obsession. I couldn't just settle down with the first flashy looker to come my way, I reasoned, already searching the LuckyScent site for the word *honey*. If I'd found something this good already, who knew what lay ahead?

I was just beginning to understand the limitations of the sample programs. There were perfumes that were available only at the dreaded department store counters or in Sephora's manic aisles. There were perfumes that required writing directly to artisan perfumers who bottled and shipped their own line. And there were perfumes—far too many, it seemed to me—that had been reformulated or discontinued or were sold in a single faraway boutique and could be obtained solely through a mysterious underground perfumista black market that I sometimes caught glimpses of in the blog reviews and comments.

And there was this: On a whim, I'd recently sent an e-mail directly to a big French luxury house whose nearest boutique was a four-hour drive away. In response they'd sent me two large, beautifully packaged samples for free—not from Dallas or New York but *from France*. Brief, cynical thoughts about high prices related to overhead and inefficiency did little to dampen my delight in the foreign stamps and the handwritten note—*Bonjour, Madame*—that accompanied the perfume. How could I stop now and let my mailbox go back to being a sad, ordinary receptacle for grocery-store coupons and used-car ads?

There was one more reason I wasn't ready to stop with that first bottle. It was an embarrassing reason, one that I was trying unsuccessfully to ignore. I was worried—how shall I say this?—I was worried about my inexperience. No, that's not quite it. I was worried about taste—my taste—and about beauty, and most of all about sweetness. I am very sorry to report, dear reader, that I was worried about my perfume cool.

I blame the power of scent to conjure memory. After all, the last time I'd been really serious about perfume was also that magical time of life when we all learn to worry about being cool.

Perhaps you remember clouds of Alyssa Ashley and Drakkar Noir, or Anais Anais and CK One. In my junior high, Ralph Lauren reigned supreme. The boys—the right boys—wore Polo, splashing it on with abandon from the handsome hunter-green bottles they kept in their lockers. Their female counterparts patrolled the halls in clouds of the original Lauren, passing that deep-red square bottle from girl to girl until all were fully anointed. Andy Warhol, who knew a thing or two about both perfume and cool (a serious devotee, he was buried clutching a bottle of Estée Lauder's Beautiful), wrote that perfume is another great way to take up space. Nobody knows this better than adolescents, even if they generally all want to take up exactly the same kind of space.

Polo was a swoon-worthy scent of deep, smoky-sweet woods and gentlemanly confidence, good even when broadcast at very high volume. A few years later I would fall successfully in love with a wonderfully off-kilter boy who wore it very well. But the real object of my desire was Lauren. It opened with the rusty-spicy green of marigolds and then rounded ever so slightly into wide, wax-polished planks of wood floors, clean hair, and cut roses chilled by the florist's case. Now sadly attenuated, it was a scent like the clear tone of a bell, with no hint of dirt, sex, or decay.

But though I can still identify it from twenty paces, I never wore it. As you have no doubt guessed, I was not among the girls in the hallway waiting for their turn with the red bottle. I was in the basement, eating lunch in the art room with my friends, as I did every day for three years, our sandwiches and diet sodas permeated by the comforting vapors of turpentine. There we spent hours discussing the shifting power structures of the school—who had moved up or down, who was in the center, and who was at the fringes, who was hanging on by a thread and who had been cut off for good. It seems impossible, but I dimly remember our making an actual map one sleepless slumber-party night, a magic-markered, star-stickered poster-board flowchart of the teen court.

So I wore the perfume my grandmother gave me. At least I think it was for me. It came tucked into the packages she sent us—little vials gleaned from the beauty counter of the department store where she worked. Once there was a whole mini-bottle of Bal à Versailles eau de cologne, which I tried and failed to wear for years. (And no wonder. Bal à Versailles eau de parfum is famously rich and dirty—huge, overblown roses and rotting cherries smoked with incense and mellow, aged manure. The eau de cologne is just plain dirty and is best worn by very wicked old women.) I settled instead on Oscar de la Renta's eponymous perfume, a blowsy floral oriental that required twenty years, two bra sizes, and an evening gown more than I had at my disposal to be worn properly. It went on strong and then bloomed bigger into a thick sweatiness that set my teeth on edge. I gritted them and wore it anyway, the tuberose of my resistance, sniffing past it to catch a whiff of the Lauren that teased me every time I walked from my locker to class.

Like everyone else, I did all of this blindly, compulsively, without knowing why. But when I think back to that time, trying to understand what was at stake in our battles, there is always a scene—just a moment, really—that flares up with a vivid and distressing immediacy.

I am standing in the crowded hallway, a still body in a stream of people, fighting with Courtney Drake, the toughest, longest-reigning queen. We have a grudging respect for each other that makes it impossible for us to leave each other alone. *How can she be that way?* So we are fighting again, as we have since third grade, and she is magnificent, a lean, pointed dose of acid-bright invective—until the moment, the exact moment, when a tall, broad-shouldered, dull-witted boy taps her gently on the back as he walks by.

She turns, and as she turns all the tension and electricity leave her body. She goes soft and small and sweet. Her eyes widen and her face empties out. She touches his shoulder. She giggles. She has nothing to say.

And I see it. I see her switch herself off like a light.

A moment later he's gone—he's never stopped walking, he's not a boyfriend, not even a crush, just one of the right boys. It all happens in less than a second, and then she turns back to me, mean and angular and fully alive again.

For days afterward I was furious. *Fake! She's fooling them! They don't see!* But at the bottom of my fury was a sadness I couldn't name. Sadness and fear. If that's what was required of Courtney—cruel, smart, powerful Courtney—what hope was there for me?

I know we are supposed to get over this kind of thing—or so my mother tells me—but it is my firmly held belief that we do not. The days of our adolescence stay with us, moping just outside the door of our consciousness, bending us in one direction or another, waiting for a moment of upheaval, change, or uncertainty to weaken us so they can take center stage again.

The end days of graduate school had made me gawky, awkward, as quick to take offense as any teen. Now, sitting at a desk littered with tiny glass vials, I peered through my computer screen into the new world I'd found and felt the same humming energy, halfway between panic and excitement, that I used to feel on the first day of school.

I offer this as a partial explanation of why, several months into my love affair with the perfume blogosphere, I was still lurking in the basement. The whole point of a blog is the easy conversation between author and audience—at least it was for these blogs. Long before my afternoon perfume revelation, I had been reading the comments as eagerly as I read the posts, soaking up the collective knowledge, the teasing back and forth, the learning lightly worn, and the generosity of spirit on display there. But though I was brimming over with ideas and responses and questions, and though I usually talk far too much, far too easily, I had not said a single word.

Partly, I was just unused to online life. I read the blogs more or less the way I read my books, and it took me a while to come up to speed on the culture. But another part of it—a much larger part—was that I had arrived late at a lively party already in full swing. All the evidence of backdoor communication and life offstage made my inner adolescent twitch. There were references to blogs that no longer existed, people whose names I didn't know, events that had happened before my time. Some of the commenters were clearly hanging out with each other, e-mailing each other, and—tantalizingly, infuriatingly—mailing perfume to each other. They made offers: *Would you like a little taste of that?* They touched base: *Something coming for you in the mail!* And they made sly references to their latest scores: *A generous someone just sent me some of that. I like it very much.*

It only made it worse that many of the regular readers were as intriguing as the bloggers themselves. They had screen names like Divalano, FleurdeLys, and Minette, and they knew so many things—not just about perfume but about whiskey, photography, colored diamonds, horses, chemistry, medieval fashion, welding, and Japanese tea rituals. How could I not love Violetnoir, who breezed in from L.A. with her art deco screen name, sounding as if she had just gotten done meeting with her agent? *Hey babe, don't know if this is for me, but you make it sound great. Hugs!* And what about Chayaruchama, a sort of perfume fairy godmother with endearments, pet names, and gifts of rare perfume for all the bloggers? A woman whose warmth and exuberance could not be contained by ordinary sentences and paragraphs, her comments that snaked down the page, stuffed full of all-caps endearments and exclamations, learned and lascivious scented description, and casual references to several lifetimes' worth of adventure.

I may have been a little paranoid, but I wasn't far wrong about the history and relationships in the air. At first I thought the circle of bloggers I was reading had formed around a perfume blog written by the fascinating, perfume-loving biophysicist of smell Luca Turin. Turin was the author of a French perfume guide and the subject of a book-length profile, *Emperor of Scent*, by Chandler Burr (who went on to write about perfume for the *New York Times*). He was one of the first people outside the perfume industry to take perfume seriously and critique it as an art. He did so with a brilliance and wit that would have made him a star in any other genre. Though his blog had been suspended by the time I arrived on the scene, it was available in PDF format, and when I read through it I saw that the comments section was full of names I recognized. His influence was undeniable, even if many of those who referenced his work did so as the preamble to an argument. Turin has since written an updated, English-language version of his perfume guide, *Perfumes: The A-Z Guide*. His coauthor—and now wife—Tania Sanchez, a long-standing member of the perfume community, met him through reading his blog.

But Turin had simply catalyzed a community already long in existence. Before the blogs began, Robin, Victoria, and Marina, along with many other bloggers and much of their devoted audience, had been part of a much larger perfume-obsessed community on forum sites like the U.S.-based Perfume of Life and the U.K.-based Basenotes (a forum originally created, as the name suggests, for men) and particularly the fragrance board at MakeupAlley, a forum for reviewing and discussing beauty products. It was on MUA, as it's called in the blogosphere, that my favorite writers had traded tips for niche lines, mainstream gems, and reliable discounters. It was on MUA that they first began trying to describe the things they were smelling.

And it's where they became perfumistas, chatting back and forth in a language that can't be found in any official perfumery book. They polled each other on their SOTD (Scent of the Day) and looked for their EFTs—Evil Fragrance Twins—people guaranteed to hate all the things that you love and thus the perfect friends with whom to trade unloved samples and bottles, and an excellent way to figure out whether or not the latest release from Guerlain is likely to be FBW (full-bottle worthy). They wrote reviews that gave birth to a thousand lemmings— a mad desire for a perfume praised by another perfumista. (For mysterious reasons, lemmings are born or started, but never launched. The term is also used as a verb, *to lemm*.) A lemming might lead you over the cliff into ordering unsniffed, buying a bottle online without trying the perfume first. ("Never buy unsniffed!" being the first, oft-broken, rule of perfume collecting.) Of course, you might do so anyway if it's an LE (limited edition), because it will disappear soon, and if you don't like it, it's bound to be someone else's HG, a Holy Grail, the ultimate favorite of a perfume type—iris, vetiver, rose, vanilla—the one the wearer would pick if forced, presumably at gunpoint, to limit themselves to a single bottle from that category. An HG is different from an SS, or signature scent, a single perfume that defines the wearer and to which she is faithful. In the perfumista world, signature scents are almost always referred to in the past tense, as in, "Coriandre was my SS for ten years before it was reformulated into cheap paint thinner. I discovered MUA while I was looking for a new signature, and I never looked back."

Most important, MUA facilitated swaps. MUA members post publicly viewable swap lists and wish lists—items they are willing to trade, and items they hope to own one day. Both lists are part of a searchable database. This means you can find the one person in the world looking to swap a sample of that niche perfume sold only in Taiwan for a sample of the early-1970s version of Love's Baby Soft, of which you just happen to own a backup bottle—an extra bottle of a favorite perfume. (Backup bottles are a common perfumista hedge against the industry practice of discontinuation and reformulation). Swaps are rated and reviewed. The rare MUAer who gets swaplifted—stuck with someone who doesn't hold up their end of the trade—reports the experience and the swaplifter is summarily ostracized.

In the case of perfume, swapping means trading full or partial bottles, samples, or decants—small amounts of perfume transferred to generic bottles. When things get serious but you still can't afford a bottle, you can go in on a split: get together ahead of time with a group to buy a bottle of perfume that will be decanted in prearranged amounts. Once enough people have your address and get to know you and your tastes, you might be the target of a RAOK, a Random Act of Kindness, which is what it's called when a fellow perfumista sends you an unsolicited gift of perfume she knows you love, or something she thinks you would like, or, most endearingly, something she saw you wishing for while you were chatting online.

Swapping was the primary source of the perfumista black market I had glimpsed in the comments on the blogs. The international network has had some surprisingly far-reaching effects. To begin with, it upended the logic of a prestige market. Swapping made even the rarest, most outrageously expensive perfumes relatively obtainable and affordable, and it turned something that was supposed to be about conspicuous consumption into a gift economy. It replaced French glass bottles swaddled in lavish packaging sold by haughty sales assistants in exclusive shops with utilitarian atomizers, bubble wrap, colored tissue paper, cheerful good wishes on leftover Christmas cards, and, nearly always, extras: a few pieces of candy, a small tin of hand cream, or, most important for our story, a few more perfume samples—maybe from your wish list, maybe not, but often just as interesting, if not more so, than what you asked for in the first place. All these packages and their little surprises flying around the world meant that a lot more people were smelling a lot more perfume and then writing about it and comparing their experiences with other people doing the same thing. Thus was an educated subculture born alongside all those lemmings.

Along the way, the perfumistas did what people do when they grapple with uncharted territory: They created categories, taxonomies, rankings, hierarchies. You might say they created a map—a map of taste. It was a messy, rambling kind of map full of holes and scribbled over with corrections along its many disputed borderlines, but it was, unmistakably, undeniably there.

After only a few months of reading, I was sure I knew the lay of the land. Old and French was good, especially the inaccessible vintage perfumes from the great houses of Guerlain and Caron, with all their rare ingredients intact. Among the modern designers—Dior, Yves St. Laurent, and so on, Chanel was at the head of the pack. Everyone was sick to death of the cheap, fruity floral perfumes that were flooding the mainstream marketplace, but even a fruity floral celebrity scent beat out anything aquatic (perfumes that feature the scent molecule

Calone, which smells like shrink-wrapped ocean air with a side of melon—think Acqua di Gio, Cool Water, L'Eau d'Issey, and the rest of the 1990s). In the niche world, strange, complex, and downright weird triumphed over pretty and pleasant—it was always better to be shocked than bored.

Different categories of scents, I discovered, had different sorts of personalities, and I was sure I knew how those ranked, too. Deep, earthy smells like tobacco, smoke, and leather were a mark of intelligence, sophistication, daring, and toughness—the Barbara Stanwycks of perfume. I wanted very much to love them, though I suspected my favorites would probably always be the scents associated with oriental perfumes: spices and resins, dark flowers swathed in rich, balsamic amber. Elizabeth Taylor–circa–*Cat on a Hot Tin Roof* sorts of smells, their beauty always on the edge of a voluptuous too much.

So I was surprised, and very disappointed, when I realized that the golden honey perfume I had fallen for, the one that V. had said smelled like me, was a gourmand—a very beautifully done gourmand that I am now prepared to defend, but a gourmand nonetheless, which is to say, a sweet, foodie, olfactory confection. I knew, or thought I knew, that gourmands were, if not quite reviled, a bit obvious. Too easy. A soft, brainless indulgence. I'd been hoping for a gun in my purse and I'd ended up with a cupcake.

I had enough grown-up sense to realize that I was just a beginner and that my tastes were likely to change as I gained experience, but that didn't undo the not very grown-up fact that I wished they would, and sooner rather than later, even as I hoped I would never stop seeing the beauty of the thing I had discovered. I was embarrassed by what I loved, and embarrassed that I was embarrassed, and determined not to give it up. I was ridiculously happy, and the whole thing was very funny, but not quite funny enough for me to tell my story to the only people on the planet who would have understood my predicament.

It wasn't just the perfume. I'd fought off sweetness, in all its many varieties, for a long time. Not just since graduate school, where cool reserve was a matter of professional survival (no wonder I didn't last) and where I learned to prefer my chocolate bitter dark, and my literature even darker. Nor even since college, where I learned to dress in black, drink my coffee without cream, and draw blood in casual arguments (a hard habit to break). It must have begun, it seems to me now, that moment in the hallway when I swore to myself, without knowing it, without ever saying a word, that I would keep mind sharp and tongue sharper, that I would never wear Lauren or stand around giggling in a pack of girls, that I would forswear pink, and nail polish, and window shopping, and that no matter who happened to tap me on the back, I would never, ever compromise who I was.

Smelling the scent of honey on my skin, I began to see how narrow that sharpness was, how stiff and inflexible I'd gotten, holding the same pose for so many years. And watching the way those smart, lively women in my new online dreamworld giggled with one another and cheered one another on, I began to wonder—nervously, and with a tender, prickly, painful feeling, like blood rushing back into limbs that have fallen asleep—if there might be another way.

3: THE CURATOR AND THE COWGIRLS

drove past the house twice before I realized it was there. It sat on a corner lot in a gritty neighborhood, completely hidden from the street by a tall, graying wooden fence. On my third trip around the block, I pulled over, checked the address on my map a final time, then got out and walked the perimeter of the yard. A few steps down the unpaved driveway I found a narrow gap in the fence, crossed my fingers, and slipped through, hoping that I was not about to trespass on the property of someone who obviously liked his privacy.

Once or twice a year, the artists who've colonized Austin's East Side open their studios to the public. The organizers of the event publish a thick catalog with photographs and descriptions of the work for sale, accompanied by a map and addresses, and visitors make their own way from place to place, as I had been doing all day. Most artists do their best to blend in with the neighborhood. It isn't unusual to open a front door scabbed with peeling paint and walk into a hallway covered floor to ceiling in glittering glass mosaic tiles, or to cross a weedy, half-dead front lawn into a backyard with a fishpond surrounded by wildflowers and an immaculate, newly built studio still smelling of fresh plywood.

I thought I was at one of the studios listed on my map. But standing just inside the fence on a narrow dirt path all but swallowed by an overgrown garden, I still wasn't sure. I picked my way up to the front porch of the rambling Victorian, past an open ladder and a heap of painting supplies to the open front door. I knocked. There was no answer, but the door creaked open a little farther into the house, and I went inside.

To my great relief, a short trip down the hallway brought me to a large, airy room lined with shelves of glass beakers, jars, bottles, and books. I recognized the scene from a photograph in the event catalog titled "The Factory: Expressions of Creation." "Studies in Natural Perfumery at The Factory," read the passage below the photo. "For the second year, we welcome those interested in fragrant plant extracts, the subjects of high scientific and metaphysical drama on Austin's East Side. Weekend demonstrations will cover extraction techniques and alchemical methods. Precious aromatic plant extracts will be brought out for sampling."

On one side of the room was a table with rows of overturned glasses. On the other, a woman sat at a long table, her compact frame dwarfed by an enormous bubbling mad-scientist contraption. I watched as she turned a mysterious metal knob and adjusted a length of plastic tubing. There were stacks of bangles on her wrists, her muscular arms were covered in tattoos, and she wore large circles of bone in her ears, but her trousers were tailored and her dark hair was carefully styled. I had no idea what she was trying to do, but it seemed to be giving her some trouble. Her brows were drawn together, and her jaw was stubborn. I hesitated to cross the room. But when she finished fiddling with the contraption and looked up to see me standing in the doorway, she smiled.

"Would you like to try a rose hydrosol?" She held out a small spray bottle.

I smiled back, walked over, and took it from her.

"Where do I spray it? In the air or on my skin?"

"Wherever." She picked up another spray bottle and spritzed energetically at her hair, face, and arms. "Ah!"

I gave my arm a single, light spray and sniffed. My skin smelled faintly of fresh rose petals and living green plants. I aimed the nozzle at my face, closed my eyes, and sprayed again, with more force. A cool rosy mist enveloped me.

"Oh! It's great! But what's a hydrosol?"

"The condensed steam that separates from the distilled oil. Here, I'll show you."

She bent toward the bubbling contraption. A large Bunsen burner sat in the center of the table. It gave off a circle of blue flame that jumped up an inch or two to meet the round bottom of a tear-shaped glass vessel about the size of a beach ball suspended above it in a circle of copper tubing. It was full of bubbling boiling water and clouded with steam. A tube, also clouded with steam, jutted out from its side and ran parallel to the table until it reached a second glass vessel, this one packed with dark-green leaves. A glass tube bent like a saxophone grew out of its side and ended in a separate, smaller glass chamber shaped like a long cylinder.

"We did the roses yesterday," the tattooed woman continued. "These are myrtle leaves," she said, tapping on the green sphere. "The water boils here," she said, pointing to the first sphere, "and when the steam builds up enough pressure, it forces its way through the leaves. The aromatic oils in the leaves are volatile, so they rise up with the steam. We trap the steam up here." She pointed to the small glass cylinder. "When it condenses, the oil rises to the top. See it?"

I bent in and looked closely at the small glass cylinder. It was half full of water. On the surface of the water was a layer of golden oil, no thicker than a couple sheets of paper.

"How much oil will it make?"

She shook her head briefly. "Not very much. This one's been going all morning already. Some plants make more. This is the first time we've tried the myrtle."

She pointed to the water underneath the oil. "That's the hydrosol. When the cylinder fills to here"—she tapped a short, black-lacquered nail against a red line on the cylinder—"I have to drain it off so there will be more room for the steam to collect." She showed me a small spigot jutting out of the cylinder. That was what I'd seen her fiddling with from across the room.

"This is the myrtle hydrosol." She picked up another spray bottle and spritzed several times in the air. It had a bracing, bitter, vegetal smell that vanished almost instantly.

"I don't know if I like it," the tattooed woman said, wrinkling her nose. "We did lavender a couple days ago. That was nice."

"So how much are these?" I asked, pointing to the row of spray bottles.

"They're not for sale."

"Oh." I hesitated—she wasn't smiling anymore. "Do you sell the oils?"

"No. We just make them."

"Oh," I said again. I thought for a moment. "And then you use them to make perfume?"

"We've done that," she replied, evenly.

We regarded each other a moment.

I looked around the room again, at the walls of shelves full of meticulous rows of jars and vials and the tables with their beakers and funnels and pipettes, and then back at the bubbling still.

"But what—so then—" I stuttered, "where is all this going?"

It was the wrong question. "We just do it," she said, and scowled so fiercely that I involuntarily stepped back from the table.

She stared, chin lifted, daring me to press the matter.

I gave her a weak smile, muttered something appeasing, and fled in confusion as soon as she turned away to offer the rose hydrosol to a group of women just arriving at the table. Behind my back I could hear them cooing. "Ooh, that's lovely," said one. "So how much are these?"

Safe on the other side of the room, I paused in front of the table with the overturned glasses. Now that I was closer, I could see that suspended inside each of them was a strip of paper used for testing scents. I picked one up, gave a hesitant sniff, and the room disappeared in a swirl of resonant polished wood, incense, and leather.

"Do you like that?"

I set down the glass and opened my eyes. The man in front of me was slight, handsome, and disheveled, with dark, staring eyes, a shadowy day's growth of beard, and the pallor of a chronic insomniac. Though the day was warm and sunny, he was dressed, as he would be every time I saw him, head to toe in faded black, with an old sweater over his button-down shirt. Without waiting for my answer, he launched into a detailed explanation of the essence's common and botanical names, its method of production, its country of origin, its medical and spiritual uses, and the wars, past and current, that had been fought for control of the land where the trees that produced it grew.

"It's very expensive," he concluded. "Very rare."

I picked the glass up and sniffed again.

"There goes another four dollars," he sighed, with a world-weary shrug.

I suppressed a giggle and thanked him for letting me smell it.

He spread his hands, gesturing toward the crowd in the room. "Not everyone appreciates it. But what can you do?"

I picked up another glass, sniffed, and gasped. It smelled of pine—

not the sharp burnt-plastic smell of cheap floor cleaner, but the scent of the living trees mixed with dry needles mulched underfoot, a touch of smoke and cold mountain air.

My guide raised his eyebrows. "You like that, too?"

"Very much." I sniffed again, trying to catch the lovely fleeting notes at the beginning—a hint of apple, or of tea. "These are so complex."

"That's why we keep them in the expansion chambers. If I dip a strip in the absolute and hand it to you, you get only the lightest molecules. It takes time for the heavier ones to expand. And then after a few hours only the heaviest are left. It doesn't work for something like this, where people are just wandering in. Under the glass, the molecules collect, and then when you lift it up you can smell everything at once—until it all disappears." He shrugged again. "Here," he said, picking up a glass from the back row, "try this one."

I sniffed. It smelled wonderfully of sweet tobacco and warm earth. I took a series of small sniffs, little sips of fragrant air, trying to tease out the facets of something familiar—coffee or vanilla or—*oh, that's it.*

"It reminds me of something. Part of a perfume I just tried, I think. . . ."

"You like perfume?"

Blushing, I nodded, intending to leave it at that. But then, in spite of myself, I went on. And on. I told him about the blogs and all my samples, about how much I loved the language of perfume and scent, and how I'd been trying to teach myself to recognize the notes in scents, and about all the reading I'd been doing. Halfway through my little speech, his eyebrows went up again. I wasn't sure if it was a good sign or a bad one, but either way it was too late—once I'd gotten started on my story I couldn't stop.

"Would you like to sign up for our salon?" he asked, when at last I reached the end. "We meet to smell and discuss different groups of aromatics. I'm trying to bring together people from different disciplines—cooks, artists, writers, musicians."

I hesitated a moment, then wrote down my name and e-mail address on the sheet he proffered. We shook hands and he promised to be in touch. I walked out, got into my car, and sat for a moment, dazed and bemused, wondering why I'd given out my contact info. I didn't know the first thing about these people. The whole situation was more than a little strange. What were they doing with all that stuff? And why did I keep giggling? *A smelling salon.* I giggled again. *Oh well,* I thought, pulling myself together and starting up the engine. *I'll probably never hear from him anyway.*

But a couple of months later, an e-mail arrived from the Curator. He apologized for taking so long to contact me. The salon had been on hiatus for some time, but they were starting up again next week. Would I care to join them? They would be exploring expressions of vanilla, including benzoin and tonka bean, and there would be a discussion of some interesting matters pertaining to the vanilla orchid. I was welcome to bring food to share for the optional first half hour, which was dedicated to socializing. Discussion would begin promptly at 7:30, and guests were asked not to arrive after that time. There would be wine.

I read the e-mail over again, smiling at its strange formality. What had I gotten myself into? I began to answer, then paused. It would be easy enough to say no. I could just say I was too busy. A year ago, I thought, that would have been true. A year ago I would have dismissed the whole idea as ridiculous. But—I glanced at the latest bundle of paperwork from the testing company—I wasn't busy. Hadn't that been the point of quitting my nonprofit job? To take a chance on staying open, available to whatever might come my way? The corners of my mouth twitched upward as I remembered the scents, and the still, and the Curator sighing and explaining, and I felt again the fluttering something that had made me tell him my perfume story. "Yes," I wrote, "I would very much like to attend. Thank you for inviting me."

The day of the salon, in a fit of nervous anticipation and curiosity, I bought my first real vanilla beans. They were expensive. At home, I slipped them out of their protective plastic bag carefully, like the precious things they were, and brought them to my nose. *Woody,* I thought. *Sweet.* But also *brown,* a warm, light brown, I thought, like caramel but with more liquor in it, something verging on bourbon. I scraped their dark, sticky insides into egg whites, sniffing all the while at the bowl, my hands, and then the fragrant air that drifted out of the oven as the meringues set. They were still warm when I arrived at the salon.

"Vanilla meringue?"

I held out the platter to the fierce tattooed woman like an offering. She took one from the top of the pile and told me her name was Kat. She finished off her meringue, then took another. And another.

"These are good," she declared. She inspected the dark-flecked meringue, then sniffed it. "Did you use real vanilla?"

I told her how I'd made them, and she told me I'd paid too much for the beans. We talked grocery stores as the rest of the group filtered in and sat down around the long table in the center of the room. They were a motley group—a few young hipsters, male and female, in vintage wear and skinny jeans, a rail-thin woman with sinewy arms and a deep tan who had just returned from hiking in India, and a pale, puffy woman in her mid-fifties. A woman with an open face and easy manner, as tall and long-boned as Kat was tough and compact, walked through the door. We'd never met, but I recognized her from the café where I liked to hang out with my laptop.

"Hey, I know you!" she said cheerfully, leaning down from her height above me toward the plate. "I'm Tess. Can I have a couple of these?"

"Please," I said, holding up the plate and introducing myself. The Curator had listed Tess's name and number for RSVPs on the invitation. She and Kat bustled around setting out tiny hand-labeled jars and cutting strips of paper. At the close of the designated thirty minutes of socializing, the Curator took his seat at the head of the table, looking as pale and rumpled as he had when I met him, and began to talk.

He described the smell of vanilla, the places where it has been grown and produced, its history in food and trade and perfume, the way that materials like tonka beans and benzoin have been used to extend or replace it. He told us about the sexual life of the vanilla orchid, which must be painstakingly pollinated by hand, and the slow harvest, also by hand, of the vanilla bean, whose fragrant compounds don't emerge until after it has aged, shrunk, and shriveled. He read long passages aloud from the overlapping tomes that lay open in front of him on the table, agreeing with or refuting writers whose names and proclivities he seemed sure we already knew.

He talked and talked and talked, his voice ironic and weary, propelled forward by the sheer amount of information he had to convey. And running like a bright thread through the tangled weave of facts and opinions was a reverence for his subject that ran so deep it bordered on mysticism. In the Curator's talk, aromatics were not commodities, or luxuries—little bottles sitting on the grocery-store shelf next to the fancy soaps and homeopathic remedies. They were powerful, complex substances to be treated with caution and respect. They were the distillation, the very essence, of something that went far beyond plants.

"Are there any questions?"

The pale woman wanted a few points about the orchids clarified. One of the hipsters wanted to know if tonka beans were edible.

I held my tongue. I'd heard the Curator's reverent tone before. It was the sound of one half of an ongoing debate that occasionally turned my gentle, well-mannered online perfume world into an angry firestorm, and I was fairly certain that in that room, and at that table, I was on the wrong side of the argument.

On the surface, it was an insider's fight, a spat about the methods and materials used to make perfume. But at its heart it was about nature, art, and technology, and our shifting feelings about the places where they come together. As I sat at the Curator's table, I remembered the details I'd collected over the past months.

For hundreds of years, perfume was made primarily with essential oils derived from plants and animals through distillation—steaming or boiling the raw material as Kat had shown me. In the nineteenth century, the French discovered that the aromatics of jasmine, tuberose, orange blossoms, and other florals too delicate for water distillation could be captured through enfleurage, a process in which the flowers were laid in fat (originally, pig fat). The solid aromatics were extracted from the fat and distilled further into a potent liquid. Today, chemical solvents are used in place of fat. The resulting solids are known as concretes, and the ultimate distilled liquids are absolutes.

Then, in 1870, chemists figured out how to isolate aromatic molecules and compounds, and shortly thereafter how to synthesize them. Isolates, fractional distillations (taking just the fragrant compounds desired from a natural material, rather than its oil), and synthetics radically expanded perfumers' palettes allowing them far greater control over the structure, longevity, and composition of a perfume. They made it possible to create scents that had been too difficult or expensive to capture in other ways, such as lily of the valley, violets, new-mown hay, and gardenia. When perfumers used them in combination with the older, natural materials, they opened up the facets of the natural oils, gave air and structure to the perfumes, and produced heartbreak-ingly lovely effects, like the fizz of champagne in a perfume's top notes or the velvety softness of cashmere in the base. With synthetics, per-fumers could paint impressionist portraits of flowers and woods, ex-periment with hyperrealism, or create new, abstract scents. In many ways, synthetics made the art of perfume as it exists today possible.

They also paved the way for cheap mass production. Oils, concretes, and absolutes are all still used in perfumery, but they are expensive— sometimes outrageously so—and difficult to standardize. They differ from harvest to harvest. The plants they come from are subject to drought, floods, war, famine, and the whims of politicians. Synthetics can be costly, too, but many, especially those used to scent products like laundry soap, shampoo, deodorant, and other functional products are far more cost-effective.

Companies depending on perfume to bolster their bottom line naturally prefer a stable, low-cost product, and in the battle between art and money, art has not always fared well. Often, when I confess my love of perfume to someone, I'm met with an exclamation of disgust. "Ugh! How can you stand that stuff!" she says, curling her lip in contempt. "All those chemicals give me a headache!" And though I could tell her about how really gorgeous some of those aromachemicals smell and how the flowers in her garden and the spices in her kitchen are full of the very same molecules, mostly I just sigh. Because I know what she means. She means the fug that announces to those who know how to smell it that all the money in the company budget has been spent on the bottle. It's the smell of cynicism and short-term profits and it gives me a headache, too.

In the past ten years or so, a small group of passionate artisans have begun making perfumes without synthetic materials, and they call what they do natural perfumery. Their ethics spring from many of the same longings that have spurred the growth of farmers' markets and seasonal eating, including the desire to turn away from mass production and to feel more closely in touch with the natural world. The Alice Waters of the natural-perfume world, its best known and most articulate spokeswoman, is Mandy Aftel. Aftel, who began her career as a journalist and a therapist, is a brilliant, self-taught perfumer. Her aesthetic sense and her research into the pre-synthetic days of perfumery have done much to transform the field, lifting it up from the kind of simple oil blends sold at headshops into high art. While not as well known as Waters, Aftel has been widely profiled. Her celebrity clients include pop star Madonna, and the luxury New York department store Henri Bendel carries her line.

Aftel's *Essence and Alchemy: A Book of Perfume*, with its wonderful antique alchemical engravings salvaged from her personal collection of rare books on perfumery, was one of the first books on perfume I read. It is a well-researched, wholly charming book full of wonderful literary quotes and gorgeous description. It is also a manifesto. For Aftel, the invention of synthetics was not the beginning of art, but the moment when we turned away from the joys and difficulties of fashioning perfume out of temperamental, fragile, unique living things. As a perfumer and an artist, she was devoted to the alchemical magic of natural materials. For her, synthetics could never compare.

Many natural perfumers seem to feel the same way, though, like any devotees, they exist along a spectrum. Listening to the Curator talk, it seemed clear to me that he was on the ultra-orthodox end. When he talked about vanillin—the aromatic molecule found in vanilla beans that is now derived primarily from wood pulp—he didn't just say it was inferior to the complexities of vanilla, he described it as a dangerous, contemptible facsimile that led us away from an appreciation of something important and rare and broke one of our connections to the earth itself.

I understood what he was saying—my old, pre-perfume self would have agreed. But sitting at that table, I felt nervous. I liked that perfume was both art and commodity, both science and nature. I liked learning about chemistry, a subject that until recently had made me fall asleep to nightmares of pesticides and evil men in white lab coats. I thought aromatic molecules were, in their own way, as magical as flowers. I felt confused about the boundaries between what was natural and what wasn't.

And I was, when it came down to it, very tired of trying so hard to make sure I was always on the right side of everything. I didn't want to give up this feeling of standing on the brink of something that was larger and stranger than I had imagined it could be. There were still so many perfumes—hundreds and hundreds—that I hadn't smelled. My world had just begun to expand. I didn't want to start carving it up and narrowing it down again. I just wanted to breathe it all in.

I wondered if I should leave. But then Tess began handing around the strips that she and Kat had dipped into the tiny jars gathered in the center of the table. Our job, she explained, was to smell each strip and then write down our impressions, keeping careful track of which essence we were smelling. After the strips had made the rounds at least once, we would talk about what we had smelled.

I held the first strip up to my nose, closed my eyes, sniffed, and considered. *Rum,* I wrote. *Burnt sugar.* I sniffed again, smelling the way the rum shifted and opened like—something. I waited for my mind to make the match. Ah, there it is. *Raw wood,* I wrote. The next strip smelled of coffee and chocolate as much as vanilla. The third had the sweet, flat, comforting scent of a freshly assembled cardboard box. I sniffed the fourth strip and giggled. *ROOTBEER* I wrote, in capital letters. The scents had different textures—soft, sharp, woolly, liquid, round. The cardboard stayed in the front of my nose, while the rum went to the back of my throat, and I could practically taste the root beer on the roof of my mouth. I wrote all that down, too. And next to each collection of notes I dutifully copied down the mysterious strings of abbreviations written on the strips: *Vanilla Abs Madag 25% Liberty, Benzoin 10% White Lotus, Vanilla Dist Mex.*

It wasn't until the fifth strip, which smelled of dust and cotton candy, that I noticed how noisy the room had gotten. Nearly everyone else at the table was chatting and drinking wine. I had grown accustomed to thinking about a single perfume for hours, alone in my office. I'd treated these strips the same way, and I was going much more slowly than everyone else. And, as is often the case—I glanced at the blank notebook in front of the young hipster sitting next to me—I was the only one who had paid much attention to the directions.

But something else had slowed me down, too. Nearly every strip I sniffed told me something new about my perfume. *Oh, there's that thing that smells like hay, and that's that weird sweet note that makes the back of my throat tighten, and—oh!—I thought that smell was vanilla, but it's tonka, I've always wondered about the difference between the two of them. There's that rough texture, I always thought that was the anise note*—and on and on, a steady stream of tiny revelations that could have easily kept me busy all night, if Kat hadn't broken into my thoughts to call us all to attention.

"Has everyone had a chance to smell everything? Okay, good. Let's start."

Kat called out the names of the essences, and after each we went around the table, saying what we had smelled. Most of the people at the table offered a tentative idea: *Sweet and, um, earthy, maybe?* Or they gave an opinion instead of a description: *Ugh, I hated that one.* But Kat, Tess, and a few others gave brief, precise descriptions that made me sit up straight and lean in to ask questions, or just to agree: *That one smelled spicy to me, too—would you say it smells like cinnamon? Yes, coffee, exactly, I'm so glad you smell it, too.*

It was a little shocking to me how glad I was. For the first time, after months of solitary reading and testing, I was sitting in a room full of live human beings, having the same kinds of discussions I'd been having in my head. I hadn't known I was hungry for that talk, but after my first taste I was ravenous. All the facts and stories I'd absorbed, all the little observations I'd made to myself, all the questions I'd been thinking about—the whole deeply nerdy inner monologue that had accompanied my days since that first puffy white envelope arrived in my mailbox—ballooned in my head.

In the midst of my enthusiasm, I realized how much I had been talking about my perfumes. My synthetic, unnatural perfumes. I looked down the table at the Curator—was he offended? For the most part, he had been silent since his opening remarks, breaking in only to supply an occasional clarifying fact, and he remained quiet now. Eyebrows lifted, face unreadable, he nodded slightly. Then Tess asked me a question and there was a conversation about whether or not vanilla could be sexy and what the opposite of vanilla would be, smellwise, and then, somehow, all the wine was gone and the session was over.

Everyone got up from the table and bustled around for their things. I made for the door, fending off questions as I went ("So how do you know all that stuff about perfume? Do you have a shop or something?"), but when I stepped out onto the porch and turned to close the door behind me, the Curator was standing in the hallway.

"I just wanted to catch you before you left," he said.

"I'm so sorry," I apologized. "Thank you for having me."

"No, no," he said, waving away my politeness. "I just wanted to say how glad I am that you came. I hope you'll come back for the next salon. Or anytime, really. If there's anything you'd like to smell, anything at all . . ." He trailed off.

"That's so—thank you," I said, still stumbling. "I'd love to. I will."

"And maybe you could present sometime. On perfume. If you wanted to."

There was a longish pause while I recovered from my surprise enough to answer.

"Well, I don't know if I'm really—" I started, then stopped. "I mean, I don't really know enough to—but I guess I could bring—"

I took a deep breath and tried again.

"Yes," I said. "Yes, I'd be happy to do that. Anytime. Yes."

I went back the next time, and the next, and I kept on going. Each session was as full of small revelations as the first. In spite of all its technical advances and fancy new molecules, modern perfumery retains a basic common vocabulary of scents, and the salon gave me the rare chance to smell and discuss the referents for these scents—to become more fluent in perfume's original language. Often, I'd spend the morning after a salon re-smelling my samples for notes and constructions I hadn't understood before. The voluptuous warmth and roundness that kept showing up in the heart of so many of my favorites? Roses. That touch of scratchy, dirty richness that kept showing up in the base? Patchouli. That perfume with an odd combination of dried grass and sweet cereal? An exaggeration of the notes present in vetiver oil. I chased specific notes, ordering batches of samples focused around sandalwood, or iris, the way I had done with honey. Now when

Robin rattled off a list of notes, I could conjure them up in my mind. I could even begin to imagine the way they might combine, the way I could imagine the flavors of ingredients and the dish they might create.

But it wasn't just about understanding perfume. The salon also showed me the depth, beauty, and complexity of the raw materials themselves. Extractions do and don't smell like the materials they're made from. They're like a record played at very slow speed, exaggerating and stretching out subtle facets that fly by your nose in real time. Black pepper's spiky heat turned out to be both bright and warm, with a surprisingly floral cast to it. Nutmeg had woody sweetness underneath its spice. The citrus burst of bergamot oil turned smooth and powdery, and bitter orange had a delicious funk under its freshness.

I learned something about the psychological effects of scent, too. I had never really believed in the idea of simple correlations between mood and scent—vanilla for comfort, lavender to calm, ginger to stimulate, and so on. The perception of scent is cultural and personal. What's comforting to me is often nauseating to you. But the night we smelled labdanum made me wonder.

Labdanum is a resin extracted from the woody twigs of the cistus, or rock rose bush. It was originally harvested by dragging strips of leather across the backs of goats when they emerged from the bushes with tears of fragrant sap clinging to their wiry hair, and that is pretty much what it smells like. Its rich, sweet, leathery funk gives amber perfumes their warmth and sensuality. Sniffing it straight at the salon was like downing a shot of tequila. All around the table, we rolled our shoulders and shifted our hips while the conversation turned loose and wicked.

Then came the jasmine. In *Essence*, Aftel describes the scents of white flowers as "narcotic" and writes about the drugged, dreamy feeling that overcomes her when she works with them for long hours. Tuberose and ylang-ylang are both important to perfumery, but jasmine is its heartbeat. It's revered throughout China, India, and the Middle East, and in Grasse, France's perfume capital, jasmine is called simply "La Fleur."

I'd read all that and remembered it, but it did not prepare me for my first encounter with jasmine absolute. I inhaled and was undone. People talked, but I didn't hear them. For once I had nothing to say. I just sat there sniffing, until someone forced me to pass along my strip, after which I sat there, waiting for it to come back. At the end of the night, I dipped a strip of my own and took it home—and to bed—with me.

On slow nights when Kat and Tess and I were the only ones who arrived on time, there was plenty of time to talk. Good-natured Tess turned out to be the mellowest real estate agent I have ever met. Kat, in spite of her tattoos and the circles of bone in her ears, had just quit her corporate job to train as an aesthetician. Both of them were indispensable to the Curator. When he spoke about the collection, it was always "we," as in "Didn't we order some of that last year?" The string of mysterious abbreviations on the smelling strips at each session was Kat's handiwork. She showed me the spreadsheets she kept with the name of each aromatic, its form (essential oil, concrete, absolute, distillation), country of origin, place of purchase, percentage of dilution (some essences are solid or very viscous, and nearly all are too concentrated to smell properly without dilution—it opens them up, as air does for wine) and a string of detailed notes on how it compared with other scents.

It took me a while to understand just how necessary those records were. A bottle of perfume is small, but essences take up even less space. Thousands of dollars' worth of absolutes can fit easily into a shoebox. So it was not immediately apparent that the Curator's entire house was dedicated to storing his collection.

In a tiny room to the left of the front door was a full-size refrigerator devoted to the well-being of hundreds of tiny dark glass bottles full of delicate, perishable essences, stashed and stacked in segmented trays. Sharing precious space in the fridge were the hydrosols, which all had to be given away or used before their brief lives ended.

The walls of the room where we sat were lined with labeled drawers full of resins and balsams nestled in airtight containers, slowly getting richer and smoother with age. In the cabinets were chunks of fragrant wood that could be burned for their perfumed smoke or made into oils (if we could figure out how) and coils of Japanese incense that could be used to tell the time while meditating, a different scent for every hour.

Scattered around on the shelves and tables were all the tincture projects—roots, seeds, leaves and whatever else caught the Curator's fancy left to marinate in perfumer's alcohol in the hopes that they would infuse it with their scent. Some projects were more successful than others. I once arrived to find a large jar of murky, deep-purple liquid tinged with green fluorescence sitting in the center of the table. "Blueberries," said the Curator with a grimace. "They've been going two weeks."

There were occasional random windfalls: "Would anyone like some of this Moroccan black soap?" asked the Curator, brandishing a lump of greasy, grainy, dark-gray stuff the size of a misshapen watermelon that gave way easily when we each tore off a chunk. The night we smelled wormwood, the herb that gives absinthe its bitter taste and (reputedly) hallucinogenic properties, the Curator produced several bottles of the then-illegal real thing (the ban on absinthe in the U. S.

has since been repealed). With great ceremony, and the appropriate silver instruments, he demonstrated how to drip water over a sugar cube and into the pale liquid to produce the *louche*, opalescent green clouds worthy of the most mystic bohemian souse. (It was a good night—what I remember of it.) Kat and Tess liked to tell the story of the time the Curator traveled for untold hours through several international airports clutching a slightly leaky bag full of a ceremonial tribal hair dressing composed of camel dung and Charlie perfume.

And every time I happened to mention an essence—a mysterious note I kept reading about in reviews of new perfumes, a reference I'd come across in a French novel or a news story about ancient Egypt, or—more than once—some storied piece of perfume history that was supposed to have disappeared from the face of the earth, if indeed it existed in the first place, the response was always the same: "Yes, I think we have some of that. Would you like to smell it?"

All during the time I was getting to know his collection, the Curator himself remained something of a mystery—a collection of rumors about other countries and other lives—and so did his gracious tolerance of my perfume habit. Several conversations had revealed that his feelings were even more extreme than I'd first suspected, but every time I arrived, he welcomed me to the table with enthusiasm.

I had only one guess why. The Curator was nearly as obsessed with the problem of describing scent as he was with the fragrances themselves. He often lamented that there was no separate vocabulary for smell—no olfactory version of *bright*, for vision, or *silky*, for touch. He wasn't satisfied with the professional language of perfumers. Among the string of notes on Kat's spreadsheet was a distillation of words and phrases culled from each of the salon sessions. This, she explained to me, was the point of our meetings: to build a lexicon. Thanks to the blogs and and my bookworm's vocabulary, describing scent was something I could do a little better than the average person. And I was improving.

In fact, as I grew more confident in my ability to recognize and describe what I smelled, I began to wonder if describing scent was as much a problem of translation as it was of vocabulary. Complex scents (and most scents are complex when you pay attention to them) often smell like different things to different people. Sometimes these things seem like cousins, two shades of the same color: My mushrooms are your rotting leaves, my melon is your mango. Sometimes they seem to have little connection at all: My delicious buttered popcorn is your disgusting sweaty sock. (Until, that is, you tell me about the sock and suddenly, to my utter chagrin, that's what I smell, too, because the human brain is hugely suggestible when it comes to smell and description. Go ahead. Make some popcorn and see.) At the salon, I often found myself asking some version of the question "Could that thing you're describing as x be my y?" On the blogs, I saw the same thing—varying descriptions that seemed at odds with one another but were actually like a series of dots that, when connected, revealed the perfume at hand.

Sometimes the connection between the dots could be explained by aromachemistry. The socks and the popcorn, the melon and the mango, or, to use another example, violets and raspberries, which often show up in perfume together, share aromatic molecules (in the latter case, ionones). The magic of this fact, the way it suggests an invisible map of scent linking together all kinds of unlikely things, is what inspires me to keep fighting my way past the mysterious diagrams and unpronounceable names to learn more about organic chemistry.

But even for professionals fluent in aromachemistry and accustomed to thinking about scent as an abstraction, smell remains intensely embedded in context—in who we are, what we've smelled, and how we feel about it. The most striking example of this I've come across is perfume critic Chandler Burr's description of Tonquin musk. It smells, he writes in *A Perfect Scent,* like a clean naked man sniffed "sometime around midday." The passage that follows provides a lingering olfactory tour of that man, with an especially detailed description of his armpits and genitals. "There's simply no other way to describe it," Burr concludes, with what I assume is a wink.

Because, of course, there are hundreds of other ways. Tonquin musk, a glandular product of the Tonquin deer, is very rare now, but it was hugely popular for hundreds of years. There are mosques with Tonquin musk mixed into their mortar—how did those who worshipped there describe its scent? Josephine Bonaparte was a huge fan of oils rich with musk. What image came floating into Napoleon's mind when he smelled her scent on his pillow?

Even if we can agree on a referent—*this smells like lilac*—my lilacs are never quite your lilacs. Mine are warm and spicy and grew in the summer in the suburban backyard of my happy childhood. Yours are green and wet and grew in the rainy spring, a city block down from the apartment of your melancholy early twenties. But that's not just a problem with describing scent. It's the problem, so familiar to me from my literary studies, of describing any experience in language. It's the problem literature sets out to solve—or to exploit.

The most magical thing of all, it seems to me, is that we can tell a different story. We're not trapped in our own memories and experiences. We can learn to recognize and love new smells. We can change.

I became fascinated by a version of olfactory acquired taste known on the blogs as "getting it." For every agreed-upon classic or popular new favorite, there is a contingent of perfume lovers who simply don't smell what everyone else is smelling. Some of us give up and go on—

there's a lot to smell out there. But the stubborn among us go back to try again. And again. We keep on looking for the beauty that's supposed to be there. And then, one day, the earth tilts on its axis in just the right way and *there, there, there it is!* The thing that smelled of attic dust smells of angel wings, the horse stable turns into the sexiest leather imaginable, the man-eating lilies go from cloying to voluptuous. We get it.

Why? Maybe we ate more chiles that week, or switched shampoos, or gave up smoking. Maybe the weather changed. (Heat and humidity can make a big difference in smell perception.) Maybe we read the description of what we were supposed to be smelling so many times that our brains finally gave in and agreed. Or maybe—this was the part that I kept thinking about, this was what it felt like to me—we found a slightly new way to be. We became, for those few hours, people who knew the humid jungle of those lilies, the hot excitement of a racetrack, the lightness of divine feathers.

It was one thing to talk about perfume with people who didn't wear it. It was quite another to speak up among experts. I remained silent in my online world. But I began to branch out a little, clicking from site to site, and I added the Perfume Posse to my regular rotation. I'd known about them for a while. Every few months, Marina, Robin, and Victoria teamed up with a few other bloggers to do a seasonal top-ten post, and March Moore, Patty White, and the rest of the Posse crew were always included. But it was different over there. Louder. Less formal. More—how shall I put it?—free-spirited.

Where Robin was reserved and diplomatic, Patty and March were shoot-from-the-hip opinionated—March occasionally employed a giant Mr. Yuck graphic to make things clear from the outset. On Bois de Jasmin, perfumes had lineages. On the Posse they had nicknames.

One particularly fierce amber inspired by the Russian empire, a perfume I occasionally wear and enjoy, was referred to as Rasputin's Armpit. On Perfume-Smellin' Things, there was a feeling that we all might slip into French at any moment—a quote from Camus, *un bon mot*. On the Posse, French was routinely and deliberately mangled. A particularly seductive floral called Amaranthine arrived, via MakeupAlley, as Amaranthigh. Dans tes Bras (In Your Arms), a strangely metallic and mushroomy violet, was quickly stripped of its romantic pretensions and turned, inevitably, into Dante's Bra.

And then there was the conversation. Maybe it was just the name of the blog, or the fact that Patty had grown up on a farm and lived in Denver, but whenever I arrived at the Posse, I always felt as if I'd just pushed through a pair of swinging doors into a saloon packed with regulars a few too many hours into their Saturday night. (The header graphics, two sexy she-devils straight from a Harley rider's right arm— a blonde, for Patty, and a redhead, for March—were from a different but equally rowdy kind of bar.) Urged on by March (*Go ahead,* she'd say at the end of each new polemic, *tell me why I'm completely wrong!*), a review that might have garnered a sedate string of learned replies on Bois de Jasmin or some gentle back-and-forth teasing on Now Smell This or Perfume-Smellin' Things generated dozens upon dozens of raucous, rapid-fire exchanges replete with teasing puns, dirty jokes, long asides on past discussions, mini-reviews of other perfumes, enthusiastic deployment of the fifty or so animated emoticons available (extra points for working in the clown or the pig), and links to male-model photos considerably less safe for work than those in the perfume ads illustrating the post. You could almost hear the glasses clinking and the roar going up from the table as the waitress set down another round.

All of this left me blinking in distress. It wasn't just that, coming from Robin's library, or Victoria's plush salon, I had trouble adjusting to the shift in volume and tone. (Emoticons! I was such a geeky English major, I'd only recently begun using exclamation points!) Nor was it the feeling that some of these women had been the kind of people who beat me up in grade school. (Patty was an actual former cheerleader.) What threw me was the revelation that this new thing I'd found, this treasure that I had approached with such solemn caution, such earnest studiousness (that's why I kept ordering all those samples—for study) and that I had been so tender and secretive about, could be batted around with such casual glee.

It was the writing that brought me back—March's writing, in particular. She wrote from the middle of a very full life. Her four children—Diva, Enigma, and the twins, Hecate and Buckethead, as they were known on the blog—were all young. She worked. Her husband (the Big Cheese) was often overseas. But her various stresses only seemed to fuel her perfume adventures, and she poured everything she smelled and thought and felt into her posts with a rare natural warmth and verve that was a kind of party unto itself.

She had a particular talent for weaving deliriously between extremes—high and low, poignant and piquant, earthy and angelic— and she had a soft spot in her heart for perfumes that did the same thing. She loved unapologetically trashy sexpot perfumes that turned cuddly in the dry down, room-clearing musks that were downright chic in their stinking furs, the grand old high-couture French perfumes with their erotic base notes smelling frankly of sex and dirty panties, and the big white flowers, especially gardenias and jasmine, with all their natural ripeness intact. One of her many contributions to perfumista vocabulary was the use of the term *skank* as high praise.

Her posts, likewise, had a kind of dual personality. Most of the time, March wrote like a hedonistic mad scientist. She went pell-mell

through the samples on her desk ("the candy"), was willing to try layer-
ing any combination of perfumes together—including the already
outrageously complex and rare vintage classics—and doggedly returned
to perfumes that repelled yet compelled her (*I decided to get X out and
torture myself with it again*). She conducted experiments inspired by
discussions, taking them further than any of us had imagined: *Do you
remember that exchange we had in the comments about wearing tropical
flowers in the heat? It was 90 degrees yesterday and I tested eight of my
skankiest jasmines at once, four on each arm, just to see what would happen. It was so wrong. I can't wait to do it again. Maybe I'll layer some of
that big musk from last week on top. Do you think my nose will drop off?
If I go to the bank, will they arrest me for public indecency? The last time
I was there, I swear the teller was backing away from the window.* That's
a composite example, but it is neither parody nor hyperbole. No one but
March could think this stuff up.

But then, after a string of similar posts followed by discussions of
the scent of afterbirth, the overlapping facets of honey and urine, and
the particular stink of teenage boys, she would write something that
wasn't about perfume at all. A tribute to her late mother-in-law's style.
A report on which roses in her garden had survived the fiercest storm
of winter. A story about the pleasures and travails of buying her teenage
daughter a dress. And it would be so intimate, so lovely, so startlingly
openhearted and honest, that all I could do was dab my eyes and shake
my head in gratitude.

I told myself I was only reading in the hope that the next post
would be by this other March, the one who could make me tear up
before my first cup of tea. But the truth was that for me, the Posse was
like one of those perfumes March kept torturing herself with. I didn't
think I liked it, but somehow I kept coming back. And back. And back

again, just once more. And on one of those days, the world, as was beginning to happen more and more frequently, tilted just a little and I got it.

Reading Robin, Victoria, and Marina, I was still a scholar, a student. They had allowed me to come to perfume the way I came to everything: headfirst. All heart, guts, and gonads, the Posse was about process, about experimenting, about taking risks and—why not?—going to extremes. Participation was everything. *Go ahead, tell me why I'm completely wrong!*

I was careful. I was hesitant. I was irritated and taken aback. And then, one day, I was a little less so. I wrote down what I thought, and pressed a button, and there it was: the thing I had written, on the screen beside all the other comments. Such a small thing, so ordinary, something thousands of people do all day long, but it was new to me.

Over the course of the next few weeks, I joined in the conversation on the blogs. I learned to speak emoticon. The line between my online life and my everyday world grew thinner, more permeable. I ventured onto a few of the forums, bought my first decant—one of those available-only-in-France perfumes—and was astonished when, after giving my money to a complete stranger, it not only showed up but arrived wrapped in purple tissue paper, surrounded by caramels and extra samples. A few months in, I won a sample of perfume in a draw on the Posse, which meant that March not only e-mailed me but sent me a package in the mail. The day it arrived, I showed it to V., then walked around the house with it, looking at the address, feeling like I'd just received a present from a movie star.

The alphabet soup of abbreviations that had once bewildered me became magically intelligible, the references to other perfumes that had once flown over my head were now all vaguely familiar. And though I still felt a little like I hadn't been invited to last weekend's slumber party, I couldn't help noticing that when I described the way something smelled to me, there was a chorus of agreement. Occasionally there was even a thank-you. Somewhere along the line, it seemed, I'd learned a bit about perfume.

So when the Curator asked me again if I'd like to present some of my perfumes, I said, without hesitating, that I'd bring them to our next meeting. I was still just tucking samples—and the occasional decant—into my cigar box. But since the Curator didn't want any perfume sprayed in the air, I needed only enough of each perfume for people to dab a little on their skin. And since we agreed that it would be best for me to wait until the end of the regular session, so that, as the Curator put it, people wouldn't ruin their ability to smell by sniffing harsh aromachemicals, there would only be time to share three or four. In fact, the Curator seemed altogether ambivalent about actually having commercial perfume in his house, and I remained just as baffled as ever about why he persisted in asking me to bring them.

But he had asked, so at the end of the next session I fished out a few vials from my bag and, heart beating a little faster than usual, passed them around while I talked.

I spoke about the houses that had made the perfumes, their histories, reputation, and misadventures. I talked about the perfumers and what had inspired them. I described the perfumes themselves, their notes, the categories they belonged to, the way they connected to other perfumes or tried to capture a moment, a memory, or a place. I expounded on the importance of warmth and skin and time. I told them that sniffing a perfume from the vial or on paper was like catching sight of a painting out of the corner of your eye while walking fast. I described, in detail, the heart and base notes waiting for them. I offered my own skin as a testing strip. *Please,* I said, *please try a little. Just a dab. Give it time to unfold.*

Some of them did and some of them didn't. The ones who did got up and walked around the table, extending their arms like strips for everyone to sniff, and I did the same. The session ended much too soon for the perfumes to develop. But the brave ones, Tess and Kat among them, left sniffing at their skin, curious about what was coming next.

After nearly everyone had filtered out, the Curator asked me to wait a moment, and disappeared into the back of the house. When he reappeared, he was carrying a large cardboard box. He set it down on the table, opened it, and began taking out plastic bags full of perfume samples, one after another. "Do you know this one?" he asked. "How about this one?" And I nodded: Yes, I knew them, or had heard of them—nearly all of them, I realized.

"They're old," he apologized, "and I used to have more, but I got rid of some of them. I haven't been to a trade show in a while. That's where I used to pick them up. There's just too much to keep up with, but you know," he said, gesturing in that weary way I'd grown familiar with, "if you want to try any of them . . ."

I looked at the chaotic pile on the table and then back at the Curator, touched and puzzled, trying to fit this new piece of the collection in with the rest of the things I knew, or thought I knew, about him. I moved a few of the bags, pretending to look, but there were so many, and it was getting late. He'd already been so generous, I said, meaning it. And with thanks and apologies and promises of a next time, I made my way to the door.

Was the Curator more like me than I thought? I wondered, walking through the dark to my car. Did he want to make a place for everything in his collection? *It's so hard to keep up.* Maybe. Then again, maybe not. I grinned, thinking of how nervous he'd gotten when I suggested I could spray one of the perfumes on a test strip instead of dabbing it. I unlocked my car door, got in, put my keys in the ignition, then stopped, my hand still on my keys, and burst out laughing. *Oh— oh dear,* I gasped, still laughing, leaning back in the seat, bringing my hands to my face.

I'd had a vision of myself as the Curator must have seen me, sitting at the end of the table, talking about my perfumes, introducing each one, taking them out of carefully labeled individual bags. And I'd seen what he must have seen that night. What he'd seen at that first salon, what he'd seen, maybe, the first time he'd met me, long before I'd seen it in myself: The Curator wasn't like me. I was like him.

PART II

THE PROBLEM OF BECOMING A BRIDE

4: THE GRANDMA BOX

The year I fell for perfume, a second completely unlikely thing happened to me: I became a bride.

It is possible to get married without becoming a bride. I know women who have accomplished this feat. I am not among them. I tried, but I am too in love with spectacle, and have too much respect for the power of theater and ceremony, to commit to a really big ritual like a wedding in a small or ironic way, one that would deny everyone their lucky charm, their temporary diva. Their star. For that is what a bride is, whether she wills it or not.

The problem is that it doesn't end there. It seems so simple—a dress, a walk, a few repeated words. Perhaps some flowers. But beware, beware. Deep magics are at work. The old stories lie in wait. For a bride is also: a virgin, a princess (never a queen or an empress—they have armies), her father's property in tender human form, her mother's emissary, carrying the customs of her people to a foreign land, even if that land is only a few blocks away. And though this is all very old news, the bride herself is always new—a new beginning, the bearer of hope and the hoped-for bearer of children, the means through which families and countries combine wealth, settle old scores, and seal the peace.

She is, at the very least, a gift. All wrapped up and ready to go.

At thirty-six, with fifteen years of feminism under my belt, having attended weddings of almost every description, I knew all this and more, and it did not help me one bit. As I navigated through fantasies of virgins in white dresses, registered for sheets for a marriage bed I'd been sleeping in for more than a decade, and tried to broker a peace between rival religions, languages, customs, and countries, I kept thinking, in a distracted, bewildered way, *But I'm too old for this.* I thought I'd outwitted the stories by waiting so long, as though there were an expiration date for all that ancient silliness. Yet there they were—along with everything I thought I'd abandoned or escaped when I lived long enough to forget, at least a little bit, what it was like to be fifteen.

But, as usual, I'm getting ahead of myself. Let's have a bit of romance first.

V. and I met when I moved to Austin to go to graduate school. No, that's not quite right. I met him just before I officially moved, when I'd come down to find a place to live. In one of those fateful coincidences that always attend the beginning of a love affair, I had run into Andrew, a friend from college I hadn't seen in years, and was staying with him. Andrew is a poet, and the last time he'd seen me I'd been a poet, too, so he took me along to the meeting of a poetry discussion group he'd organized.

We parked on an ordinary busy street, but when we walked through a door in the high stone wall that ran along half the block, we found ourselves in a secret, green-shadowed courtyard. On one end was an old mansion. Scattered throughout the yard were four low stone cottages. The one our hostess lived in was encircled by the wide fronds of palmetto palms. I would not have been surprised to see a peacock walk by. In fact, I often add a few peacocks when I'm thinking of that evening—two ordinary peacocks for the evening dusk, and one rare white one, luminous among the fireflies, for the dense Southern dark that followed. The group sat in a circle on the lush grass in the center of the courtyard, beneath a grand old magnolia tree. It had rained earlier in the week, and the tree's huge creamy blossoms were open, their silken lemon-apple sweetness hovering around us in the humid air, as much a flavor, or a feeling, as a scent.

There we were, reading poems aloud and talking about them. You can decide which poems they were. I don't remember, because I was distracted by the good, handsome face of the man sitting across the circle, smiling at me. A quiet, soft-spoken man who was also, for the moment, a poet. Andrew introduced us briefly at the end of the meeting—they were good friends—and I talked about him on the way home.

It would be another four months before V. and I had our first real conversation (at a Halloween party, out on the porch—I was in costume, he was not), eight months before our first date (in the middle of a rare Texas ice storm—we made fried wontons and drank a lot of bad red wine, and he juggled the oranges my grandmother had sent me from Florida), three years before V. was one of two best men at Andrew's wedding (wearing wrinkled khaki pants, just like the other best man, but very gorgeous all the same), six years before V. began writing a novel, and ten years before we got engaged and began planning the wedding that threatened to distract me from my pursuit of perfume.

If you are, say, my mother, my grandmother, or any one of my in-laws, ten years seems like a very long time to wait before getting married. But if, like me, you never really planned to get married at all, it might not seem like quite long enough.

I read my first perfume review several months after V. proposed. By the time I met the Curator, our wedding day was a little less than a year away. Only a short span of time, my mother insisted, just barely long enough to get everything done. I had no doubt she was right. But as I sat at my desk, sniffing through my latest set of samples, reading two or three reviews of each one, comparing them to similar samples from my collection and then looking up the history of the house in the latest perfume book to arrive, I was doing my best not to think about it.

I have never been ambivalent about love, just about the way the love story of a man and a woman is supposed to go. I would like to be someone who has rewritten that story in a bold way, but like most people I have traded true innovation for happiness and small repairs. Still, I can dream. Austin is full of wonderful old bungalows that have been split into duplexes, and for a long time I had a fantasy about living in one of these with V. We would be able to arrange things exactly the way we liked and have our own kitchens (very important) but still be within easy reach. When I was feeling flexible, I provided us with a shared front porch and an adjoining wall, so that we could each hear when the other was at home and have the comfort of each other's presence and the comfort of solitude at the same time.

One day, after V. and I had been living with some success for several years in the same house, I found an article on a couple, both writers, who had married and divorced and remarried several times. Finally, they stayed married, fired their lawyers, and used the money that freed up to split their townhouse into two flats. He got the top one, she the bottom. This was practical, not symbolic. She was a gardener, and the yard was her domain. Perhaps he liked to stargaze, and smoke on the roof. I believe they shared an entrance, which seems important. They met each other coming and going.

I showed this article to V. as evidence that I was not alone in my fantasy, and that it might even be a good thing for some people. He sighed and, in a voice people usually reserve for showing small children how to tie their shoelaces, reminded me that I had been the one to ask him to move in with me. This was true. We shuttled back and forth between my sunny rental house and his tiny, dark apartment for two years until suddenly the whole thing seemed silly, and a little demeaning. Such is the way of fantasies. Sometimes you long for a house when all you really need is one good room.

Our wedding came about in a similar way. First I had reasons—good ones, some political and idealistic, others personal and idiosyncratic—why we shouldn't get married, and reality seemed to support them. Then, while I went about living my life, that reality gradually changed until I could no longer remember why I had been clinging to my reasons so firmly in the first place. (Of course, V. had reasons of his own. But you'll have to ask him about those yourself.) We'd had a running joke for years that we'd get married on our tenth anniversary. Then, suddenly, ten years had passed. So we gathered up our courage and got really, officially engaged instead.

Which left me with the problem of becoming a bride.

Between the ages of fourteen and twenty-two, I had a little business, cooking and serving at parties, and in my role as kitchen maid I witnessed many, many weddings and many, many backstage brides. They did not inspire romantic dreams of a perfect day. The bride I remember best was from the deep South. She and her party brought with them a boozed-up flamboyance, a glamour that was foreign to the Northwestern modesty of my hometown. Her bridesmaids wore exquisite wasp-waisted tea-length dresses of bright, crisp silk in saturated colors—orange, fuschia, deep violet. Teetering on their matching heels, their full skirts fluffed out by petticoats, they flocked around the bride like so many agitated tulips.

She was a work of art. Stiffened and molded by corsetry, wound around with yards of ivory satin and lace, she was painted, pinned, powdered, and sprayed to within an inch of perfection, and she intended to stay that way, no matter how badly she wanted a drink. "Here, sugar," said one of the older tulips, proffering a can of beer with a straw in it, "this is the way we did it at my wedding. I'll hold it so you don't muss yourself, and you just sip as much as you want. If that doesn't work, I have some pills in my purse that will."

I thought I knew why the bride was sucking bad beer from a straw held between her teeth. Her groom had been in the kitchen twenty minutes earlier, drunkenly trying to coax a phone number out of my pretty co-worker while his best man made a pass at me and toasted his friend's last-minute play for whatever was available. She was hardly the only doomed bride I saw in those years. But I'd never seen one so beautiful, so stubbornly loyal to her role, or quite so clearly part of a long tradition of brightly polished, iron-willed despair.

What a fool, I thought. *That will never be me.* But she haunted me, so straight and still in her gown. Without my fully realizing it, she became one of the women I fashioned myself against when I had to make one of those endless small feminine choices—stilettos or sandals? lipstick or ChapStick? patchouli oil or perfume?—that add up to a style, to a kind of woman, to a life.

And where did all those choices leave me? It's an important question, maybe *the* question, the one running along underneath this story and a lot of other stories besides.

If the center of the Kingdom of Women is a gleaming white-walled city built by movie executives and ad agencies, where supermodels, screen goddesses, and all the perfect girls we knew in high school fill the streets, I live far outside the city limits, beyond the suburbs, a few counties over, in a country village founded by a lesbian feminist collective in the mid-1970s. (Before that, it was a summer retreat for bohemians, and there's still a strong artsy contingent.) I like it there, away from the glitz and the glare. In our softer, plainer light, it's easier to see how many ways there are to live as a woman, how many forms and shapes there are of beauty, energy, work, and wisdom. There's a lot of fresh air, and I'm surrounded by people quietly and not so quietly staking out new territory on the map, so that there are days, sometimes weeks, at a time when the category *woman*, as an immutable opposite of the category *man*, doesn't mean much, and it's easier to use the word *person*, which is a word I've always liked. It's a place where small details are important—a new pendant, a line of silver buttons, a charmingly crooked tooth, a pair of particularly fine clear eyes.

I didn't always live so far from the center of the kingdom. I started out more or less where my mother lives now, in the neat, well-kept suburbs just outside the city walls. In the Kingdom of Women (and sometimes in real life, too), the suburbs are all about being what my mother once called, with great approbation, *well groomed*. You've *made the most of what you have,* as though you were a country whose raw materials have been properly exploited. You've done a great job of *putting yourself together*, as though you were a chair or a car. It's a learned skill, this self-creation, the territory of endless tips and tricks. Anyone who works hard enough, the theory goes, can be pretty (the corollary being that those who are not pretty do not work hard enough). To be well groomed requires an instinct for limits, boundaries, dividing lines. Money helps. (There's a lot of shopping.) And free time. But for that mythical creature, the truly well-groomed woman, everything is effortless. The endless small adjustments and daily rituals of maintenance are as natural to her, and as expected, as breathing, walking, or using the telephone—say, to make a hair appointment. She notices her own polish as little as a former ballerina notices her perfect posture. Both are the result of years of practice.

I'm being a little mean. There's a hissing, a little meow in my voice, that tells you how much that world frightens me, and how much I admire it. How I have to go on escaping it because it is a part of me. Its rules are a test I will go on failing all my life.

Because I was never a rebel, or at least I never meant to be one. (I may have refused to wear Lauren, but I longed for it all the same.) I wish there were a single story I could tell to explain what happened, but there isn't. It was just a long series of negotiations, a *no-I-won't* here and a *yes-I-will* there. An absurd number of these arguments had something to do with hair—all that cutting, combing, straightening, curling, waxing, shaving, plucking, bleaching, and spraying that was required of me, as though the moment I let my guard down I would become a snarling, thick-pelted animal.

And it's true, I always had a wild streak, a taste for drama. All through my growing-up years, even when I matched my socks to my turtlenecks and blew my thick, curly hair straight and then set it in hot rollers for good measure, I was always a bit too much. It was as though I were wearing a costume I couldn't take off. A loud, curvy, dark-eyed girl in a land of cool, slim-hipped blondes, I spent a lot of time onstage, where I made more sense. There, and elsewhere—the lines between life and stage aren't always clear—I played the roles that were available to me: the tough showgirl, the exotic gypsy, the lusty wench, the Egyptian queen, the madwoman. Even at fifteen, the ingenue was beyond me. By the time I was seventeen I was singing "Big Spender" at the local charity auction, and though I have no memory of doing so, my mother loves to tell the story of how I came down off the stage, microphone in hand, to sit on the seventy-eight-year-old lap of J. R. Simplot, the billionaire potato king. In college, I played prostitutes, unfaithful wives, and, once, a blues singer named Honeypot. It was pure instinct, all of it.

So I went, skating along on this thin ice until the moment in my early twenties when feminism came along and plunged me into the cold, dark waters below. Dripping wet, but wide awake, I looked upon my double life with horror—prim constraint on the one hand, a series of self-betraying stereotypes on the other—and in my usual earnest, censorious way, chucked the lot. It never occurred to me that I might be throwing away some things I wanted to keep.

And that's where I was, more or less, fifteen years later when, having long forgotten most of what I've just told you, I sprayed on a bit of Paloma and went home to lie on the bed and ignore my mother's e-mails about whether the napkins at the wedding reception should be brown or gold.

Perfume for the bride: That's the tagline for the 1950s magazine ad on my wall from the great French house of Caron (for a most un-bridelike perfume, their fiery take on the clove-pepper scent of old-fashioned carnation flowers, Poivre). Perfume ads are still full of brides, and there are many perfumes designed specifically to appeal to brides, with names like Beautiful and Love in White. Many women buy perfume for the first (and only) time for their weddings, hoping for a scent that will capture the day and their groom. They anoint themselves with precious oils like the brides of antiquity, unconsciously linking themselves to a tradition that stretches around the world as well as back through time.

And yet I was so unconscious myself that it was a long time before I could see any connection between my growing obsession with perfume and my upcoming wedding. In fact, I found it difficult to think about both of them at the same time. Perfume was my secret, sensual, private dreamworld. The wedding was public, hard to grasp, and far off in the future. It, too, was a kind of dreamworld, but one already thickly crowded with other people's dreams, rules, and expectations. I could imagine the ceremony—what V. and I might say to each other and to our beloved guests, how we might make that particular kind of magic our own. The rest was a blur.

So it's only now that I can see how my perfume story—or, at least, the magic of that year—began, not with perfume itself, nor with the blogs, but with a knock on the door, a few days after V. and I got engaged.

When I opened the door, the UPS man waved at me from his truck at the end of the walk and drove off. I picked up the small brown box from the doorstep and went into the kitchen to open it. I was expecting some books I'd ordered. But inside, swaddled in bubble wrap, was a shoebox, and inside that, wrapped in newspaper and smelling faintly of dust and old perfume, was a battered blue velvet jewelry case. There was no note. I looked at the package again—no return address either, but the postmark was from Florida. It had to be from my aunt.

My grandmother, the one who had sent me my little vials of Oscar de la Renta, had died the previous June. A month after the funeral, I got a rare phone call from my aunt. She was cleaning out the safe-deposit box: Did I want anything? "Not the diamonds," she clarified. "For those you have to wait until *I* die." I'd laughed, looking down at my rumpled clothes and the jewelry I usually wore—large, inexpensive stones with mystical powers I always seemed to know about, even if I pretended not to believe in them. What would I do with diamonds? Then six silent months had gone by and I'd forgotten all about it. Now, without warning, the package was here.

But then, my grandmother's gifts had always been surprises, unlikely flamingos dropping into my life from another world with an entirely different set of rules and customs. Most came from whatever high-end department store she was working at that year. When I was ten, she sent me a Christian Lacroix nightgown that made my mother gasp a little when I pulled it out of the box. I turned thirteen in the middle of what was, apparently, a brief vogue for knickers (but not in Idaho, never in Idaho). That year's present was a pair in periwinkle-blue velvet trimmed with plaid satin ribbon that tied in a bow, just below the knee. There was a matching jacket, too, with little puffed sleeves, frog closures, and more satin plaid in pleated ruffles at the neck and wrists. Somewhere there is a picture of me wearing this outfit, completed, if I recall correctly, by a creamy satin blouse with a huge floppy bow at the neck and white knee-high stockings. My memory is mercifully blank on the shoes.

My grandmother's gifts were her emissaries, and on the few occasions when my grandparents came to visit us in Boise, she did not disappoint. My whole family went to meet their plane at the gate, as you still could back then. My brother and I craned our necks, trying to be the first to spot them among the arriving passengers, but we could smell my grandmother before we saw her. She was announced by great savory clouds of onion, garlic, herring, pickles, pastrami, and innumerable other fatty, fishy, smoky, salty, vinegar-sharp things. It rolled toward us, this living ghost of a genuine Jewish deli, until its source appeared, tottering toward us on high heels between two enormous shopping bags overflowing with the food of my father's childhood, its smells grown stronger during the long flight, unappreciative or hungry fellow passengers be damned.

My parents joked that my grandmother brought so much food because she was afraid there would be nothing to eat in Boise, a place so foreign to her that it might as well have been another country. Sitting in our homey yellow-and-white kitchen, she seemed just as foreign to me—fancy, dressed up, in a way I'd never quite seen. She had elegant ankles, long legs, slim hips, and broad shoulders above a wide shelf of a chest that must have been spectacular when she was younger. She must have worn flats occasionally, but my memory refuses to produce an image of her in anything but the heels that eventually ruined her feet beyond repair. There were tailored skirts and slacks—she'd probably had most of them forever, but I didn't know that—and lots of black cashmere sweaters, albeit peppered with lint. There were a whole series of little jackets with brooches and, underneath them, silk blouses in cream and all those classic florid patterns—ropes, horses, giant flowers, paisley and such—worn with multiple strands of pearls and chains à la Chanel. By the time I knew her, her hands were ropy and gnarled, but her fingernails were always shiny with red polish, and long enough to clack against the table when she drummed her fingers in impatience. Several times a day, I watched closely as she painted on her matching red lipstick, fascinated by her total disregard for the actual outline of her mouth.

She looked, in other words, exactly like what she was—one of those tough, smart, hair-raisingly opinionated denizens of women's wear who can determine your dress size, income bracket, and worst neurosis from twenty paces. She was a name-dropper and a label snob, and while my sweet grandfather looked on adoringly, she told wonderfully funny, mean stories, punctuated with her own raucous laughter. The best of these were hardly stories at all, just world-weary asides. "Oh, that Ralphie." She'd sigh. "He was such a nice Jewish boy when he started out. Now look at him." "Ralph who, Grandma?" "Ralph Lauren, darling. Lau*ren*." She would snort. "It used to be Lifshitz, you know."

I set the jewelry case down on the counter and began—carefully, and with a certain sense of ceremony—to open it. It didn't budge. I pulled harder at the lid, scrabbling for a good hold on the worn velvet, but the hinges were bent and the misaligned corners were stuck fast. Giving up on dignity, I tried fingernails, then car keys, and finally a butter knife jimmied into the gap at the most crooked corner. Leaning against the counter for leverage, I pried at it with all my strength, and at last the lid flew up with a sudden snap.

Inside was a tangle of rings. I was sitting at the kitchen counter trying on an enormous pinkish-red sparkler when V. came home.

"How do you like it?" I said, waving a bejeweled hand at him.

"It's . . . very big. Is it real?"

"I have no idea." I explained about my aunt and the box.

"Wow, look at this one," he marveled, holding up an equally enormous faceted stone in a smoky brown.

"I know. But then look at all these little skinny ones. They look like something a child could have worn."

"I like this." He held out a long, flat signet ring, the initials picked out in sparkling hematite, the corners filled with triangles of jade-green enamel. "Was it your grandmother's?"

I tried to decipher the elaborate looping script. The first initial was right, but the last one was wrong. Unless—oh, of course.

"The last initial is for her maiden name. It must be from before she was married . . ."

I trailed off, distracted by a bright silver ring I hadn't noticed before, a quarter-inch band with a beautiful scrolling pattern. I picked it up—it was surprisingly heavy in my hand—and looked at it more closely. The pattern was elaborately detailed, and it was carved all the way through the ring, creating an open fretwork set with tiny crystals. The thick top and bottom edges of the ring were carved as well, so that the curving shapes seemed to float, just barely connected.

The night we got engaged, V. had given me a striking amber ring, a long, rough rectangle in a spare, modern setting. I was thrilled, but it seemed made for the middle finger of my right hand—a perfect celebration of our ten years together, but not an engagement ring. I'd been dreaming of a ring with history and meaning. Maybe something we designed ourselves, the way my father had designed my mother's ring. Something forgotten in a box in his parents' attic. An antique.

I slipped the silver circle onto the ring finger of my left hand. It was loose, but it fit.

"What do you think of this one?" I asked, proffering my hand to V.

"I think it looks like you," he said.

He was right. The ring looked natural on my hand, like something I'd buy for myself. "I think I'll wear it as my engagement ring for a while," I said, "you know, while we're still looking for one." I turned my hand back and forth, watching it sparkle in the light.

The next day, I called my aunt to thank her.

"You're welcome," she said. "Wear them in good health. Don't just lock them away in another safe-deposit box, okay?"

"Okay, Aunt Toni. But can you tell me anything about them?"

"What do you want to know?"

"How about this big red one? Where did it come from?"

"Oh, that one. That's a ruby. Supposed to be, anyway. It was mine. I bought it on a trip to Mexico. I got the smoky quartz there, too. When was that? Back in the sixties. Too long ago."

I listened to her taking a drag from her cigarette.

"What about that pretty silver one? You know, with the scrollwork, and the crystals."

"That's not silver!" cried my aunt. "That's platinum. And those are diamonds. It was your grandmother's original wedding band."

"No—really?"

"Yes."

"Oh."

"Yes. Oh."

"Aunt Toni, did my dad tell you V. and I got engaged?"

"No one tells me anything. When?"

"A few days ago. We haven't told very many people yet."

"No kidding. Well, mazel tov. It's about time."

"Thank you. But Aunt Toni, listen, I'm wearing Grandma's wedding band right now, as my engagement ring. I put it on last night."

She was horrified. That was a wedding band. I needed a real engagement ring. She would find me one. And then my aunt, the one who remembered all the longtime and temporary members of our scattered family, the marriages, divorces, grudges, and second cousins three times removed, began to describe my options—rings I could barely imagine from long-gone relatives I had never met.

I listened, saying nothing. I was thinking about the last time I'd seen my grandmother.

She was in a hospice, in a cramped room filled with medical equipment, food trays, and a hospital bed. There was a window that looked out onto a small courtyard, but the shades were drawn against the Florida sun. And there was a phone. It rang and rang, but she refused to answer it.

"They'll only want to come see me," she explained, waving away imagined visitors from her bedside.

She was tired and in pain, and she looked very small under the bedclothes, much smaller than I remembered her. All day long she flickered in and out—barely there at all for a while, then coming back in a brief flare to tease the nurses and give me advice. In one of these moments she asked me if I had a cell phone.

"Call that boyfriend of yours. I want to talk to him."

She'd never met V. in person, but somehow he'd managed to impress her. "What a nice young man," she'd say, when he passed the phone to me. V. is a nice young man—he is invariably respectful, and listens more than he talks—but he also has a deep voice, warm and slow, and he took open delight in my grandmother's outsize personality. I'd long suspected that she enjoyed flirting with him. I glanced at the time. He'd be in the middle of his workday, but—

"Go on," she commanded.

"OK, Grandma, I'll do it right now."

There was no signal in the room. I got the number of her bedside telephone and walked outside to call V. By the time I got back, he'd called and she was on the phone with him, miraculously restored to her old, wisecracking self. When I appeared in the doorway, she promptly ordered me out of the room again.

I went back out into the hall, closing the door gently behind me. I leaned against the wall, breathing in the scent of disinfectant and Florida damp undefeated by air conditioning. I listened to the Haitian nurses gossiping at the end of the hallway and then, when they were silent, the whir of ventilation and, every now and then, from behind the thick door, faintly, the sound of my grandmother's rasping laughter.

"What did she say to you?" I asked V. that night.

"Oh, I—it was sweet."

"But what did she say?"

"Well. She said I should be good to you."

"Really?"

"That's what she said."

"Was that all?"

"She said she wanted to make sure my intentions were honorable."

"After all these years?"

"She was serious. I said I loved you. She said I should take care of you and cherish you."

We were silent.

"She laughed," I said, when I could speak again.

"Mmm. Yes. There might have been a few other things."

"Like what?"

"Never mind."

I blinked my way back into the present. On the phone, my aunt was describing another ring, a cluster of pearls that my great-grandmother had once owned. I looked down again at my grandmother's wedding band. I thought I knew now what she had said to V. that day. The bright metal and the tiny diamonds—diamonds!—glimmered next to the dark-red garnet I'd worn on my middle finger since my early twenties, a gift from my other, quieter grandmother.

"Aunt Toni," I interrupted, as politely as I could, "I think I should wear Grandma's ring."

It would have been enough—more than enough—but that wasn't the end of the story. A few months later, the morning after my last day of work at the nonprofit, there was a second knock on the door, followed by a loud thunk. The box was much bigger this time, and so heavy that when I bent to drag it inside, I only made it as far as the front hallway before I sat down on the floor to open it.

I folded back the top flaps and pulled out the piece of paper sitting on top, thinking it was a note from my aunt. A long moment went by before I realized that I was holding my grandfather's death certificate. Below it was a yellowed Passover Haggadah dated 1949. Then a white lace apron, then a baby's blanket, covered in tiny yellow flowers. And underneath the blanket were boxes and boxes and boxes, and inside them were other boxes—jewelry cases for necklaces and rings, zippered travel cases in gold lamé and red crocodile, the odd curio still in its original package. I unfolded and refolded the blanket and the apron, my throat tight. I come from a forward-looking family, the children and grandchildren of immigrants, people who moved from world to world, reinventing themselves along the way. We are rich in many things, but heirlooms are not one of them. I had before me more tangible family history than I had ever seen in one place.

I began to pull things out, digging down through the decades of my grandmother's life. There were long beaded necklaces from the sixties and seventies and huge, bright clip-on earrings from Miami circa 1993, big brooches from the fifties and a fragile antique circle pin set with tiny seed pearls, a few missing. Each time I took a box out, the ones left inside seemed to multiply. After an hour I began packing it back up instead.

The first box, arriving so soon after our engagement, had felt like a blessing. The second felt like an assignment. I was sure it needed something from me and I was prepared to do whatever work was necessary. Every few days, I took things out and looked at them and then put them away again. Like the good scholar I still was, I tried to catalog them, but I was never quite able to find a system that worked. I had to know more about our family, I thought, and I sent my aunt an e-mail with questions. I researched the history of department stores in the 1960s and 1970s. I brought in experts. My friend Lois, a design professor, cooed over the chunky pop-art rings that spelled LOVE. An antique collector I befriended at my café told me the brooches were collectible. The owner of an old-fashioned jewelry store downtown with display windows full of diamonds and dusty china dogs peered through his loupe and said *yes* and *no*—mostly no—to the question "Is this real?" I took the box out. I put the box away. A little terrified by my new freedom—I should be *doing* something, shouldn't I?—I very nearly made the box my new job.

When I finally figured out what the box wanted from me, it was so simple and so obvious it made me blush: It wasn't an assignment; it was a gift. I didn't need to study my grandmother's jewelry—I needed to wear it.

I began picking out one piece every day, sometimes more than one. I started with the easy ones, things that looked like they already belonged to me—a strand of tiger's eye beads, a square silver ring. Then I got a little bolder, pinning the brooches that reminded me of my grandmother's jackets to my own slouchy cardigans, wearing the LOVE ring instead of my usual large, simple stones. Soon enough, I had a small collection of favorites.

I grew especially fond of a pair of oversize costume pearl earrings. They were unlike anything I had ever imagined myself wearing, but when I put them on, they glowed against my tan skin and dark hair and gave me cheekbones I'd never had before. They turned my habitual French twist into something that looked deliberate, chosen. They made me reach for deep V necklines that exposed my collarbones, and on those days I found myself standing up a little straighter, with my chin lifted, to make my neck as long as possible. They made me feel like someone slightly different from myself. Not someone like my grandmother, exactly, but someone a little closer to the glamorous bygone world of gloves and hats—and perfume—that she came from. I liked feeling that way. I was surprised how much I liked it.

5: THE **JAR** EXPERIENCE

My mother was being very restrained on the subject of the Dress. I could tell it was difficult for her. I'd like to say I tried to make it easier.

"So," she was saying, very casually, at the end of a phone conversation about something else entirely, "have you thought about what you're going to wear?"

"Yes," I said.

Then I closed my mouth and let the silence go on for as long as it liked, which was, it turned out, a long time. Long enough, finally, to make us both giggle. Encouraged, she tried again, lowering the stakes.

"You don't have to know what kind of dress it is. But it would really help me to know what sort of color you're thinking about."

"I don't know," I said. "I don't even know if it's going to be a dress."

"What do you mean?"

"I want to be able to wear it more than once, and I don't really wear dresses. I was thinking maybe I would just wear a suit."

"A suit. No. Really? What kind of suit?"

"I don't know. Something I could wear to a job interview."

I was improvising—an interview for what job, exactly?—but it wasn't a bad idea. I tried to picture myself standing in front of my friends and family in a suit, right next to V., also in a suit. I was having a little trouble. So was my mother.

"What color would this suit be?"

"I don't know. Black?"

"Black! Come on. Be serious."

I took a deep breath and tried to comply.

"Mom, I don't know what I'm wearing. But I'll let you know when I do, okay?"

"All right, all right. It's up to you."

"It really is."

"I know. I was just asking."

"I know."

She wasn't the only one. My friends wanted to know. My hairdresser wanted to know. Perfect strangers who knew nothing about me besides the fact that I was planning a wedding wanted to know. They told me fond, elaborate stories about the dresses they had worn, or hoped to wear, or dresses that other people they knew had worn. (It was always a dress. It had to be a dress.) Some of them, usually the strangers, gave me advice on what I should wear, including—and here there would be a pause while the speaker cast a significant eye over the generous expanse of my hips and bustline—tips on the importance of proper foundation garments.

There was something ceremonial about these exchanges. I could feel the members of a tribe surrounding me, drawing me into the circle. I was fair game—a group project. It was making me very worried.

Because I felt sure I was going to disappoint them—my mother, my friends, the lady at Walgreens who had recommended a long-line bra (whatever that was), and maybe you, too. I was a fraud. A spy in the House of Brides. I hadn't planned on answering all these questions. I had planned—if denial can be a plan—to ignore the whole thing until the last possible moment. I knew the questions were just an opening gambit, a prelude to the long and satisfying conversation that was supposed to follow. And it wasn't that I didn't want to talk, exactly. It was just that I couldn't be the thing they were inviting me to be: a girl, dreaming of a dress.

When I close my eyes and think of girls dreaming of dresses, I see my mother—young, and very beautiful, with her long black hair hanging down her back, going down the stairs at Filene's to that first, original discount basement. She's taking a dress from the rack where she found it and hiding it among the wrong sizes and styles on another rack, halfway across the room. Store policy is to lower the price every week a garment remains unsold. She'll come back for weeks to tend to her bargain, checking to see if it's still there, moving it again, until the lucky day when she can afford the number on the ticket.

That was one way to get your dream. Then there were the days when everything was discounted at once and the women waited for the doors to open and then rushed inside in a frenzied mob. *You had to run like this,* my mother shows me, elbows jabbing out to either side. They tore through piles of clothes on the tables, stripping down to their underwear right out in the middle of the mayhem, for speed's sake, and because there were no dressing rooms, and because standing half naked in a tornado of flying dresses was just part of the whole humiliating, exhilarating thing.

For years, listening to these stories, I was so dazzled by my mother's wily persistence and ingenuity that I hardly noticed her pride and her poverty. I tried, and failed, to imagine myself in the scene. I felt sure that I was missing some crucial genetic material.

It's not that she didn't try to teach me. I spent my adolescence trailing my mother in and out of discount-store dressing rooms. She showed me how to identify my flaws and features, and then dress to flatter them. She demonstrated how to pick out the bargain from a rack of clothes by looking at labels and seams and linings. She coached me in the art of pulling together an outfit, or a whole closetful of them, that could be taken apart and put back together in a dozen different ways appropriate to an equal number of occasions—a marvel of art and economy.

But I was, for various reasons, a sulky, poorly motivated student. It was the mid-eighties, not anyone's best fashion moment, really. I was short, with an hourglass figure that leaned toward pear, a shape wholly at odds with the clothes I wanted to wear. The few trendy things I did end up with, carefully chosen according to my mother's rules, assured that I would stay in the art-room basement. (To this day I harbor a deep resentment against shoulder pads and wide belts.) But the most important reason for my resistance was the gap between what I could imagine and who I was. I wanted to listen, I wanted to get it right—I really did. But every time I looked in a mirror, it told me I was hopelessly wrong.

Over the years, I had tried various ways to make my peace with the rules of getting dressed—and with that mirror. Things got better, as they usually do, but I'd never completely gotten the hang of it. My long, unhappy years in grad school had completed my transformation from hourglass to pear (really, something closer to a plump butternut squash). I shopped for clothes no more than once a year, a trip that I conducted like a commando raid: My goal was to get in and out alive.

On one of those rare occasions, I was standing in front of the shared mirror outside a row of dressing rooms when I saw a dark-haired woman walk toward me in what she hoped—she wasn't sure yet—was a beautiful red dress, something that might really work. Her face was open, vulnerable, lips parted, eyes shining but unseeing. She almost walked into me, so focused was she on the delicate task of keeping her balance in front of that mirror. I watched her moving back and forth between pleasure and critique, hope and fear—*yes, that looks all right from the front—better than all right—but how is the back, and my hips, oh God, forget about it, and what about when I bend forward like this—* adjusting and smoothing, twirling just a little, back and forth, looking and looking, comparing what she saw with the images of other women, and other versions of herself, lurking just behind her eyes—bargaining, the way women do, with the noise in their heads.

By the time everyone was asking me what I was going to wear for my wedding, I had lost the will, and then the ability, to do that kind of bargaining. When it came to shopping for something that required as much hope and longing as a beautiful dress, I was like a child raised by wolves—or some other, more nervous animal. Rabbits, maybe.

Nevertheless, five minutes after I'd gotten off the phone with my mother, I was clicking through pictures of white gowns on my computer. After all, I'd reflected, sitting down to my computer to work after I'd said good-bye, I had to have *something* to wear. Probably not a suit. It wouldn't hurt to just look at a few Web sites, I told myself. It's not like the salesladies were going to come out of my computer and force me to try things on.

I did a search for bridal shops in Austin and began clicking through their photo galleries. There they were, the Creatures from Planet Bride: slender, laughing girls in yards of satin and lace, most of them blond and blue-eyed, all of them well under twenty-five, so fresh and new it was impossible to avoid the word *dewy.* Ignoring the slight buzzing ache behind my eyes, I tried to look past the girls to the dresses. Failing, I ignored the pictures and read the descriptions. They were full of words that smacked of architecture and royalty—*a-line, empire waist, princess seam.* I tried to understand how many shades of white there were in the world. *Ivory, bone,* and *chalk. Almond, ecru,* and *cream. Cloud. Snow. Antique.* And something called *purity.*

Then my mind went entirely blank and I decided to check my e-mail instead.

There, under the subject line "Wedding," was an invitation to a wedding. Our friends David and Anna, who taught at the local university, were getting married at City Hall in New York, the first week of February. Anna had taken a job at Parsons, and they were sneaking in the wedding just before the start of the spring semester, the same weekend that Anna had a gallery opening. It was going to be a small gathering, just relatives and close friends—would we come?

I called Anna immediately. "So," I said, after hellos and congratulations, "what are you going to wear?"

"Well," she confided, "my dream would be to wear felt."

Anna was a professor of interior design. Felt was one of her scholarly interests. (To tease her, V. had once proposed an academic panel: "Felt Felt: Material Emotions." She laughed, then paused and said, "You know, that's not so bad.") I tried to push away the visions of grade-school craft projects that filled my head. Circles and triangles and squares of dark green and bright red and jack-o'-lantern orange cut with dull scissors. Bags full of soft, tantalizing scraps.

"What color?" I asked.

"Dark gray."

"Gray?"

"Yes, you know, that gray industrial felt. I think it's so beautiful."

I recalled the last time I'd had a flat tire. When I lifted up the plastic lining in the trunk to dig out the spare, beneath was dark-gray felt, flecked with cottony bits of white, blue, and pink—soft, but thick enough to stand up on its own.

"Like the felt in the trunk of my car?" I asked, describing it for her.

"Yes, exactly."

"Would it be a jacket?"

"Oh, no. I was thinking of a jumper. That way I could put a shirt under it and wear it to teach in after the wedding."

Anna is a small, pale person, with a generous, worried mouth, slightly snub nose, and large hazel-gray eyes. Most of the time, she wears her straight, light-brown bob pulled back at the nape of her neck. I pictured her in a sleeveless, round-necked triangle of gray felt with patch pockets on the front, holding a bouquet of flowers. She would look like a child's drawing of a bride.

"I think that would be great," I said.

And I meant it. I was, in fact, jealous. Anna seemed to have stepped past all the obstacles I was facing as though they weren't even there. She didn't sound like a Creature. She just sounded happy. Why wasn't I getting married in a felt dress? (Never mind how it would look on me.) Why wasn't I flying to New York to get married at City Hall like something out of one of those classic Hollywood wartime films? (I'd always *loved* those films!) Well, why not? (It wasn't too late!)

I said as much to V. that night when I was lying in bed, not sleeping.

"Sweetie, we talked about this," he said gently. "I could see doing something like that if it was just about us. But that's not what we talked about, remember?" He grinned at me in the dark. "We're not classic Hollywood. We're Bollywood."

He was right. We'd been over it all before, not just the kind of wedding we wanted but why we wanted one at all. We'd spent many of our years together building a life that we thought was different from the lives our families led—different, maybe, from the life they had expected us to lead. We'd felt separate, independent. But now that we were older and more settled, we saw that our little circle of two was a fiction. Every person in the far-flung network of our friends and relatives—V.'s innumerable aunts and uncles and cousins, the Mexico relatives, the loving crowd of my parents' friends in Boise, my father's college roommate from Philadelphia, the friends who had moved all over the country and the friends still in Texas, the people we talked to every week and those we barely spoke to once a year—had helped to make us the people we'd become. We wanted the wedding to be a moment when we could gather everyone, turn to them and say thank you.

So we set out to plan a celebration that would be more about them than it was about us, and we made our peace ahead of time with the rich and happy chaos that would ensue when we brought so many dramatically different people together. We thought of our future wedding as a cross between an amusement-park ride and a Bollywood musical—a huge, noisy, brightly colored production with bells, whistles, and flashing lights, mountains of food and flowers, and a cast of thousands, all of which, once set in motion, could not be stopped.

It was V. who had come up with the idea. "I can hear the sitars tuning up," he'd crowed after we made those first phone calls to our parents to tell them about our engagement. "The very first dancing girl is coming onto the screen. Hang on, sweetie! There's no turning back now!" Like most of his dead-on jokes it seemed to come out of nowhere—when we first got together, I'd nearly despaired of V.'s long silences. But I soon learned to listen when he did talk—though occasionally he had to remind me, as he was reminding me now, what he had said.

"I remember." I sighed. "The first dancing girl."

"Good. Now, let's go to sleep. If you still want to wear felt in the morning, we can talk about it then."

I sighed again, snuggled in, and closed my eyes. But a moment later

I opened them again. *We were going to New York!* Somehow, distracted by dresses, it hadn't dawned on me that I'd be in the city for the first time since I'd fallen for perfume. I had research to do.

There are only a few truly great perfume cities. Some say only two—but why be so narrow about it? London and Florence have their own traditions. I know just enough about the deep history of perfume in India and the Middle East to keep my mouth firmly closed until I know more. Surely there are cities and traditions I have yet to discover. But if we are speaking of the business of perfume, of shopping, and of the West, then we are speaking of New York and Paris. I am an American, and a little afraid of the French, so my perfume city is New York. I love the city as much as I love its perfume. Some days—many days—I love it much more.

It was not always so. I've always rooted for the underdog. For years I railed against New York, that bully, a city so arrogant and so greedy for the spotlight that it had fooled the entire world into believing it was the center of everything. It seemed so sure it had my attention, I felt determined to ignore it. That's what I said, anyway, talking and talking about it to anyone who would listen, but especially to the many displaced New Yorkers who happened to be my friends.

I came by my ambivalence honestly. My parents had grown up on the East Coast, and their running commentary on the relative merits of East and West was the background music of my childhood. Out West, where we lived, was clean, safe, beautiful, friendly, and a great place to raise children, but a little slow on the uptake when it came to irony, local news, decent Chinese and Italian, and—well, it was just a little slow. Back East, which I imagined as a web of lesser cities radiating outward from New York, was a dirty, noisy, dangerous place full of status-seeking, money-grubbing snobs who talked too fast and sent their children away to boarding schools at just the age when kids needed their parents the most. But it was also, mysteriously, superior in almost every way. When they could, my parents sent my brother and me away to bigger cities. *We just want them to get a taste of the real world,* they explained, as though Boise were only a bright and pleasant dream.

When I began visiting New York—to see a friend or go to a conference, or on some other handy excuse—I made lists of the places I wanted to go and mapped them out ahead of time. I filled my suitcase with my darkest clothes, shoes I never wore anywhere else and first-aid supplies. I checked the forecast once, twice, three times, trusting neither nature nor myself to behave predictably. I told my friends, not really joking, that I was afraid the city would swallow me up—that I would cross the wrong street or turn a bad corner, the earth would open beneath my feet, and I would never be heard from again. Obviously, the subway, which required a willingness to be swallowed up on the dubious theory that one would be disgorged at a chosen location, was out of the question. So I walked everywhere, in all kinds of weather, in my terrible shoes, clutching my map (because my mother had warned me against walking into the wrong neighborhood) but never looking at it (because my father had told me that looking at a map on the street would mark me as easy prey). When I could walk no more, I took cabs. I was always either exhausted or broke or both. I never went out after dark alone.

At the time, I thought I was afraid for life and limb. But looking back, I can see it was something else, something not unlike what I felt when I first fell for V.—the heart-pounding terror that signals the beginning of a great romance. All my arguing was for naught. The city had already swallowed me, probably before I ever set foot on the island of Manhattan. But though I kept finding reasons to return, I hadn't been able to see it, hadn't even allowed for the possibility. When I looked at a map of the city, I saw something like one of the popularity charts I'd made in junior high, with famous neighborhoods where the various cliques should be, and the grid of the streets as a series of velvet ropes, locked doors, and concealed entrances.

The list of perfumes I wanted to smell when we got to New York had begun as a pleasant way to procrastinate, but by the time February rolled around, it was a masterpiece of nerdy cross-indexing that included the names and addresses of the stores where I could find the perfumes, complete with opening and closing hours and a possible route from place to place. But looking at that route, I could see it was going to take me away from the narrow, crooked streets where I'd achieved a modicum of ease and bring me up to the wide avenues full of thin, exquisitely groomed women clicking by on high heels that cost more than my monthly rent, and straight on through the doors of the fine, fancy department stores that were their natural environment. In short, deep into enemy territory.

I suppose I could have stayed downtown. There were other places to visit. Aedes de Venustas, where I'd been ordering many of my samples, was right in the heart of Greenwich Village. But there were perfumes—indeed, whole houses—on my list that were available nowhere else in the city: Guerlain, the crowning glory of French perfumes past, beside which every other house else looks like an arriviste. Frederic Malle, herald of the future, the first modern house to turn traditionally anonymous perfumers into art stars by providing them with money and artistic freedom and then featuring them alongside the perfumes they had created. The über-exclusive JAR Perfumes, which didn't advertise, didn't offer samples, didn't even list the names of the perfumes on its Web site, and flatly refused to describe what its perfumes smelled like, lest mere words interfere with the direct experience of the scents. All of their boutiques were tucked inside the largest, most luxe department stores.

I looked at my list and tried to imagine the perfumes in the places where they were kept. I had—JAR's efforts notwithstanding—read all about them, so I wasn't thinking of cold, inanimate objects, a series of glass bottles lined up on a counter somewhere. I hardly knew what those bottles looked like. I was thinking, instead, of their lively imagined presence in the air and on the skin—fruits and flowers, woods and spices, tapestries of memory and color. I pictured them as magical, shimmering beings. Not quite genies in their lamps. More like old-fashioned stars of the silver screen—regal, temperamental, surrounded by a phalanx of handlers and guardians. I tried to imagine the guardians, too, the men and women who worked the floors, counters, and customers of those fancy stores. I saw them as imperious—intimidating to the point of rudeness, but tough, savvy, knowing the score. And then, to my surprise, I saw my grandmother.

I saw her not as I had known her, sitting at our kitchen table, with her raucous laugh and her red nails, but as I had never known her—ten or maybe twenty years younger, crossing the crowded floor at a good clip in her ever-present heels to meet a favored customer, with a quick wink for the manager along the way. I saw her in front of a dressing-room mirror, giving some poor woman who had asked for her opinion the once-over. And before she disappeared, I saw her waiting, just standing behind a counter, her eyes scanning the room.

I tugged at one of her heavy pearl earrings—I was still wearing them almost every day—and looked at my list again. I imagined myself walking down the avenue and through those doors.

When we left for New York, Austin was on the brink of spring, the wildflowers just beginning to emerge, but we arrived to find the city deep in the grip of February chill. The afternoon of the wedding, V. and I peered out the cab window on our way to City Hall at a steady stream of wedding-bound New Yorkers with odd bits of finery peeking out from their winter armor—a lacy sleeve, a white satin heel, a red carnation on a black woolen lapel.

We arrived to find Anna and David and the rest of the wedding party in a long, festive line. Ahead of us were three brides in full glittering regalia, with three skinny, woeful grooms and a Russian couple with shaved heads, horn-rimmed glasses, and matching fur coats. Haughty, beautiful, and bald, they held hands and stared straight ahead, saying very little. Behind us was a large Korean party, already toasting and teasing the shy couple in the center of their circle. We waited peaceably together for our numbers to come up, momentarily part of the same party. When the time came, we crowded into a tiny meeting room where a bossy, grandmotherly judge stood on a raised platform and led David and Anna through the short ceremony. Afterward, we cheered and took pictures of the two of them, standing underneath the government sign in the hallway that read WEDDING CHAPEL 2.112. David with his shaggy ponytail and rumpled shirt, Anna in a short gray shift she'd ordered through the mail, the lines where she'd unfolded it from the package still faintly visible, both of them shining with happiness.

Anna had been too busy preparing for her gallery opening to find the felt she'd been dreaming of, and someone to sew it. It didn't seem to matter, just as the fluorescent lighting in the meeting room and the cold gray skies outside didn't matter. It was all, I thought vaguely, taking V's hand as we walked out to the street with some Canadian cousins, part of the ceremony. The people in line, and the bossy judge. The city itself.

"It was perfect for them," I said to V.

"Yes," he agreed, giving me a little squeeze. "For them."

The Canadians hailed a cab to take us to the restaurant where we were all meeting for dinner. "Ready?" V. asked me.

"Ready," I said.

The next day, after a crowded lox-and-bagels brunch in Anna's sunny one-bedroom apartment, V. went off to see a friend, and I was, at last, on my own for the rest of the afternoon. I would meet back up with everyone at the gallery downtown for Anna's opening.

I looked at the map, at my list, thought about the time, took a deep breath, and decided to begin with Bergdorf's. To get there, I took the subway. I'd been riding it all weekend, and all weekend I had been quietly thrilled. After years of habitual fear and avoidance, suddenly it was easy—laughably, childishly easy—to find the friendly green lampposts marking the entrance, go down the steps, and come back up a short while later into an entirely different world. I'd mastered only the two simplest trains, but it felt like a magic trick all the same, one that shrank Manhattan to the size of a toy in the palm of my hand. I arrived at the department store full of courage, good cheer, and a sense of possibility in spite of a long crosstown walk against a bitter wind.

Before I went in, I paused a moment in front of the famous display windows. I had to admit that they were worth looking at, even in the cold. Wrapped around two sides of the building were a series of baroque dioramas so layered with luxury goods, eccentric objects, and intricate, feathery, glittering bits of stagecraft that the couture-clad mannequins were just one decorative element among a hundred others. They had been created with such obvious love and care that they seemed less like advertisements than gifts, *un petit cadeau* from *la grande dame* of department stores to the streets of New York. Still, the windows did their work. Some of the stories they told were witty, others swooningly romantic, but all of them suggested that heaps and heaps of the world's rare things were within—empires' worth of plundered riches, a pile so high that no one person could ever own it all. You, too, could have a piece—why not, when there was so much? All you had to do was brave the guardians at the gate. And pay for it, of course. There was always that.

I touched my grandmother's earrings once, for luck, and went in the door. A little dazzled by the sudden warmth and riot of color, I made my way through the purses and silk scarves and around the glass cases of gleaming jewels to the escalator, which I rode slowly, majestically, down to the basement, where the perfumes are kept.

It's a big basement—big enough to have spa rooms and a café. The prime acreage in the center of the room is given over to brightly lit makeup counters. The perfume boutiques live in a series of nooks around the perimeter. There are a lot of nooks. I was creeping along the edge of the room, trying to get my bearings, when a green-eyed beauty gave me a smile so lovely I couldn't help but return it.

"Is Madame familiar with the Clive Christian line?" she asked, vowels twisting to accommodate an earlier life spent somewhere in Eastern Europe.

Her thick, dark hair was smoothed back into a chignon, the slim, elegant length of her clothed in expertly tailored black, from the sharp collar of her silk shirt right down to the tips of her rather high heels. I stood up a little straighter and tucked an errant curl behind my ear. Yes, I said, I knew of the line. Their perfume, No. 1, had a diamond-encrusted bottle that lent credence to their claim that it was the most expensive in the world.

"Perhaps Madame would like to try our newest perfume, X?"

I hesitated—there were too many things to try, and I only had an afternoon. I demurred and asked where I might find the JAR boutique.

"Ah, JAR." She sighed. "Yes, of course. I like these perfumes very much. Let me show you."

Taking me gently by the arm, she led me into a tiny alcove off the main floor and delivered me to an immaculate, silver-haired man with a broad chest, large, square hands, and the bearing of a career diplomat.

"This is Robert," she said, gesturing toward the diplomat. He shook my hand solemnly. "Robert, this young lady would like to have the JAR experience."

She was at least ten years my junior, but I didn't protest. Instead I stepped forward, feeling every inch the young lady—wide-eyed and ready to be taught. At Robert's request, I sat down on a soft, low chair in front of a small, black-lacquered table that held a collection of old-fashioned bell jars. Everything was swathed in shadow: the chair a maroon velvet, the carpet dark lilac gray, the walls covered in deep mauve. A mural of storm clouds hovered above us on the ceiling, a single bolt of lightning streaking across their moody grays. Two small spotlights punctuated the sepulchral gloom, glinting off the glass domes on the table and the silver in Robert's hair.

Leaning forward slightly, Robert began to talk. First he told the story of the room and the mural and how many times JAR—who had flown in himself from Paris to oversee the work—had it repainted to meet his strict standards. That done, Robert reached beneath the table and pulled out a large leather binder. I squirmed and snuck a look at the unlabeled bell jars. If the blogs were to be trusted, each of them held a square of cotton soaked in perfume. Robert ignored my glance and continued telling me, in the same unhurried, respectful tones, the story of Joel Arthur Rosenthal, from the Bronx, and how he found his true métier in Paris as a jeweler for the very discriminating (and very rich) and became the capital-letters-no-periods figure he is today.

Then, turning the binder around to face me, he began to page slowly through a series of glossy color photos of JAR jewelry. Dazzling pavé surfaces floated up to me under the bright spotlight. Thousands upon thousands of tiny diamonds, emeralds, rubies, amethysts, citrines, and sapphires set in tiny hand-drilled holes made swirling patterns, unearthly flowers, shimmering butterflies and insects. There were lilac blossoms, made to scale from clusters of gems on slender wires of precious metal, rings carved from a single precious stone, necklaces whose metal settings, made to rest against the wearer's neck, had been as intricately and obsessively worked as the jewels that met the viewer's eye. Robert was dropping the names of movie stars and the wives of politicians and billionaires, and I was thinking about compulsion, perfectionism, and patronage—czars and pharaohs, Napoleon and the Medicis. And occasionally, it must be admitted, of Las Vegas: Pavé is not a technique that lends itself to sleek, modernist restraint. I recalled a story I had read about one of the only exhibitions ever mounted of JAR's jewelry. Frustrated with the lighting, he had supplied visitors with flashlights and sent them into a darkened room to find and illuminate the vitrines themselves. I was beginning to understand his obsession with context.

At last we arrived at the moment when JAR decided to create his own perfumes—perfumes worthy of the name JAR. Robert paused, leaned back in his chair, and moved the bell jars to the center of the table. We regarded each other.

"Are you ready to experience the perfumes now?" he asked. For a moment I thought I saw a glint of irony in his eyes, though it may have been a trick of the spotlight. Resisting the impulse to wink, I inclined my head gravely.

One by one, he slid the jars in front of me, whisked off the glass, and tipped the base forward for me to sniff at the accumulated vapors as they escaped into the air. They went by like a series of fever dreams: a cloud of fiery clove-and-cinnamon-edged carnations thick and lush enough to drown in. Dirty hay and ripe animal—the filthiest, sexiest, most expensive barnyard in the world. An acre of gardenias blooming furiously in moist dirt and humid air. Carnations again, but lighter, touched with a sparkling chill and trailing other flowers and something like incense behind them. Berries and wine at the end of a perfect sunny afternoon. Something dark and sharp, smelling of dust, roots, caves, and cellars. And then something—

"Could I smell that one again, please?"

Obligingly, Robert tipped the jar toward me a second time.

And there it was again. The smell of the air just after a summer thunderstorm—an astonishing scent of trampled grass, broken branches, bruised flowers, and electricity. I closed my eyes and inhaled a third time, grateful for the dim quiet of the little alcove.

With a start, I remembered that Robert was holding the jar for me. I opened my eyes and leaned back. We looked at each other again. This time, fortified by the perfume, I grinned, and was rewarded with a faint smile, the gentle irony on clear display now.

"Would you like to try one of them on your skin?" he asked.

Of course I did. I wanted to try all of them. But I knew my greed would only make it impossible to smell any of them properly.

"May I wait a moment and then smell them again to choose one?"

"Of course."

We waited. Feeling that some kind of conversation was required, I leaned forward and confessed that I had come all the way from Texas to smell the perfumes. Then, still giddy from so much beauty, I told him about my list, and about how much I had read and thought about the perfumes I was there to smell.

"They're like celebrities to me," I said. "I can't believe I actually get to see and meet them in person."

His smile widened, "Oh, yes, I know what you're talking about. I'm from Oklahoma. I remember feeling that way about a lot of things in the city." He paused and sighed, his mouth twisting in his wide, handsome face. "Some of them lived up to my expectations. Some did not."

We had a moment of silence, thinking about cities and dreams.

"Again?"

"Yes, please."

And we went through them all again, though I already knew which one I would choose. I told Robert, and with great ceremony he anointed the back of my hand. We rose, I thanked him, and without a trace of self-consciousness we bowed slightly to each other, two courtiers taking their leave. Neither of us said a word about money.

I floated back out to the main floor, sniffing at the summer storm unfolding on the back of my hand, blinking a little at the bright lights, and nearly walked straight into the Clive Christian assistant.

"Hello, Madame. Did you enjoy your JAR experience?"

"Yes, thank you. I enjoyed it very much."

"Madame?"

"Yes?"

"I just wanted to say. Your scarf. I have never seen anything like it. It is so nice to see something fresh. Do you mind my asking—where did you find it?"

Fresh? My scarf? I thought of the couture-filled windows upstairs and put a hand up to touch the large, simple felt flowers in rusts, maroons, and browns. They were held together, a little precariously, by a single strip of felt running behind them. They had been made by hand from recycled sweaters by a woman I knew in Austin. I'd bought them at the elementary-school Christmas bazaar two blocks from my house.

"Thank you. I bought it at home in Austin. I'll pass on your compliment to the artist."

"Oh, I see." She bowed her perfect, sleek head, then flashed another brilliant smile.

"Well. Please enjoy your day."

Puzzled but gratified, I continued on out to the floor. As I made my way around the room, I was surprised and thrilled to find half of the perfumes on my list, a city's worth of boutiques shrunk to a single room. It was dizzying, and I walked and stopped almost at random. At L'Artisan, I sniffed at a perfume that smelled of saffron, roses, and sandalwood and talked pleasantly about transparency with a tall blonde. At Le Labo, I let a bespectacled assistant in an official-looking white coat ply me with nonsense about how the perfumes must be mixed on the spot to ensure they are fresh. At Jo Malone, the perfumes, so properly, Englishly named after legible, recognizable things—nutmeg, orange blossom, cedar, lime—called out to be layered over one another, and the enthusiastic, very un-English young sales assistant gave me sample after sample to try on later because, I kept explaining, I didn't want to interfere with the JAR experience still at work on my skin. And each of them said, as I was arriving or about to leave, *What a wonderful scarf.* The Jo Malone assistant asked if she could touch it. I let her try it on.

Maybe there had been some kind of training session recently. *Find something unusual about the customer and compliment her on it. Accessories are good for this.* If so, it was a good tip. Between the perfume and the compliments, I was feeling witty, a bit magical, even a little bit beautiful. I felt I could talk to anyone about anything. It was time to tackle Guerlain.

I approached their brightly lit corner boutique with a nervous reverence. One side was open to the floor. Two of the remaining three walls were lined with the modern releases and limited editions, the make-up line relegated to a single counter. In the center of the small room was a round table where the classics were displayed on graduated steps, a shrine to the great days of perfumery. Standing between me and that table, arms folded, was a small, thoroughly French woman who looked as if she knew everything I knew about Guerlain, and quite a bit more.

"May I help you?" she asked without smiling.

Completely forgetting what I had come for, I stammered the names of two classics and watched as she sprayed two smelling strips for me, her movements quick and efficient. I sniffed eagerly at the paper, but what greeted my nose was completely illegible. I put the strips down and waited a moment before trying again. I wanted to ask for L'Heure Bleue, whose beautiful name I loved, but as I looked at the assistant's face, my mouth refused to shape the difficult French vowels. I tried the strips again, and was defeated again. They needed time, and skin, but I didn't know that yet. A corner of the assistant's mouth twitched briefly, and she raised an eyebrow.

"Perhaps one of our more recent releases?"

And then I remembered. "Yes, please. If I could—I would like to smell Plus Que Jamais."

Her face went blank. "You mean, Plus Que Jamais?" she said, correcting my accent. I breathed a sigh of relief that I had not attempted L'Heure Bleue.

"Yes, please."

"But this is not available yet. How did you know it?" she demanded.

"Oh, I'm sorry, I didn't know it wasn't out. I read about it. It sounds lovely."

Both Marina and Victoria had given it glowing reviews. It was a farewell gift, as another blogger put it, from master perfumer Jean-Paul Guerlain, one of the perfumes launched in the brief moment before he retired but after the family company had been acquired by the luxury conglomerate LVMH and was flush with money.

"It is lovely," she said simply.

She stood still for a moment, then, without another word, turned and walked to the back of the boutique, where she knelt, opened a hidden cupboard, and retrieved a small tester in plain glass with a white label. Spraying a test strip, she handed it to me, pausing almost imperceptibly to sniff at it herself first.

The prickle of aldehydes reached me first—not the sharp attack I got from Chanel No. 5, just champagne bubbles rising up from the glass to tickle my nose. Beyond them hovered something like toffee and pearls and raw silk, at once rich and light, with a pleasing roughness to the texture.

"I think—I need—I'm going to—" I was stammering again, but for different reasons. "I want to let this unfold for a while," I managed. "I'm going to go walk around."

And I turned and left her standing there with the tester in her hand. I got halfway across the room when a honey note billowed forward, and I had to stop moving and close my eyes. "Oh, my." I sighed as the golden sweetness unfurled around me, still light and effortless, but a tangible presence now, wrapping me in a gentle glamour. When I opened my eyes, the Guerlain assistant was standing in front of me.

"If you feel that way," she said, "you must have it."

It was far too expensive for an impulse purchase—too expensive, really, to imagine owning a whole bottle. I already knew the most I could manage to do was buy a decant from someone.

"But I can't—I mean—I haven't even tried it on my skin. I would want to wear it for at least a few days first," I said. "And I'm already wearing something from JAR," I added lamely, waving my right hand.

"I see," she said, with a Gallic shrug. But she didn't sound angry.

Instead, there was a grudging respect in her face. "Here is my information," she continued, presenting me with a business card. "If you would like to preorder, please call."

She began to leave, then turned back.

"Madame?"

"Yes?"

Another shrug.

"Your scarf. It is very nice."

Out in the street, giddy with triumph and perfume, I breathed in the fresh, frigid air and walked quickly in no particular direction, grinning to myself. Any sane person would have stopped there for the day, and I meant to, I really did. There is only so much one can smell in an afternoon. I had barely an hour or so left before I needed to be on my way to Anna's opening. I meant to stop for coffee. I meant to go back to the hotel for a nap. I'd missed lunch, and I needed to eat something. But then Barneys' front door suddenly appeared before me like an offering, and it seemed ungrateful not to open it and go in.

In a moment, I was tripping lightly down a flight of wide steps to my second beauty basement of the day. At the foot of the stairs was a long perfume counter. Behind it stood a forbidding line of assistants in black, staring up at me like a panel of judges. For exactly six steps I thought I had made a terrible mistake. Then I was safely on the floor, the Frederic Malle line was right in front of me, and I forgot everything but the perfume again.

"Hello!" I cried, coming to a stop in front of the Malle assistant, "I've been looking for you!" He was a short, powerful man with a square head and tremendous arms, like a wrestler, or a small-time crime boss.

"How can I help you?" he replied in a voice that matched the rest of him.

"Wait, wait!" I fumbled in my bag. "I have a list!"

I produced my crumpled sheet. There were two I wanted to smell. First, perfumer Olivia Giacobetti's En Passant. The tender lilac more than lived up to the reviews I had read. It wasn't the smell of the flowers in a vase, or the spicy, honeyed lilac of a sunny afternoon. It was, precisely, the scent of lilacs *in passing*, a rain-freshened breeze carrying the scent from somewhere down the block, a scent of mercurial spring, made all the more lovely by the cold gray day. The second, Le Parfum de Thérèse was a love letter from perfumer Edmond Roudnitska to his wife, rescued from obscurity by his son, Michel—ripe melon and plums, jasmine, and buttery soft leather. It was a more complex perfume, a richly pigmented oil painting to Giacobetti's watercolor, and the wrestler didn't seem sure I was ready for it. He kept offering other things, and I sniffed and described while he agreed or amended. The more enthusiastic I got, the warmer and more responsive he became, until it was clear that he loved the perfumes as much as I did.

While we talked, another assistant looked on silently, giving an occasional nod of approval. She was a wan, listless woman with long, bedraggled hair, her gash of dark lipstick strange on her otherwise colorless face.

"Which one is your favorite?" I asked her, leaning in on the counter.

"Musc Ravageur!" she replied without hesitation.

I saw my surprise mirrored in the wrestler's face.

"Oh, yeah?" he said, turning to her. "I wouldn't have picked that one out for you."

"Yes," she said, smiling to herself, her dark lips pressed together. "I love it."

She smiled again, this time at me, and her face was transformed. "So spicy!" she exclaimed, and went off to stock the shelves.

I thanked the assistant for the notoriously hard-to-get samples he had given me and made my way down the counter, sniffing a few random things along the way. I was truly lightheaded now, and the world was beginning to go a little fuzzy around the edges. I knew I should leave, and I was trying to do just that, edging past the makeup artists at their glass counters, when one of them, a petite woman, vibrant as a hummingbird, called to me in a warm, lilting voice straight out of the Caribbean.

"Well, hello there, my darling. What a wonderful scarf! You are looking a little tired. Why don't you sit down here with me for a moment and let me make you beautiful?"

The idea of sitting down was very appealing—I hesitated a moment. That was all it took.

"Come, come," she said, patting the cushioned leather stool in front of her. "It will not take long. I am Ynolde. And you?"

I introduced myself, and obeyed, protesting all the while, "But I don't want to waste your time. I don't really wear makeup. I have to be somewhere soon. I'm only here to smell the perfumes, and"—I leaned in and lowered my voice—"I can't really afford to buy them, either."

"Please," she said, gesturing to the empty floor. "Do I look like I'm busy? You are a beautiful girl. Now let's have a little fun. Hmmm . . ." She leaned in, casually brushing my thick eyebrows with a tiny comb as she examined my face. "Are you a hot girl or a cool girl? I think you are a hot girl. Yes, definitely hot. Never thin these brows, darling, they are wonderful. Look this way, please."

As she turned my head to the side, I saw what I had missed and nearly leapt out of the chair.

"Serge Lutens! I didn't realize they were here!"

"Oh, yes. He does wonderful lipsticks. Very deluxe."

"But the perfumes! I'm here to smell the perfumes. I only have an afternoon. I'm sorry," I pleaded, "but I need to go."

Ynolde pursed her lips and put a hand on one hip. "Don't be silly. Look—this is Janine," she said, drawing out the French *zha* of the first syllable. "She will get whatever you want. Now sit down."

Beside her stood one of the most striking human beings I've ever seen. Janine was at least six feet tall in her flat shoes and trousers, with glowing mahogany skin, a long, elegant neck, and a close-cropped head of black curls. As Ynolde introduced her, she inclined her head gently in my direction, the thick fringe of her eyelashes brushing against her high cheekbones.

It seemed absurd that such a person should run errands for anyone, but I was too dazzled to refuse. I named a few of the perfumes from my list and watched, riveted, as she walked across the room to the counter. Ynolde smoothed foundation onto my face and answered my question about how long she had lived in New York.

"Oh, I've been here a few years, darling, a few years. I love my family, but I had to get off of that island. I am telling you, heat makes you stupid. No, really—I believe it! That is why I have to stay here. Every winter I make plans and get things done. Then summer comes and I get stupid again. But at least it is cold for part of the year, you know?"

I thought of the long Texas summers—how easy it was, in Austin, to let the days and months and years go by. I thought of graduate school and the drifting years that followed it. I knew she was telling only part of her story, but I believed her, and said so.

"I'm from Texas. It's hot down there, too. Sometimes I feel like I have to go up north just to wake up."

"Oh, my. That is it. Wake *up*! That is it, exactly!" She reached for a tray of eye shadow. "Now I am going to wake up those eyes of yours. Not too much, not too much," she reassured me as I began protesting again, "just a little color now. . . ." I sighed, and was about to close my eyes when Janine arrived, holding a fan of smelling strips. She handed them to me with a gracious nod.

Any perfumista worth her salt would surely remember her first encounter with a Lutens creation—would know exactly which perfume she had smelled, would be able to regale you with the tale of its weird but beautiful top note, its shocking twists and turns, the beauty that emerges from that shock. Alas, I cannot remember a thing from that first handful of strips—not the names, not the notes, not a single spice or flower.

What I remember instead is how, when I passed that first strip to Ynolde to ask her opinion, she sniffed cautiously, drew her mouth into a little moue of disgust, and handed it back to me—"Oh no, that is not for me. I need light, air, sparkle!"—and how, when I handed it on to Janine, she bent her beautiful head over it, sniffed once, then again, thoughtfully, and then, flashing an impish grin, made a little dumb show of tucking the strip into her jacket pocket. There was a beat—it was so unexpected—and all three of us burst into laughter.

That was how it began, and that was how it continued. By the second round, all pretenses of formality were over. We were stealing strips from one another, arguing, and making an increasing amount of happy noise. Heads began to turn in our direction.

"You girls are having *waaay* too much fun," a fussy assistant scolded, shaking his finger at us as he walked across the floor. We quieted momentarily, leaning in toward each other to giggle like fifth-graders at a slumber party caught talking after lights-out. But then I brought the next strip up to my nose and smelled something that made me yelp and twitch with delight, and Ynolde and Janine laughed at me so loudly that the Lutens assistant came over from the counter to find out for himself what was going on.

I had seen him on my way in. He was hard to miss—tall, thin, and stoop-shouldered, all knees and elbows, with an unhealthy pallor, a day's growth of beard, and an enormous beak of a nose made even larger by his severe, Caesar-style haircut—a latter-day Ichabod Crane of perfume. By the time he arrived, I had slipped out of my chair without realizing it and was almost dancing. He stopped short, staring at me open-mouthed.

"I don't think I've ever seen anyone react that way," he said.

"It's the honey note," I explained, gasping a little. "I don't know why it makes me do this, but it does."

"Well, I'm going to have to start using honey more often," he replied. And I understood that after he was done selling other people's perfume for the day, he went home to try to make his own.

Then, like the Guerlain assistant, he said, "I think you need a bottle."

"I'm so sorry," I said, going into my own part of the routine. "I know you're probably right, but I can't afford to buy one just like that. And I've been smelling so many things. I would need to try it on my skin for a while to be sure." I sat back down on my stool, calm now. Ynolde and Janine watched the assistant.

"I see. But I don't have any samples of that one." He seemed disappointed. "Can you come back and try it later?"

"Ah, well." I sighed. "I live in Texas. But I'm sure I'll be back sometime." The minute the words were out of my mouth, I knew they were true.

"Let me—" he said, "let me just—" and he went off excitedly back to the counter.

The three of us looked at one another. Ynolde leaned in to whisper, "I've never seen him like that." Janine tapped her on the shoulder and tipped her chin in the direction of the Lutens counter. He was busy doing something I couldn't quite see. He came striding back over to us with a tiny round jar, like the kind used for makeup samples, in his hand.

"I made you a mini!" he said excitedly, handing it to me. "Please tell me how it turns out for you."

"Oh, thank you!" I said, genuinely touched. "I will. Thank you," I repeated, not knowing what else to say. Was he blushing?

He nodded once, then turned on his heel and retreated to the counter. We watched him go.

"Well, then," said Ynolde when we had taken a few deep breaths to recover from all the laughter. "Let's finish up that pretty face of yours." She put the final touches on my lips and eyes and handed me a mirror.

I was a gaudy, Technicolor version of myself. My skin glowed under a patina of foundation and bronzer. My lips gleamed with gold shimmer. My brown eyes had deepened to black under lids painted with chartreuse shadow and layer upon layer of thick mascara. I would never have chosen any of it. I would never look like this again. It was perfect.

"It's wonderful," I said to Ynolde, and was rewarded with a proud smile.

"Well, of course," she replied, hand on hip. "What did you expect?"

Back out on the street again after hugs and good-byes, I gulped at the freezing air and tried to re-orient myself. I should have been worried about being late for Anna's opening, but I wasn't. Hungry, giddy, shocked by joy and the sudden cold, I walked down the wide avenue suffused with the sense that everything would be well. The locked doors of the city grid I'd carried in my head were giving way to the slip and renewal of chance and possibility, and they were taking me along with them. I thought of the woman at Barneys saying, "Musc Ravageur!" and of Janine, pocketing the test strip. I thought of Anna, a woman too in love and too busy with her work to iron her wedding dress, and of my mother in Filene's. I thought of Bollywood dancing girls and of Indian silk. I thought about the Dress, and I thought, Maybe—

And here, through the haze of hope, I saw before me the green lamppost showing me the way to my subway stop. I gathered myself together and picked up my pace, falling in step with the people around me. We rushed together down the street to the top of the stairs, where I came to a sudden halt, to the great displeasure of the man just behind me. He cursed and stepped around me. I wanted to apologize, but I was laughing again, and he was gone before I could recover.

The thing that had stopped me in my tracks was a smell—the gorgeous, completely unlikely scent of flowers, as though the winter air had suddenly broken into blossom. For a moment, I was mystified, and then I laughed. It was the JAR experience, all but forgotten, revived by the heat of my quick walk and the closeness of the strangers all around me, the contrast of warm bodies and cold air. I sniffed once, twice, three times, and then I let the crowd carry me down the stairs.

6: THE KIND OF WOMAN WHO WEARS PERFUME

I stood on one leg in front of the mirrored wall at the gym, arms outstretched as though for flight, leaning forward, then back, then dangerously to the side as I tried to keep my balance on the Bosu ball, a jiggly, inflated, flat-bottomed half sphere that looked and felt like a gigantic blue vinyl breast. In the mirror, I could see my friend Parker behind me, crossing the room in a series of deep lunges, swearing under her breath each time she swooped down toward the floor.

"Perfect!" said the small woman walking alongside her. "Your form is much better this week. You're really getting stronger. How about, let's see . . ." She peered at her notebook through a pair of reading glasses. "Twenty more."

The woman began walking over to me. Parker scowled at her retreating back, then continued her swooping and swearing.

I don't remember whose idea it was to hire a personal trainer. Up until the exact moment when we checked the alumni rates at the university gym, I thought of trainers as an unimaginable luxury, the provenance of celebrities and reality shows. But it turned out to be cheap. So cheap—especially when we split the sessions—that before I could remember my gym teacher–induced childhood traumas, we were meeting twice a week at the small, windowless basement gym to be questioned, encouraged, and ordered around by Deb.

Unlike most of the fatally perky young women on the staff, she was in her mid-fifties, so her enthusiasm was tempered by understanding, and her kind, watchful face was lined with worry and experience. Disconcertingly, she looked half her age when viewed from behind, and she had to eat every two hours to keep up with her racing metabolism. I sometimes thought of her as one of those fierce, tiny animals who have to consume twice their weight in food daily to survive. Most of her clients were elderly, sedentary professors, so we seemed young and strong and flexible to her, and she was sure we could accomplish anything we wanted to do. After all, she told us, she herself hadn't started working out seriously until her late thirties, after several dark years of thinking it was too late to change.

She was a natural teacher, an explainer who loved to talk, and while she put us through our paces, we discussed everything from public-health policy and celebrity breakups to existential crises. There was always a study she had just read that she wanted to tell us about, usually while we were rendered speechless by trying to keep our heart rates up. Once, she cheered us on by explaining that it's better to be fit and well upholstered than thin and indolent, since thin people who don't work out often have fat on their internal organs, an idea that made me laugh so hard I had to get off the elliptical machine until I stopped. (Sure, you're a size double zero, but your *liver* is fat! Behold my slender kidneys, my svelte and fetching pancreas!)

I'd laughed the last time Parker and I had worked out together, five years earlier when we were both working toward PhDs in different departments and her name was still Lynn. She'd talked me into training for a triathlon with her—just a short, gentle toddler of a triathlon, but still a project so preposterous for someone like me that I was unable to take anything about it seriously, even as I trained in earnest. I laughed every time I got up at six in the morning to walk or swim or ride my bike. I laughed at the looks on the faces of sales assistants in sporting-goods stores when I said I was training for a triathlon. I was still laughing when I finished the race, just behind a seventy-year-old woman in a leg brace.

I am a kind of anti-athlete. The mindset required to keep track of all those miles, minutes, grams, and repetitions is completely foreign to me. Since this is also the mindset that best facilitates becoming and remaining thin, that state is also foreign to me. Yet there I was, bobbing gently up and down on the Bosu ball in front of the mirror—on both feet now—listening to Deb's directions as she passed me a set of hand weights, a smaller set than last week's, she explained, because they would feel heavier since I'd be using more muscles to keep my balance.

I took the weights and looked in the mirror, the ever-present mirror—sometimes I think the hardest part about going to the gym is that mirror—to check my alignment. I squared and dropped my shoulders, drew in my belly, made sure my knees weren't locked, and began a set of curls, drawing the weights up toward me. Left, then right, then left again. Watching. Working. Wobbling.

We weren't training for a triathlon this time around. We were training for—well, we each had our own reasons. Mine, to my chagrin, had mostly to do with the wedding, and what I had started thinking of as my performance.

Everything in me rebelled against the cliché of it—the bride slimming down for the big day—and I had already ruled out the idea that there would be some miraculous transformation. The wedding was just one goal along the way, I told myself. A catalyst. The piled-up damage from all those years of sitting and misery in graduate school would take a lot of time to undo, more time than I had. But every time I looked in the gym's wall-length mirror, the words of my friend Rubi rang in my head. "Everyone looks and looks," she had explained to me in her Chinese-inflected English, her face a mask of horror. "This is why I did not want to be a bride."

I'd always resisted working out for beauty's sake. Instead I tried to work out for what I was sure were the right reasons—to be strong, to have more energy, to live longer. My attempts to do so lasted as long as noble, high-minded intentions usually do. This time around, I was experimenting with a kind of practical vanity. Instead of trying to think of myself as one of those sporty, golden-retrieverish people who climb mountains on their vacations, I envisioned myself as a retired showgirl from an old movie, gearing up for one last hurrah, sweating and complaining and cracking wise. Instead of imagining myself bicycling up a hill with ease, I imagined needing the strength to push a manic James Cagney out of my dressing room. So far it was turning out to be a much more effective strategy.

But it was tricky. I felt the need for caution, for treading with care. I'd had good reasons for turning my back on the endless project of improving my looks. Returning to the fray, I had the feeling of walking along the edge of a roiling swamp thick with the poisonous air of impossible expectations. There were things I wanted, things I needed, from that swamp. But it was going to be difficult not to fall in.

"Good work," said Deb as I finished my second set and began a third. She looked me up and down carefully. "Your posture looks great. You stand like a dancer!" She held a cautious hand in the air behind the small of my back, but my wobbling was at a minimum. The mirror and my muscles were doing their work. "Beautiful, beautiful," she encouraged. "Next week you can try doing it on one leg!"

*　　*　　*

The showgirl—the idea of her, the comfortable space she made for me at the gym, and her down-but-not-out attitude—had come from my perfume. Perfume fans often talk about perfumes as though they were women: a difficult diva (Mitsouko), a proud dominatrix (Bandit), a good-time girl (Tocade). And we talk endlessly about how different perfumes suit, or even create, different moods: Take-no-prisoners perfumes and come-up-and-see-me-sometime perfumes. Tough perfumes that wear like armor, and fragile, melancholy perfumes for a broken heart.

What we talk about less often, because it is harder to explain, is the way a perfume can give breath and body to the phantom selves that waft about us as we go through our days—not just the showgirl, the femme fatale, and the ingenue, but all the memories and dreams of the taller, meaner, sharper, sweeter, softer people we have been or long to be. With the smell of dark roses and smoke on my skin, I knew what it would be like to stomp through a rainy city very late at night, reckless in black leather. Breathing in black pepper and incense, I was cool and contained, and my hair, without ever having come near scissors, was short and chic. Trailing the golden sweetness of raw honey and milky sandalwood, I remembered all day long what it was to wake up knowing I was loved.

And there were certain perfumes—it was hard to explain what they shared in common besides a certain refined complexity, perhaps a certain French something, though several were Italian—that continued the story my grandmother's pearl earrings had begun. Wearing them, I thought of words like *polished* and *gracious*. They made me think of Mrs. Dalloway going out to buy her flowers. They made me feel like a lady.

I had plenty of time and space to imagine things that spring. At the beginning of March, a few weeks after we returned from New York, V.

began a six-month writing fellowship that required him to live on a ranch two-hours outside of Austin. He was planning a short break in June for us to visit his parents, and then mine, but he wouldn't be back home until the second of September, a week before the wedding. The plan had been for me to visit on weekends, but the ranch had a creek that ran between the primitive dirt road and the house. There was no bridge—you just drove through the creek with a wish and a prayer for your engine. When it rained hard, the road washed out and the creek became impassable. It rained a lot that spring. Pretty much every weekend. Record-breaking amounts of rain. The rainiest Texas spring in ten years.

So I was often alone. And while I was alone, with no one to remind me every day of who I was supposed to be, something began to happen. Something to do with those perfume phantoms, and with all the time I was spending at the gym.

I was still very much my rumpled, squash-shaped self, but I was standing taller and walking with a longer, looser stride. My muscles and tendons were forging electric new connections to my brain. After long neglect and abuse, my grateful body was shaking itself awake, and it began to respond, in small, subtle ways, to the little stories, those lost or forgotten parts of myself I was carrying around in my head. Bit by bit, though the mirror told me I was more or less the same person, the phantoms—especially the lady—were becoming visible to the people around me. They were there in my posture and gestures, my breath and my stance. The way I got out of a car or up from a chair. The way I picked up my grocery basket or reached for a ripe fruit. The way I turned my head to smile and say thank you when—as seemed to be happening more and more often—a stranger complimented me or stopped to hold open a door.

*   *   *

"Is that you who smells like lemons?"

Deb had come through the doors of the gym sniffing, and had made her way, with unnerving accuracy, over to the elliptical machines where I was dutifully putting in my time.

"Probably," I said.

Inwardly I cringed. Perfume in the gym is a terrible idea. I'd put on a light cologne that morning, sure it would fade before my late-afternoon workout.

Deb leaned in toward me and gave another enthusiastic sniff.

"It *is* you. I could smell it out in the hallway and I was going crazy trying to figure out where it was coming from!"

Out in the hallway? Oh, no.

"I'm so sorry. I thought it would be gone by now."

Deb looked surprised.

"Why are you sorry?"

"I just—I don't know. I don't want to bother anyone. It's a small gym."

"Are you kidding? It's way better than what I usually smell in here all day. I *love* lemons. They're one of my favorite scents. I collect essential oils, but I could never find a really good lemon."

"Wait—" I let the machine slow to a crawl and turned to face her. "You collect essential oils?"

"Oh, yeah." She nodded emphatically. "Not as much as I used to, but I still love all the ones I have. I like to play with them. I just love *smells*, you know?"

"Yes," I said. "Yes. I think I know what you mean."

When Parker arrived for our session, I was in the middle of telling Deb about every lemon-scented perfume I had or knew about and offering to put together a packet of samples for her. As Parker lowered herself onto the mat to join us, she listened, and then broke in—

"If you're looking for a beautiful lemon, you should really try Cristalle by Chanel. Do you know it? It's a classic. Very crisp."

I turned to stare at her, my mouth open in disbelief.

"Cristalle?"

"What?" she said, nonplussed. "You don't like it?"

"No, no," I said. "I haven't even smelled it. I was just—I mean, I didn't know you wore perfume."

"Oh, sure. I love perfume." She bent forward toward her toes, her legs straight out in front of her. "Just love it," she repeated, leaning into the stretch, holding it. "I always have."

I looked at my friend. We'd known each other ten years and running. She'd been a brilliant student, a star in her field who'd gotten a plum internship, and then an enviable job. But though she loved her colleagues and her work, she was miserable. So miserable that to save her own life she'd left her position, and then the academy altogether. That was when the changes she was going through now had begun, or, at least, when she knew they would begin.

For a long time, I didn't notice. She'd always worn her dark hair short and spiky. She'd always dressed in black, always looked a little punk when she wasn't in her professional drag. So I didn't think twice when she began to wear her hair a little longer on top—brushed forward, across her forehead, or gelled straight up in the air—and buzzed to bristles at the nape. When she traded sleeveless shirts with plunging necklines that showed off her gorgeous cleavage for big crewneck T-shirts, I chalked it up to a change in style, or a passing mood.

It was only when she told me that she was going to legally change her name, and explained why, that I saw what I hadn't seen: that her breasts were bound flat under her T-shirt. That she wore her jeans slung low and loose. That her stance had widened. That the set of her jaw and the way she held her head had changed. I blinked once, twice. I looked again. And there, standing where my friend had been, was a very beautiful boy.

I saw him for only a moment. Then he opened his mouth, my friend began talking to me, and he flickered and vanished. That was the way it still was: I saw him, and then I didn't see him. Every now and then I said *he,* but most of the time I said *she.* I was getting used to the new name, but sometimes I forgot that, too. Ten years is a long time.

Parker laughed and told me she understood. It was confusing for her, too. She said that there were things she liked about living in between, and that she might stay there awhile. That whatever happened next would happen slowly. Hormone treatments, probably. Surgery, maybe, but she wasn't sure when, or how much. The process was expensive, difficult, irreversible—and hard on the body. In the meantime, she was at the gym. She was in training.

I thought about how important perfume had been for me over the past few months. How it had conjured up my phantom selves, and given them weight and substance.

"So," I said as we got up from the mat and walked over to the weights, and the mirror, "Cristalle. What other kind of perfume do you wear?"

"Oh, I haven't worn Cristalle in years." She waved away the notion. "That was the eighties. I've moved on." When I pressed her for an answer, she named a string of popular men's colognes.

I raised an eyebrow. "I think maybe you can do better than that," I said.

"Oh, yeah?" she said, laughing at me again. "What did you have in mind?"

A few days later I was sitting on the living-room floor in Parker's apartment, laying out a series of samples from my precious stash and asking her questions. We talked about the perfumes she'd worn, and the smells of her childhood, and what she wanted to feel or do when she wore perfume, and a dozen other things. In between rounds of conversation, I paused to introduce her to one or two trial scents, describing them as I went.

"Ah, this is great!" Parker sighed, leaning back against the couch, relaxing into the attention. "It's like a cross between therapy and going to a spa."

Looking over my perfumes the night before our smelling date, I'd been surprised to realize how well prepared I was for exactly this kind of challenge. In the United States, perfume has traditionally been considered feminine frippery. Scents for men are carefully labeled as cologne, or aftershave lotion, or "fragrance"—anything but perfume. But this is mostly a matter of bottles and marketing. More than once in my testing, I had fallen in love with a fragrance and then, to my bafflement, realized that it was supposed to be for men. I'd had the opposite experience, too—finding flowers and powder where I'd been expecting stubble. One of the most popular mass-market men's scents of all time—your father probably wore it—smells bracingly of carnations.

Much of niche perfumery is intended to be unisex, and the catholic tastes of my fellow perfume obsessives had quickly disabused me of the notion that any smells were off-limits. It helped, too, that our community was so international, since, in the end, perceptions of scent are always a matter of culture, memory, and context: Roses lean feminine in the United States, masculine in the Middle East. Italians feel macho in smells that might once have gotten an Englishman arrested.

So far, my own tastes had veered away from the stereotypically feminine—no pastel florals or big, heady white flowers—and the superclean, frat-boy masculine. Everything in my collection was fair game. But, thinking about my friend—about who Lynn had been, and who

Parker might become—I'd had a few ideas about what might really work.

We began with a handful of citruses, because of the Cristalle, and because citrus is so easy—familiar, bright, cheerful, universally beloved. I started with the perfume I'd been caught wearing at the gym, sparkling with basil and cypress as well as lemon. Then a juicy orange matched with the bitter green of crushed leaves. Then a well-salted sparkling lime. And finally, a grapefruit softened with vanilla and patchouli that left clean and bright behind for something dirtier and more interesting.

"They're nice," said Parker, sniffing each in turn. "I really like them."

"But maybe a little boring?" *Nice* wasn't the reaction I was looking for.

"Maybe a little," she admitted. "But I still like that first one a lot. And that grapefruit one is so weird, but I think I like it anyway."

I set those two aside and we continued on with more conversation and one or two things from the opposite end of the spectrum. First, a fantasy of black leather, asphalt, rubber, and smoky vanilla.

"Whoa!" cried Parker, reeling back from the strip, then coming back again, cautiously, for another sniff. "Well, it's not boring, that's for sure." She sniffed again, thoughtfully, giggling a little. "It's kind of hot, actually."

"But not something you would wear."

"Not yet. Try me next year."

I smiled to myself—she'd reacted almost exactly as I'd suspected she would—and handed her a rich, boozy amber.

"Ugh. No." She held the strip at arm's length. "Sorry. Too sweet."

"No need to apologize. I just wanted to be sure."

Holding my breath, I handed over the perfume I'd thought of first, the one that had seemed like it might be the perfect thing, at least for right now. Parker bent toward the strip and sniffed quietly. Once. Twice.

Vetiver is one of my favorite smells in perfume. The natural oil comes from the massive root system of the tall, clumping vetiver grass, grown throughout India to control erosion. Unlike most perfume ingredients, it is relatively cheap and plentiful, but that is not the only reason it shows up in so many perfumes. Vetiver is a chameleon. It can be used to make a classic cologne, or to ground lush florals with a touch of earth. It can smell green and citrusy—in India it is often used to make a refreshing tea—but in a perfumer's hands it can also smell of salt, of peppery wood, of earthy roots, of smoke, leather, wool, even sweet, nutty cereal. Yet vetiver is always distinctly, recognizably itself, so much so that perfumers carefully control how much they use, lest it overwhelm the blend. Once you know it well, you can pick it out in any of its guises.

I'd collected several vetiver-based perfumes to bring along, but the one I'd handed Parker was a recent favorite. The perfumer had woven together bright citrus and pepper top notes and a striking mineral heart with a sensuous, woody vetiver base. The result was something that wasn't quite any of those things. Something that went beyond the sum of its parts. Something new. It had been marketed to men, but it struck me less as masculine than tailored—a perfect white shirt of a scent—seasonless, sophisticated, appropriate for any occasion, ready to become whatever its owner required. And sexy as hell, the way the right white shirt can be on the right person.

I tried to say some of this to Parker, but she wasn't listening.

"Oh my God." She groaned.

"Do you like it?"

She lifted her head and gave me a wicked smile—the boy flickering into view again.

"You can leave now. I think we need to be alone together."

"Don't you want to try it on your skin first?" I asked, laughing, handing her the vial.

She struggled with the cap for a minute, cracked it, dabbed some perfume on and assumed the position that was so familiar to me—eyes closed, nose pressed to wrist.

"Oh my God!" she said again. "It's like a drug." She laughed. "Where can I get some? Are you sure it's legal?"

"I'll send you a link. I think you'd better hang on to that sample. And here—keep the citruses, too." I put them all in a small bag, tucking in the black leather, too, just in case. "Try them out for a few days before you buy anything."

"But these are yours. Are you sure?"

I waved a hand at the long line of vials on the floor.

"I think I'll be all right."

"Oh, this is so great. Thank you." She leaned back, arms spread along the back of the couch.

I put the vials away in their box. She lifted a wrist to her nose for another sniff.

"It's changing."

"Oh, yeah. The base notes are great. I think you'll like them."

She watched me as I gathered up the strips and put the box of samples in my bag.

"Can we do this again in a few months?" she asked.

"Sure," I said absently, thinking of how much closer the wedding would be then. I really had to do something about my dress. "It will be summer. We can try out some hot-weather scents."

"Mm. And my body chemistry will be different."

I stopped what I was doing and looked at her.

"Testosterone," she said. She laughed again, nervously this time, bringing her arms in across her chest. "It changes the way you smell." She grimaced briefly, then sighed. "What do guys do about that kind of stuff? I have no idea."

In the silence, I had a glimpse of how it would be—how she would disappear into a world neither of us could quite imagine. Then the boy gave me another wicked smile.

"Hey, maybe you could be my smell consultant."

"Like a trainer," I said.

"A personal perfume trainer! What do you think?"

We grinned at each other.

"Will you keep working out with me?"

"Of course."

"Then it's a deal," I said.

And we shook on it, our gentlemen's agreement.

Not so long after my afternoon with Parker, I walked into my living room on the evening of a small dinner party and smelled something green and delicious and unfamiliar in the air. I walked back out, and raised a wrist to my nose. Had I forgotten what I was wearing? No, my skin still smelled faintly of saffron and roses. I walked back in and made a circle around my friend Erica, sniffing gently.

She was one of my steadiest, most generous friends, the one whose phone number I always wrote down when asked who to contact besides V. in case of emergency. She was also a talented, well-respected graphic designer—though she was so modest, she'd sooner die than hear anyone say so to her face. She preferred to stay in the background, getting things done. I had never seen her dressed in anything besides what she was wearing that day—a unisex, vanity-defying uniform of nerd cool: baggy pants, sneakers, an ironic T-shirt layered over a loose long-sleeved shirt, her horn-rimmed glasses the only dramatic touch on a face free of makeup.

"Are you wearing perfume?"

"Is it too much?"

"No," I said, "it's wonderful. Wonderful." She told me that one of the other designers at her office had picked some up at a hip little retro grocery store nearby. That it made her realize she'd always wanted to wear perfume. I sat down and told her that I, too, had gotten very interested in perfume lately. Within a week I was over at her house with my samples.

Then I had coffee with my former academic adviser, an activist and sometime go-go dancer for her girlfriend's rock band, and when I told her what I'd been up to, she confessed her love for Joy's regal jasmine and roses. V., reporting on my activities to his family, discovered that one of his most macho South Texas uncles had a huge cologne collection and dreamed of importing perfumes from Mexico. Prickly Rubi, who had not wanted to be a bride, told me, blushing, that she wore Clinique's Happy but maybe would like to try something else. I introduced her to Erica, and together we spent a giggly afternoon touring Austin's best perfume counters.

After that, I got bolder. I told Julia, one of my oldest graduate-school friends and my comrade-in-arms for many an activist scheme. She did her best not to look at me like I was crazy. "Oh," she said. "That sounds interesting." Undeterred, I asked her if she'd like to come over and let me introduce her to a few things. "I'll make dinner," I added, knowing her weakness for a good meal.

A few nights later, she sat on my couch, wary but, as usual, game for anything. The things I'd gathered for her were all clear, direct, outdoor smells. Before graduate school, she'd spent two years in northern Colorado, living out in the woods with her husband, Alex, in a yurt with no running water or electricity. They still lived frugally, on principle, and she avoided driving, pedaling along the unfriendly, SUV-choked roads every day, no matter the hour or the weather on a bike tricked out with a long trailer and a tall flag.

I handed her the first strip—beginning with citrus again, this time matched with dry woods. She sniffed, leaned back, and closed her eyes.

"Oh," she said, before I could launch into my usual description. "Oh. It's my grandfather's shed. He used to keep these wooden crates full of lemons and oranges in there in the winter." She sniffed again, deeply. "Oh, that's so strange." She opened her eyes and looked at me. "I didn't know it could be like that."

We continued, and every time I handed her something to smell, she reeled off the notes without clue or prompting, her descriptions precise, her nose, I suspected, far more acute than my own. She was startled, then curious. And then, on the fourth try, she wriggled with delight.

"It's the trees!" she cried. "The trees around the lake—what were they? Cedar trees." She sniffed again. "And the water, too. Trees and water."

"It's called Cedarwood Tea," I said, unnecessarily.

She left on her bike, dabbing some on before she slipped the vial into her backpack. "So Alex can smell me when I come in," she said with a giggle, adjusting her helmet and turning on the blinking light on the back of her seat before she cycled away into the dark, a tall flag waving in the wind.

Then I told my mother, who told me the story of the Texas heiress and her bottle of Femme. (But not right away. First she said: "You're kidding." And I said: "I know it seems strange." And she said: "I'm just surprised. Perfume. I never would have thought." And I said, trying to translate: "No calories, no sizes: What's not to love?" And she said: "That sounds like the title of a book you should write.")

And then it was time to tell Sam.

If you are lucky—and brave—you have a friend like Sam. Someone who knows you better than might be wise. Someone whose voice you hear in your head at those moments when you are tempted to repeat old mistakes or turn away from something you want, for lack of nerve or stamina. Someone who makes you want to meet your own highest standards, to be your best self.

Like Julia and Parker, Sam and I had met in graduate school, but she was older than we were. She'd had many lives before she knew us, and has had several more since. This seemed perfectly unremarkable to her, as did the number of startlingly diverse projects she had carried out and the vast network of friends and admirers she had acquired along the way. I had no idea what she would think of my new perfume life. She was always insightful and honest—terrifyingly so—but that did not mean she was predictable. What I did know was that if any of the things I sometimes feared were true—that I was escaping from myself, running away from the real work I should be doing, that it was all a frivolous waste of time—she would ask me one of her famous questions, the ones that cut casually through all chattering self-deception, and I would have to turn and look at that truth and act accordingly.

We met for dinner at the tiny, boat-size house where, for the moment, she lived alone, everything arranged according to her liking. The table was set with beautiful earthenware made by her sister. She set out olives, good cheese and bread, wine, and a salad fragrant with herbs cut from the pots on her front porch. A rich, meaty stew bubbled on the stovetop. We drank, and ate, and talked. And when, in the middle of another conversation, trying to pretend it didn't matter, I confessed my secret life, she nodded her head and smiled.

"Oh, sure," she said. "I love perfume. I've never gotten into it like you have, but I can see why you would." She took another sip of wine. "I have a signature scent."

"You do?" I asked, astonished, trying to remember if I'd ever smelled perfume on her.

"Uh-huh. I found it when I was traveling in Europe."

"When was that?"

She laughed, remembering. "A long time ago—oh, God, almost thirty years now. I was a roadie for a band at the time." She laughed again. "Christian rock and roll, if you can believe it. We were touring, and there was plenty of time to wander around during the day. I walked into one of those fancy department stores in Paris, sprayed some on, and just about died. I have a friend who lives there. He still sends me a bottle every year. Here, I'll show you—hang on a second."

She returned bearing a bottle of Grès's Cabochard, one of the greats from the pantheon of dirty-leather perfumes, the kind of thing I had hoped I would love. It was a perfume designed, when it was first launched, for the newly liberated woman, the one who had cut off her long hair, thrown away her corsets, and taken up divorce, driving, cigarettes, and sex with equal enthusiasm. The perfume of an adventuress.

I sniffed gently at the neck of the bottle, thinking of how its rough magic suited my friend. She would be the last person to call herself a great beauty—you would never pick her out in a crowd. But once you had heard her laugh, and looked into her face, it was difficult to turn away. She'd worn this perfume through a marriage, a divorce, the women and men who followed, motherhood, solitude, and all the rest of her tumbling changes.

"It doesn't smell the same as it did back then," she said, "but I still like it." She lifted her glass and smiled at me. "I'm not the same as I used to be, either."

Not everyone was so understanding, of course. "No, no, no" said a friend a few weeks later. "It's just not for me." She sipped at her cocktail but left the food on the table untouched. She'd often told me how hard it was for her to cook, even with a recipe. *It all tastes the same to me. I can't tell when something's bad.*

"You might be surprised," I said, leaning in. "I could find you something to go with those boots."

She laughed, and crossed one slim runner's leg over the other, rocking her foot back on the high heel, running a hand over the soft raspberry leather that crept just above her knee.

"No, really," she said. "I'm sure some of it's very beautiful, but I just—" She turned to face me, hesitating to finish her sentence. "I just don't want to be the kind of woman who wears perfume. You know what I mean?"

I leaned back. Paused. Smiled. Thinking, *No, I'm not sure I do. Not anymore.*

"Ah, well," I said. "If you're ever curious, I'll be here."

The spring rains continued. All over town, creeks and basements flooded. The park trails turned to mud. The radio announced the latest storm warnings and repeated its warning mantra about flash floods: *Turn around, don't drown!* The rural areas around Austin were full of roads that ran across creekbeds, like the one out at the ranch where V. was staying. In a storm, a wall of water could come rushing down on a driver without warning, lifting the car up, turning it over, even carrying it downstream.

V. and I talked on the telephone, the connection full of static and delays. He missed me, but he had gone deep into his work in the way that only a gift of concentrated solitude and time can allow. I updated him on the latest wedding plans I'd made with my mother—the e-mails and phone calls were coming thick and fast now—and he thanked me, his voice coming from far away, and gave his approval for everything. I told him that Julia, who was one of our officiants, wanted to meet with us together to talk about the ceremony. We'd try to make it up when the weather cleared. We'd tried once already, but we'd been caught in a sudden storm. The road disappeared in a rush of water and we had to drive backward for twenty minutes in the blinding rain before we found a spot to turn around.

At the gym, Parker and I went through our paces while Deb cheered us on and thought up different ways to torture us. She had to keep changing our workouts, she explained, because muscles adapt to new information so quickly. Ask your body to do something for the first time and it works hard, hesitating, making mistakes, catching and correcting itself. Soon enough, though, it figures out the easiest way to get the work done and relaxes into habit. The fastest way to get in shape was to keep surprising ourselves.

It wasn't difficult. Those weeks were full of surprises. I bent to heft a bag of heavy groceries and they floated up from the ground, buoyant, practically weightless in my hand. I braced myself to work through the afternoon fog that had always descended on me, only to find that it had evaporated, burned away by the warmth of all that newly oxygenated blood rushing to my brain. After years of forgetting to eat, or eating too much of the wrong thing, I was shocked by my hunger, and then shocked again to see how easily it was satisfied.

And I was surprised, though perhaps I should not have been, by the changes in my friend. First by their subtlety, and then by a sudden shift, a crossing of some line I hadn't known was there. *Can you tell? Can you see?* That's what he kept asking. And now, more often, it seemed right to say *he,* though with my friend's blessing I still switched back and forth. (Deb, with her typical heartfelt enthusiasm, had switched permanently weeks ago.) Could I see the prickle of hairs sprouting along a jawline growing more square? The slight flattening and broadening at the temples of that familiar face? Could I hear the gravel in a voice roughening, deepening? I looked. I listened. I couldn't, I admitted— sheepishly.

And then—a week, or a day, or an hour later—I could. It was like watching a blurry photograph suddenly snap into focus. The boy who had flickered in and out resolved into someone slightly older, trading some of his ephemeral beauty for a still unsettling handsomeness. The occasional rasp that at first sounded like nothing more than morning allergies took on a resonance that startled me when I called on the phone.

"I should take a picture of you every week," I teased, "to keep track." And then I thought about how I never do take photos. I wondered if I had any from five years ago, of Lynn.

Distracted by my friend's changes, I almost missed the beginning of my own, quieter transformation. It was Deb who pointed it out to me.

"You're getting more balanced," she said.

She was watching me carefully in the mirror as I pulled on a long, taut rubber cord, bringing it in across my chest and slowly bringing it out again, strengthening my shoulder joint so it could take the rest of the abuse I was dishing out. Deb was big on preventive measures.

"What do you mean?" I asked, confused. I was standing firmly on the ground, feet apart, knees slightly bent.

"Your shoulders are getting broader. You've built up the muscles there. You have more core strength, so you're standing upright and holding them square. And you've lost some weight in your hips." She looked me up and down with satisfaction. "More balanced."

I had noticed my shoulder muscles. They were a new and unexpected curve, one I'd been enjoying, just as I'd enjoyed how many more push-ups I could do. But as usual, I'd missed the bigger picture. I looked in the mirror, trying to see what Deb saw.

I wasn't sure I could. But I left the gym feeling lighter and stronger than usual anyway. Walking back to my car, I ran into Julia.

"Well, hello!" She greeted me with a hug, then stepped back and looked at me a moment.

"You're . . . emerging," she said, looking for the word. She traced a hand along her own collarbone.

"Am I?" I told her what Deb had said.

"Maybe that's it," she said, considering. "I don't know. You just seem more *here*."

I continued on my way, newly conscious of the set of my shoulders, the straight, supported line of my spine. I imagined my newly conditioned heart thumping slow and strong—calm, unafraid, ready for whatever came next. When I got to the car, I pulled my phone out and made a call I'd been meaning to make for a long time.

"Hi, Erica," I said when she answered. "I need a big favor."

"Thank you so much," I said, for the third or fourth time. "You have no idea how much I appreciate your doing this. And thanks for driving, too," I added. "Every time I come up to this part of town, I get lost."

"Sure," said Erica, calm and amused. "I went with my friend Kim when she picked out hers. It was fun." She looked at me, sitting bolt upright on the edge of the passenger seat. "Nice posture," she said. "You make me want to stand up straight."

She pulled off the busy highway, crossed four lanes of traffic without blinking, and pulled into the vast parking lot of a strip mall lined with big-box stores that looked exactly like the last three or four we'd just passed. And there it was, at the end of the row: Bridal Warehouse.

Well, it's about time, the more sensible among you may be muttering—especially those of you aware of what a bridal gown generally entails. *She should have taken care of this ages ago.* Dear readers, you are not wrong. But you see, I had a plan. It would turn out to be a foolish, wrongheaded plan, but it was, at least, a plan.

"Ready?" Erica asked as I paused at the front door.

"Remember, we're just looking to get an idea. In and out."

"Sounds good."

"Okay, then." I took a breath and opened the door. "Let's go."

Inside, it was exactly as advertised—a vast fluorescent-lit warehouse, carpeted from edge to edge in the kind of close-napped pattern you might find in an airport, and crowded with rack upon rack of wedding dresses. I stood there, momentarily paralyzed.

"Why don't we find your size and look through the rack," Erica suggested, leading me gently in the right direction.

Right. My size. That was why we were here.

In New York, walking past all those laundries with tailors sewing away in their front windows, I'd had an idea. Maybe I could skip the whole panic-inducing scene of paging through catalogs of laughing girls and wedding-cake dresses, and then shopping for hours, trying on dress after dress as my blood sugar and confidence plummeted. Maybe, instead, I could buy some fabric and find a tailor. And then I did a dangerous thing: I started to dream. Not of some fabulous gown, but of a very simple dress that truly fit me. Just once, I wanted my clothes to accommodate me, instead of forever trying to accommodate them. If there was ever a time for such a thing, I reasoned, this was it.

I knew just enough about clothes to realize that I should choose a basic shape and style, and that the best way to figure it out was to try some things on. We'd picked the Warehouse for its range. My goal was to be there less than an hour.

"And how are you two ladies doing this afternoon?"

Almost before we could answer, the saleswoman had plucked four dresses off the rack and begun to herd us over to the dressing rooms. Her name was Joanna. She wore her graying hair pinned back in a loose, straggly bun, and her glasses hung on a chain around her neck. A tape measure trailed over the edge of her cardigan's deep pockets, like a doctor's stethoscope from a lab coat, and she chewed peppermint gum all through her stream of chatter.

"I think you'll like these—they're the right styles for you. Of course, there's plenty to choose from here. You know, we're getting a lot of older brides in here these days. My daughter—she's up on the base in Killeen, you know—she just got married the second time. Thank God, I like this guy a lot better than the last one. And I just got married myself for the first time a few years ago. I thought, why rush, you know? You rush in, you rush right back out. My daughter learned that one. When's your wedding? Really. Not to worry, not to worry, we've still got time. That's the dressing room right over there, that's right, and if you'll just wait one minute I'll be back with a bra and a petticoat. I really recommend a petticoat. A lot of girls won't wear one these days, and then they come back here and complain to me when the wind blows their skirt between their legs while they're trying to get their pictures taken."

"Now, you"—she turned to Erica—"you wait right out here on this couch. It's very comfortable. I'll tell you, I've put my feet up every now and then, when we're slow. Management doesn't like it, but I've been here a long time, you know? Be back in a flash, ladies!"

True to her word, she was at my side a moment later, hooking me, with some struggle ("Hold your breath now! You want it tight, otherwise it won't hold you up"), into a long-line strapless bra—essentially, I now realized, a modernized corset—and zipping me into a stiff, floor-length white polyester skirt, that highly recommended petticoat. She showed me how to find my way through the multiple layers of the first dress and slip it, heavy and rustling, over my head. I heard the long zipper come together behind me in one swift motion, and that was it. I was in.

She led me out of the dressing room and up onto a round platform, about two feet high, situated in front of a bank of angled mirrors. To my right and left were women of all sizes, colors, and ages, each on her own round platform, each transformed by her dress into a bride. We looked like a row of jilted cake toppers.

I took a breath and turned to the mirrors and my own multiplied reflection. The floor-length skirt and the additional height of the platform made me toweringly tall. The doubled boning in the bodice of the dress and the bra nipped in my waist, flattened my stomach, and made my bust smooth and high, stretching me still further. The A-line skirt skimmed the handspan between my waist and the place where my hips widened and then swung out into a triangle down to my feet, held out by the petticoat and the lining of the dress. Gone, as if by magic, were all my familiar lumps and ripples, smoothed by layers of heavy satin and panels of filmy patterned organza that came together at the high empire waist to make a V shape that echoed the skirt's triangle. The halter strap that wound around the back of my neck and back down the other side highlighted the line of my collarbone and shoulders and lengthened my neck, balancing out the modest swell of décolletage it had created. Only my head and bare arms remained imperfectly, recognizably my own. That, it was starting to dawn on me, was the point.

Erica made a circle around me, crossed her arms, and nodded slowly.

"You clean up good."

"Pretty shoulders," said Joanna. "That looks like the one, but why don't you try on the others just in case."

I went through the same routine three more times, with slight variations. Then I tried the first dress on again. Joanna and Erica, who were by now fast friends, agreed that it was the best one. I couldn't disagree.

"Do you want to do it?" Erica asked, ready for any answer.

This was not the plan. But I had to admit it was an appealing idea. I stroked the elaborate folds of fabric. It was white. It was built like a tank. It was everything I thought I didn't want. I turned to one side, then the other, looking in the mirrors. *Not bad.*

"When's the latest I can decide?"

"We'll need a twelve-week turnaround," Joanna said, "unless you want to pay extra. But the fastest they can get it is eight weeks, and you'll need time for alterations."

Alterations. I thought about the gym, and my shifting shape. I thought about tailors. I still had a week or two to try and make my idea work. I put Joanna's card in my wallet. We said our grateful thank-yous. And then we left.

The bolts of Indian silk shimmered and glowed like jewels in the dark, cluttered fabric shop. They hung horizontally, one on top of another, in a dazzling double row that took up one full corner. I ran my fingers over the colors, luxuriating for a moment in all that piled-up beauty. In graduate school, I had often come just to dream over the imported colors and patterns, or poke through the dishes of exotic buttons—silver, bone, ceramic, and wood. Sometimes I left with a precious scrap of fabric, though I didn't sew and I had no idea what I would do with it. When the English department finally gave me a little closet of an office, I immediately bought a brilliant saffron length of that silk—dupioni was its proper name—shot through with scarlet threads, and pinned it up like wallpaper over the chipped industrial paint. No matter what else happened, I had always been glad to open the door to my tiny cube and walk into the embrace of that color.

In my scattershot research on wedding dresses, I'd come across several made from dupioni, and had immediately thought of these rows of color. I imagined myself in a dazzling deep blue, a rich orange, a gleaming emerald green. But standing in front of the fabric, I hesitated.

I had been thinking more and more about what the wedding would look like, and about how I would fit into that scheme. It would be early fall in Boise, and my parents' backyard would be full of silvery sage, dusty purple flowers, and tall grasses. The foothills that surrounded their house would be covered in the same soft colors—sagebrush and shining dried grasses under, if we were lucky, a clear blue September sky.

And there was something else. As we talked over what we wanted from our ceremony and the celebration to follow, V. and I had realized how important it was to us to have a wedding that would be satisfying not just to us but to our parents and other guests used to far more formal, traditional rituals. There were some things we couldn't do—get married in a Catholic church, get a blessing from a priest. But, I thought, turning away from the more vibrant colors, I could look a little more like a bride.

I pulled out a bolt of wheaten gold I had looked at the day before.

It wasn't white, or cream, or ivory. But it was far closer to those colors than emerald green. It was, in fact, very nearly the exact color of the blond grasses that covered the Boise foothills, a color I had known and loved since childhood. Yes, I thought, looking at the way the silken threads glimmered in the dim light of the shop: that blond grass, but touched by glamour and magic.

Anything remotely yellow was a risky choice for my coloring, but as I stood in front of the shop's only mirror, holding a length of it across my chest, I thought I might just be able to get away with it. I saw myself walking toward our wedding guests under the blue sky, with the hills behind me. I wouldn't wear a veil, and there would be no prayers in our ceremony, but the silk would dazzle in the sun.

"That's not for you," said a woman behind me.

I ignored her, but she continued on anyway, coming closer.

"I'm an artist," she announced. "Women pay me to tell them what their colors are. You'd be much better off in something stronger."

Irritated, but hoping she'd leave if I gave her an explanation, I told her a little about what I was trying to do.

"I see. I would try a pale pink, then."

"I'm doing all right, thanks," I said firmly.

Our eyes met for a moment in the mirror and she began to back away.

"Well, there's nothing I can do about it then," she said loudly as she walked to another corner of the tiny space. "Until a woman accepts what her true colors are, there's just nothing I or anyone else can do."

Who was this woman? I snuck a look at her, reflected behind me in the mirror, a bundle of patterns and wild gray hair. She looked vaguely witchy—an evil, uninvited fairy. I could feel the heat in my face and my pulse beating fast. I closed my eyes in exasperation, and for just a moment I was back in junior high, standing in front of the dressing-room mirror next to my mother while she explained why the skirt I'd picked out was all wrong for me. Then I opened my eyes and looked in the mirror. I thought about the gym, and about all the other ways I'd changed that rainy spring. Nearly every week, something that was supposed to be all wrong for me turned out to be just what I needed.

Still, I hesitated. She was right about the pink—it would be a safer, more flattering choice. I didn't want a pink dress, but she was right.

Then I shook it off. It was too late for nerves and second thoughts. Yesterday I'd stood out in Erica's front yard draped in half a dozen different colors of silk so we could see how they looked in the sunlight and pick the best one. And I'd already been to see a tailor recommended by the shop—a small, confident woman named Hope who had the same soft, polished Mexican accent as V.'s mother. I had watched a string of contented customers streaming in and out as I waited my turn, then showed her what I wanted. "No problem," she'd said. Then she'd handed me a small folded piece of paper with a number a third the size of the one on the price tag of the Warehouse dress. She was waiting for the fabric now.

So for a second time I turned away from what I saw in the mirror and, with a head full of blond grasses and September sun, I brought the golden silk up to the register.

A month or so later, I stood in front of another mirror in another changing room. It was a small room, and the pert young woman standing next to me was taking up a lot of room. She was very tall and very bossy, and she was staring steadily at my chest. She crossed her arms over her own and pronounced her judgment.

"That's about as good as it's going to get."

"I'd like to try on another, please," I replied, more firmly than I felt. I hadn't expected to encounter this kind of resistance.

I'd been buying my bras here for years. Usually, the saleswomen displayed the rare combination of expertise, kindness, and tact that had made me a fiercely loyal customer. When it became necessary to buy what I thought of as Serious Underwear for the wedding, I'd come here blithely, sure of myself. I even thought it might be fun, or at least funny. I'd been looking forward to putting myself in the hands of a trustworthy expert.

I was growing increasingly mistrustful of Hope. In its current state, my wedding dress looked like a craft project gone badly awry. When I saw it on the hanger, I gasped. When I tried it on, I blanched. Hope sternly dismissed my fears, and then proceeded to pin the dress in so many places that when it came time for me to take it off, she had to stand on a stool and lift it up over my head so I could duck out from under the skirt. Week after week she had missed deadlines we set together, suddenly discovering some crucial something that I needed to go buy or order. I was beginning to suspect she didn't really know how to make the dress we had planned, and was trying to buy time while she tried to figure it out. In the meantime, I was here, making sure she'd be able to fit the dress around whatever I'd be wearing underneath it on my wedding day.

The sales assistant popped back into the little room without knocking, two more of those strapless modernized corsets in her hand. As she hooked me in, I drooped in fear, and muttered a fervent little prayer that one of them would fit better than the last three I had tried. The assistant tugged sharply at me from behind and commanded me to stand up straight. I sighed inwardly and complied. If only I hadn't told her I was shopping for my wedding.

I'd quickly noticed the effect this news had on the average sales assistant: the stiffening back, the set jaw, the steely look of determination in the eyes. The situation, their faces said, called for immediate discipline, before it—or, rather, I—got out of control. Once they'd made up their minds, my usual inability to make a decision became a bride's well-known tendency to change her mind. My normal habit of asking questions became a bridal interrogation. My politest, most carefully worded requests sounded like querulous bridal demands.

I have to admit, the assistants weren't entirely mistaken about me. At this point in my wedding preparations, I was beginning to feel a touch of bridal madness. The basic retail message to brides is a one-two punch: First there is the encouragement to dream impossible dreams. *Anything you want—it's your special day!* Then the experts step up to channel all that desire. *Since you have no idea what you're doing, why don't you let us take care of this for you.* It's an excellent sales strategy, and a perfect recipe for insanity. I suspect a lot of us really don't know what we're doing when it comes to a wedding—I know I didn't—so it's easy to lose sight of what's possible and what isn't, where the dream ends and the reality must begin. We try to defy the laws of budgets, time, and gravity. The people selling us stuff are the ones who have to break the bad news. After a few rounds, some of them must come to relish the task.

Certainly the young woman towering over my shoulder while I looked at myself in the mirror seemed to be enjoying herself as she explained to me, in words that were surely plainer and more pointed than they needed to be, exactly what it was about my anatomy that required the kind of garment I said I didn't want, and why it was never going to fit the way I had hoped it would. (You might notice I am not telling you exactly what she said. I made that mistake once. After I finished telling my story, my friend stared at my breasts for a full silent minute. Then she said, "I see what she means.")

Did I draw myself up to the full length of my newly improved posture and answer in kind? I did not. Standing half naked before a badly lit full-length mirror in a garment that is impossible to put on or take off without help does not encourage snappy comebacks. I wilted under her onslaught—or would have, if wilting had been an option in what I was wearing. I felt very small, and at the same time entirely too large. In the mirror, the strong, shapely body that I saw at the gym disappeared and was replaced with something I scarcely recognized and could not look at for very long.

Clutching the last shreds of my dignity and a bag with my hard-won purchases, I made it out to the car. But once I was safely inside and out of sight, I gave in and wept like the hysterical bride I had become. I had waited too long. It was too late. The vast unknown territory of all things wedding yawned open, ready to swallow me up. I felt the full weight of my ignorance. There were probably whole networks of blogs—I thought mournfully, as I searched for something to wipe my nose on besides my sleeve—devoted solely to the art of buying and wearing Serious Underwear.

Then I dried my eyes, took a deep breath, and went shopping for shoes. I had to. Hope wouldn't know how long the dress should be until I had them. Anyway, I had already fought my way through traffic to the part of town where sparkling new malls lurk on either side of the snarling highways. I might as well, I thought grimly, finish the job.

Still a little wobbly from my recent encounter, I pushed through the doors of the department store and paused at the entrance, trying to orient myself. A sea of brightly lit mirrors and glass counters stretched out in front of me—the beauty department. If I squinted, I could see shoes and purses at the far end of the room. And directly to my right were shelves and shelves of perfume.

I drifted toward them. *Just a few minutes,* I thought, *to catch my breath.* I browsed, surprised by the selection compared with what I could find at the downbeaten mall near my house. There were new releases, too. I stopped in front of a bottle whose name was familiar. I searched my memory for the notes and came up blank, but remembered the glowing tone of the reviews I'd read—even Robin had swooned. I picked it up, the glass cool and heavy in my hand, and sniffed at a faint, delicious sweetness around the neck. Forgetting my usual caution, I sprayed some on—one full spray at the wrist and then, when that didn't horrify, another at the throat.

The scent rose up all around me in a soft cloud. The sweetness expanded, lush and narcotic. I stood quietly in the middle of it, breathing. Then it roughened with a dusky bitterness that brought me back to myself just enough to open my eyes and begin walking.

I floated over to the nearest makeup counter, sat down, and let the assistant brush some powder over my reddened cheeks, enjoying the feel of the silky bristles against my skin. By the time she'd put a coat of mascara on my damp eyelashes, the perfume had changed again, the bitterness receding, melding into the whole. I thanked her, took her card, and stood up, my silken, invisible cloud swirling gently around me as I moved.

As I walked through the rows of counters, finally ready to begin my errand, I could feel my shoulders coming down from my ears, my hands unclenching, my hips loosening and beginning, ever so slightly, to sway. I couldn't quite name what I was smelling. A memory of something teased at me, and I let it go. It was not the kind of perfume that encouraged thinking. I was not entirely sure it wanted me to be upright at all, though it didn't seem to be in a hurry to get me anywhere in particular. I would have to remember to pick up a sample on my way out.

I stopped. Looked. And looked again, unable to believe my luck. Spread before me were rows and rows of pale-gold shoes, the exact color of my dress. "Oh, sure," said the salesman who appeared magically at my side, "metallics are huge for fall." It was the work of a minute to pick out a few pairs of heels. The salesman brought my size.

"Got a formal event?"

I smiled and nodded with my mouth firmly closed.

No to the first pair. Maybe to the second. I circled slowly around the floor in the third, making sure I'd be able to keep them on long enough to walk to the altar. Long enough to stand through a ceremony. Long enough to hug all the guests on our guest list, including the cousins from Mexico, my father's college roommate, and my best friend from junior high. Long enough to dance at least two dances, one with my father and one with my groom.

Walking in those tall shoes was much easier than I remembered from the last long-ago time that I'd worn heels. I could feel my new muscles working, adjusting. Moving me forward. Catching me when I wobbled. Helping me keep my new balance.

"Those look great on you," said a woman with a pair of silver sandals in her hands.

I thanked her, meaning it, and kept walking, my perfume trailing behind me.

When Austin finally emerged from the unseasonably late wet and cold, everything quickened along with the weather. The grass and trees turned a vivid green. There were street festivals and backyard parties, the music echoing out into the street. I could feel the restless good mood of the students and professors—the end of the semester not quite there, but in sight—whenever I crossed the campus to go to the gym.

Things were moving faster there, too. It was as though I had been trudging up an invisible hill and, without knowing when I had reached the top, was now coming pell-mell down the other side. Workouts that had once been laughably impossible, then just difficult, were now almost enjoyable. I found myself trying to go faster, hold a pose longer, swim just a little farther for the sheer novelty of it. The showgirl put a hand on one hip and grinned at these extra high-kicks, momentarily without complaint.

Parker was speeding down the same hill in a very different direction. Every time I looked at him, his shoulders seemed broader, his hips narrower, everything about him more angular, more defined. "It's the testosterone," he told me. "It speeds up your metabolism and makes you lose fat." "Cheater," I complained. My waist was shrinking rapidly but my hips and bust remained stubbornly inflated, and my silhouette leaned toward the cartoonishly feminine—Jessica Rabbit, the later, much shorter years.

Working out together, side by side in front of the mirror, it was easy to feel like we were changing together. Both of us stretching into new shapes and walking into rooms in a new way. Both of us a little bewildered and giddy to see, when we looked at our reflections, something a little closer to the picture of ourselves that we carried in our heads.

But I knew that, outside the cocoon of the gym and our friendship, this was not how it looked to the rest of the world. I was walking toward the center of things, into a story that had already been told a thousand times. Parker was walking away, out to the edges and beyond, into something new. To the average stranger on the street, I was ordinary and growing more so with every pound I dropped, while Parker grew more striking and harder to place. We had stopped meeting up to swim at the big public pool downtown. "I wouldn't know which dressing room to use," he'd said when I suggested it.

While I'd been trying on dresses, mooning over silk, and trying to avoid looking too closely at the bridal books my mother had sent, he'd been researching doctors and procedures, gathering scarce facts and plentiful gossip, and considering the options for what might come next. By the time he told me about it, he had already scheduled a date for the operation, and found a friend who'd already been through it to take care of him after it was done.

"Just top surgery," he said. "That's all I want right now. Maybe that's all I'll ever want." He talked about the reputation of the doctor, the number of hours it would take to drive to the clinic, the number of weeks it would take to heal, looking nervous but happy.

After that, when we worked out together, I could feel his new urgency as the deadline for the surgery drew near. It gave us both more discipline and focus. Because of Parker, there were more push-ups, more weights, more of everything that would strengthen the muscles in his chest and make recovery faster, less painful. We got stronger together.

I never questioned his decision. I had watched all the slow, careful deliberation, the long pauses and meditation that led up to it. I had ached to see the months of daily binding and flattening. I knew there was much more that I would never know or see.

But the other changes had been gradual, hard to imagine until they appeared. They had settled like a translucent scrim over the familiar face and body of my old friend. They were an addition, a new invention. The operation would be a removal—a sudden, sharp loss. I could see the surgeon's knife all too clearly in my mind's eye. My hands flew up to cradle my own breasts in protection and protest, fending off the thought.

If it had been any other friend, my imagination might have stopped there. But it was Parker. We'd been struggling in and out of swimsuits and workout clothes together for years on end. These were not breasts I had to imagine; these were breasts I had seen and, on more than one occasion, envied. I have never mourned the loss of Lynn—I see her too clearly in Parker. But I felt a kind of yearning protectiveness, and a quiet, persistent sadness, for that soft, unwanted flesh. In my head I heard my mother sighing, and saying what she used to say every time she saw a boy with a fluttering fringe of long, dark lashes. *So pretty. What a waste.*

When at last Julia and I went to see V. and talk about the ceremony, the day was clear and warm, the sides of the roads thick with late wildflowers that had flourished in the rain. Following V.'s directions, we turned off the main road at the sign for a private zoo for rescued animals: a lion from the circus, a bear caught marauding Dumpsters, a family of peacocks from a bankrupt estate, a tiger from the apartment of a convicted drug dealer. After twenty minutes of narrow, winding country lane, two gates, a slow half-hour easing down a few miles of deeply rutted dirt road littered with boulders, and—at long last—a quick, swooshing trip across the creek, we were there.

V. walked out from the small white house to meet us, smiling, thin, and dark brown from his daily hikes. He showed us around the grassy yard, pointing out the place where the wild turkeys liked to eat berries and the spot where the foxes came looking for wild hares and quail. We admired the tiny peach tree, already putting out blooms and fruit, and stood awhile under the enormous old fig. I crumpled a leaf in my hand, sniffed, and smiled at the smell of coconut—I'd never understood before why it showed up in so many fig perfumes.

After a quick tour through the house to see the kitchen with its slanting floor, a few rooms furnished with Texas antiques, and the bedroom, with its old wooden bed raised up high above the floor, out of the way of the occasional scorpion, the three of us settled on the long galley of the front porch for a comfortable couple of hours to talk about our wedding ceremony. Julia asked us questions about why we were getting married and what we wanted from our wedding. V. said, without prompting, all the things I hadn't quite known how to say. We talked about how to translate all that into a ceremony. And then, just when we had gotten as far as we could get for the day, Alex drove up in their battered truck and we all went down to the creek for a swim.

I had developed a grudge against the creek for keeping me away from V. for so long, but as soon as I plunged into the cool, clear water, I felt nothing but gratitude. V., Alex, and Julia climbed the giant rock that rose up out of the water and rode the currents that shot out around either side of it. I floated downstream on my back, looking up at the high cliff walls that rose up on either side of the water, and at the deep blue of the sky, letting the sun dazzle my eyes.

I thought about the wedding. Then I thought about Parker and wished he could be there to swim with us. I remembered the last time we'd swum together, how I had rested at the end of the pool and watched him slicing through the water—first in long, smooth strokes and then, pushing himself harder, propelling up out of the water with a powerful back kick and hovering above the surface, arms outstretched, before he dove under and came bursting out again, and again, flying and diving his way to the end of the lane.

I turned over, put my head down in the water, and started swimming, just to see how far and fast I could go. Everything went silent and deep green. I could hear my own heartbeat and see straight down to the bottom of the creek to where the sun dappled the rocks along the bottom. I went farther, past the deep roots of a tree and then right over the edge of an underwater cliff, and for a moment I was flying, too.

Later, after Alex and Julia had gone home, after we'd eaten dinner together on the front porch and the evening light had faded, I washed the river water off my skin, dressed for bed, and dabbed on some perfume.

It was the perfume that I'd found the day I bought my shoes. I had, of course, looked up the notes the minute I got home. The reviews told me it was all white flowers: sweet frangipani, full-blooming jasmine, and rich tuberose, resting on a soft bed of sandalwood and vanilla. I should not have been surprised. After all, it had cast the same narcotic spell over me that the jasmine absolute had at the Curator's salon.

But somehow I'd always assumed that true white-flower perfumes were out of my reach. I thought of them as the bare-armed, creamy-throated center-stage divas of the perfume world. They were heady. They could be overwhelming. And very often, they were beautiful. Not quirky or cool or exotic or jolie laide or any of the other crooked side paths I'd aligned myself with over the years. Just beautiful. The way a bride is supposed to be.

I stepped out onto the front porch to turn off the light, and closed my eyes as the tropical blooms expanded in the humid night air that was their birthright. I could hear the creek rushing past, and the frogs and cicadas trilling, and beyond them, every now and then, I could hear, just as V. had told me I would, the cry of the peacocks and the roar of the lions in the zoo. I stood there awhile, listening, and then I went back inside to join him in that tall bed while the noisy night sang on.

7: THE PERFUME SHOWER

It was January, long before I began to think seriously about my dress, when my mother first called about the shower. I was happy to pick up the phone. The wedding was still nine months away. Most of our conversations up to that point had been about party planning, and in spite of my grumbling reluctance to think too hard about napkins and table arrangements, when it comes to parties, my mother and I agree. We like strong flavors, bright colors, music to sing along to and talk over, simple dinnerware that can be dropped and broken without regret. We share a relative indifference to alcohol (my mother regards wine as a waste of calories better reserved for dessert), though we understand it is important to other people. We understand the subtle architecture that supports a good party—the placement of ice and flowers, the flow between rooms, the careful timing of salt and sweet, and all the rest of the behind-the-scenes details that can mean the difference between comfort and delight, or chaos and misery. Our greatest fear is running out of food, not just because someone might, God forbid, go hungry, but because when platters aren't heaped to overflowing, people think twice about helping themselves, and stingy servings undermine the deep purpose of a party, which is the creation and celebration of abundance.

All these things I learned from my mother, but my parties are never quite like hers, and they never will be. In the time I spend breathing in the scent of the fresh basil I am chopping for a summer pesto, my mother could conquer a small island nation. Under a slightly different set of circumstances, she might have been a five-star general, a Hollywood producer, or the CEO of a multinational corporation specializing in mergers and acquisitions. Instead she has spent her life as an unpaid but highly effective member of Boise's city government. While I was growing up, she ran for, and won, three consecutive six-year terms on the school board while simultaneously serving on a series of special committees tackling everything from teen mothers to the expansion of the local art museum.

Her parties were big, theatrical productions, campaigns waged from the official headquarters of her kitchen. I grew up perched on a stool at the kitchen counter, pressing the dough for tart shells into dozens of molds, sealing hundreds of delicate wonton skins together with water and cornstarch, stuffing thousands of fat brown mushrooms, and skewering strips of beef soaked in soy sauce, vinegar, and garlic until my fingers were numb and wrinkled from the ice-cold marinade. When I got a little older, I made mosaics out of trays full of vegetables, fruits, cheeses, and canapés while my mother put roses of tempered chocolate on cakes robed in glossy ganache, dug out another set of tablecloths and runners from under the guest bed, and dragged the rental tables into the most congenial formation, all the time thinking of the next six things.

My father lobbied for quiet dinners, little conversational groups of eight, but my mother didn't see the point in doing all that work for such a small audience. Why cook for four couples when you could triple the recipe, freeze it in advance, and invite fifty instead? Besides, her friend Ross, from the meat department, had called to let her in on a deal—half a lamb someone ordered and didn't want—and her friend Dee, the florist, just got an extra shipment of gladiolas in, exactly the right color of red, and besides she'd promised the hospital, or the museum, or the library, or the teachers, or the women's shelter, or someone else I've forgotten about that she'd do a reception for them just this one more time.

In a town like Boise, these kinds of things add up over the years, and lately there have been awards in her honor, and profiles in the local press. The last time I was home, a city bus pulled alongside me at a stoplight and there, on the side of the bus, was my mother. Or rather, my mother's head, four feet high, gazing down at me in all-seeing beneficence with the same dark eyes and strong brows I saw in the mirror every morning, from an ad for a local magazine that had featured her in its last issue. The photographer had posed her against the brightly painted wagon wheel from Costa Rica that hangs on the wall of our family room, and the arc of the wheel glowed behind her thick black hair like a folk-art halo.

Considering all this, and a few other things, V. and I decided soon after our engagement that the wedding would be in Boise, in my parents' backyard, and we happily handed over executive control to my mother, reserving only the right to plan the ceremony. Not long afterward, I got an e-mail from her saying that she had found some wedding books. (My family begins all big projects with a trip to the bookstore. We like to do our homework.) She was sending me a set, too, so we could be on the same page. *They look really useful,* she wrote, *but I have to warn you that one of them is a bit much.*

There were two books. One was a pale mint green, and small enough to slip into a purse. Its cover featured a rough sketch of a bride—just a white dress, a veil, and some stick arms holding something that looked like a cross between an anaconda and a gigantic tape measure. It reared up above her head and piled up in coils underneath her feet, taking up twice as much space on the cover as she did. It was a to-do list, I realized when I opened the book. And so was the book itself. The whole book. Hundreds of urgent tasks, each with its own box to check, broken down by the month, week, day, and, on the date of the wedding itself, by the hour. I flipped back to the opening pages and swallowed, my mouth suddenly dry—I was already months behind. I closed the book.

The second book was very large and very, very pink—a bright, saturated, Barbie pink. It, too, featured a bride on its cover, a large, glossy photograph of a bright-eyed brunette roughly half my size and age, clutching a bouquet of pink flowers tied with pink ribbons. She gazed at me coyly over her shoulder, a pose that showed off the corsetry lacing on the back of her long white dress, and the length of her white veil. I grimaced back at her, sighed, and opened the book.

The elaborate world of rules and rituals inside didn't look anything like the one I knew. In my world, it was nearly impossible to plan a real dinner party, because, to my mother's horror, none of my friends understood the concept of an RSVP. And in fact, it was my mother's voice I heard in my head that day as I flipped through the chapters on engagement announcements and parties (whoops, guess we skipped those), wedding invitations (who knew there were so many ways to address an envelope?), guest lists and place settings (so many ways to offend people!), and all the other minutiae of wedding etiquette.

I heard her explaining when to unfold my napkin on my lap, how to begin with the fork that was on the outside. I remembered how she'd taught me the mnemonic she'd learned as a waitress: *Serve* the *right* way, *take away* what's *left*. And I could hear, as though she were right there in the room with me, the conversation we'd always had before the parties we attended together in the sulky period when I had begun my long drift away from the center of things: "Be nice tonight." "I'm always nice!" "You're nice when you want to be nice."

She was right, though, I thought, to send me this book. I needed a manual. I still can't eat a meal without unfolding my napkin on my lap first, but when I moved away to go to graduate school, I missed a lot of lessons. I had learned a different set of rituals and manners, ones I couldn't see because they were my own. That is, until I went home, and my mother and I looked at each other, appalled by our mutual faux pas—*How can she be that way?*

Of course, the pink book wasn't really my mother's world. With the possible exception of the creature on the front cover, it wasn't anyone's world—that's why the book existed. My first thought was to hide it away someplace and forget about it. But just as I was about to do so, my skimming brought me to the chapter on the one thing I really cared about: the ceremony.

I read about the All Night Wedding, where guests are presented with bagels and newspapers at dawn, and the Politically Correct Wedding, with invitations on 100 percent recycled paper, tree saplings on the tables, and leftovers donated to a homeless shelter for "that special touch." I learned that it was the custom in Fiji for the groom to present the bride's father with a whale tooth, and that Ukrainian brides are kidnapped by their bridal party so that everyone will remember the many times their country has been invaded. And then, after I had imagined myself as a Shinto bride, bowing gracefully to my ancestors, and as a Hindu bride, in a red sari with wreaths of flowers around my neck, I found myself reading, slowly and with great attention, the step-by-step instructions for a formal Jewish wedding.

We'd already decided to plan our own civil ceremony. V.'s parents are devout Catholics. Mine are Jewish, but I'd grown up blissfully free of any religious training. Up until that exact moment, I'd had no interest in a Jewish ceremony. But there I was, with my nose pressed up against the window of tradition, reading about how and when my groom should crush a glass with his heel and who should hold up the temporary shelter of the chuppah, taken aback by a sudden sharp longing for something impossible: to have grown up with a ceremony, to already know a tradition in my bones, to be part of a pattern that would carry me forward as it linked me back and back and back.

I took a breath and closed the book. The brunette gazed over her shoulder at me, as infuriatingly fresh and composed as ever.

For weeks afterward, the book traveled around the house to various out-of-sight, out-of-mind locations, until finally, one afternoon, when I dug it out to look up some technical question about invitation envelopes, I took the Sharpie I used to label my sample vials and gave the blushing bride a neat mustache, a goatee, and just the barest suggestion of armpit hair. It suited her surprisingly well. Now, instead of looking smug and dewy, she looked devilish, aware of her own costume—Puck in a white dress.

After that, things got easier. V. and I began to plan our ceremony. My mother planned everything else. I looked up what I needed to look up in the little green book and the big pink book. I forgot, for a while, that sulky teenage feeling of wanting and not wanting to be nice.

And then, at the tail end of January, nine months before the wedding, I picked up the phone and my mother said, "We need to talk about your bridal shower."

"Oh, that's all right," I said, as images of drunken sorority girls in miniskirts, fake tans, and toilet-paper veils came unbidden into my head. "I don't really need a bridal shower. I don't think I'm really a bridal-shower person."

There was a pause on the other end of the line, in which I could hear my mother marshaling her forces.

"Well, that is up to you," she replied crisply, making sure I understood that it wasn't. "But you need to decide one way or another, because people are asking me about it."

"It's only January!"

"I know it seems far off to you. But in my world, people plan ahead."

"What people?"

I was genuinely puzzled. Weren't bridal showers supposed to be organized by and for friends of the bride? I had exactly one good friend left in Boise, a brilliant lesbian artist named Gertrude, who spoke fluent Japanese and had recently taken up the study of avant-garde electronic music. I loved Gertrude, but she seemed unlikely to either plan or attend a bridal shower. I tried to picture the two of us, sitting quietly with my mother in Gertrude's tiny apartment, sipping ceremonially prepared Japanese green tea while we listened to the blips, screeches, and shimmers of her latest composition.

But my mother wasn't thinking of Gertrude, or of underage sorority girls. My mother was thinking of the aunts.

They aren't my real aunts, and I didn't call them that while I was growing up. I didn't need to call them at all, because they were always there: on the other end of the telephone line with my mother, sitting next to her on the school board, and on the committees and once a month at the bridge table. There were ten, or fifteen, or thirty or more of them, depending on the year and how you counted. I went to school with their children, I worked alongside them as a volunteer on some of my mother's projects, and, occasionally, I worked for them, serving at their parties or handing over a sandwich from behind the deli counter. But mostly, all through the years of my childhood and especially later, when I lived elsewhere and only came home for holidays, I saw them at parties, where they were always warm and gracious and interested in my latest adventures. When I fell in love with V. and took him home to the parties, they were warm and gracious and interested—very interested—in him, too.

"What a doll. So sweet. And *so* cute," said Liz, in a low undertone, leaning in close to me in the kitchen at that first party. Her black eyes sparkled. "You know, some of us are wishing we were a little younger tonight." "I really, really like him," said Frances the next year. Her round, intelligent face was serious, and she rested a hand on my arm for emphasis. "I finally got a chance to talk to him for a while tonight, and I'm very glad I did." "Where is he? I need him," demanded Shirley a few years after that. Spotting V. across the yard, her long, thin arms shot up in the air as she waved him down: "There you are! Come with me, I have something to show you!" She turned to me, cackling happily: "I just want to borrow him for a little while. We'll be right back!"

"These women have watched you grow up. They feel like they know you," my mother had said to me dozens of times over the years. She was saying it to me again, now, on the phone.

"I know, Mom," I said.

And, maybe for the first time, I really did know. Most of the aunts have never seen me outside of Boise. Every now and then, a few need to be updated on the basics. *No, I'm not in graduate school anymore. I got my PhD three years ago.* But I can see now, in my late thirties, what I couldn't see in my teens and twenties: the virtues of the long view.

The aunts have a bird's-eye perspective on my life that makes the spark of plot twists and the brightness of continuing threads clear to them in a way they will never be to the people I see every day. It's an increasingly rare thing, to have so many people keeping track of your life story—not for the flash of an hour or a day but for decades at a time, the years sliding into one another to make a single, smooth arc of time. V. comes from a large, tightly knit Mexican American family—

writing the guest list, we passed fifty just listing siblings, aunts, uncles, and cousins—and he is surrounded by people who keep track of his story and everyone else's, living and dead. His parents had been asking me if they would finally get to meet my family at the wedding. "Well," I said, "my parents and my brother will be there." My grandparents were gone, my aunt Toni was unwilling to travel from Miami, the ghostly circle of second cousins and people-once-removed remained mere rumors. But we had to talk my mother into limiting her guest list, lest the aunts and their husbands outnumber the other guests three to one.

For most of my life, the aunts have been family characters, defined by overheard conversations and a few telling details: Lily M. has a secret intellectual life—she's read all of Boswell and is working her way through Gibbon's history of the Roman Empire. June will wear a costume to any party at the slightest excuse. Miranda is half a head taller than her husband, a neat, bow-tied man who looks continually pleased by his good fortune. As I've gotten older, I've grown to know a few of them on their own terms, and I can see, now, how much I don't know, how many stories of work, illness, divorce, and scandal I haven't heard, or have only half understood. But—perhaps because nearly all our conversations take place against the festive, chattering backdrop of one long, continuous party—no matter how much I learn, I will always see the aunts through the soft-focus lens of my childhood, as a single net woven together from disparate strands of hope and well-wishing and ties to home, part and parcel of the thing I tried for so many years to escape, and of my great good fortune in this world.

To my mother I said, "I feel very lucky."

"You *are* lucky," she said, not quite mollified.

"Look," I continued, "maybe I just don't understand what a shower is."

"Honestly"—she snorted in disgust—"how can you not know what a shower is? Don't your friends have bridal showers?"

"Most of my friends don't get married at all," I retorted. Then I took a deep breath and tried again. "I swear, Mom. I've never been to a bridal shower. I don't even know anyone who's had one. Just think of me as completely clueless."

"Well, *that's* not so difficult," she replied, but more gently, as she shifted into instructional mode. "All right, then. There's usually around twenty or thirty women—any more than that and things get out of control. Usually, everyone arrives all at once and stands around chattering. There's some food—nothing heavy, you know, things for ladies. After a while, we all file into one room to watch the bride open presents. Everyone pays attention for about five minutes before they get bored and start talking again. And then we have cake."

"Presents?"

"Of course, presents. There are always presents. That's why you need a theme."

I began to feel a little worried. "Are you sure I need presents? I mean, that's really generous, but the shower will be more than enough. I can't really imagine what people would give me."

My mother, sensing my weak position, continued her instructions. "Lingerie is traditional. Don't worry, I know you probably won't want to do that. Hardly anyone does anymore. But I went to a really cute shower this summer that was all about gardening. Lillian hosted—she's always so good—and she made these favors out of little ceramic pots with cactuses in them, because the couple is moving to Arizona after the wedding. And lately the Hours Showers have been popular."

"The Hours Showers?" *Surely not the movie?* I drifted off for a moment, thinking about Virginia Woolf–themed shower favors.

"Hours of the day. You assign different hours to each guest. So, if you were nine A.M., you might give someone a French press, or a really nice toaster oven. But these are just options," she said generously, switching tacks as she clinched the deal. "It's your party. It should be about you and what you really want."

I was about to point out that I'd already said what I really wanted at the beginning of the phone call, when a thought occurred to me.

"Anything I want?"

"Anything you want," my mother reassured me, magnanimous in her victory.

It was a greedy thought. A slightly outrageous thought that really was all about me. Something I almost didn't dare to ask. Almost.

"Could it be perfume?"

"Perfume! Well."

I waited.

"What on earth would you do with twenty bottles of perfume?"

I thought of my carefully hoarded samples, resting gently in the cool dark of their cigar box. I knew there were more than fifty of them at this point. I'd stopped counting after I'd ordered the last dozen.

"I know it sounds crazy, Mom. But believe me, I would love it. And," I waffled, "if you think it won't work, you can tell me."

"Huh. How much are these perfumes anyway?"

I cringed. "Well, they're kind of expensive."

"How expensive?"

"Most of the ones on my wish list are between fifty and a hundred dollars," I said, seeing no reason to explain that some of them were more. "That's why I don't have any bottles yet."

"They're too much," she declared. "A shower present shouldn't be more than thirty-five dollars."

"Oh, okay, I didn't know. I can—"

"But," she went on, before I had a chance to retreat, "that's the kind of thing it should be. Something kind of frivolous. Something you wouldn't buy for yourself. Maybe we could get the ladies to team up . . ." She trailed off, not quite ready to begin planning yet.

In the silence that followed, I could hear her thinking on the other end of the line.

"I'll tell you what," she said finally. "I honestly don't know. I'm going to have to think about it and call you back."

I set down the phone, pleased and baffled. My mother, who was always so sure—I couldn't remember the last time she'd said she didn't know something—had been undone, just a little, by perfume. Who knew what would happen next?

But, distracted by that small triumph, I missed the real news. For years I had watched as my mother hosted a seemingly endless series of graduation parties, bridal showers, weddings, and baby showers, inducting each new generation into the circle. All this time, the aunts had been waiting. Now, at last, it was my turn. In the space of one phone call I had become a bride.

The following week, my mother called again.

"We have a problem."

"Hi, Mom. What's wrong?"

"Did you promise Lainie she could host a shower for you?"

"Um . . ." It seemed unlikely, but I couldn't completely rule it out. I had a long history of having conversations at my mother's parties in which I said slightly inadvisable things that I immediately did my best to forget.

"She says she talked to you at the anniversary party."

"Last June? That was six months ago, Mom. I didn't even know I was going to *have* a shower back then."

My parents' thirty-fifth-anniversary party had been happy chaos.

Guests hunkered over plates of spaghetti and seafood boil—a tribute to the New England beaches of my parents' youth—danced and sang to fifties rock and roll and big-band jazz, and played six hours of cutthroat bocce following my father's Wimbledon-inspired system of elimination rounds, in spite of the fact that most of them, not being old Italian men, had never heard of bocce before the evening began. My brother and V. refereed the game in bright-yellow shirts that said TOURNA-MENT OFFICIAL while I filmed the party and interviewed people about my parents. It was the first time I had seen my parents' friends since V. and I had gotten engaged, and many of them had congratulated and questioned me as I made my way through the crowd.

Then I remembered: I'd been filming when I heard Lainie's throaty rasp purring in my ear: "Well, hel-*lo* there. I understand you're getting *married*. Congratu-*la*-tions!" I lowered the camera and turned to her. Lainie is slim, blond, and elegant, qualities that normally make me uneasy, but she has a pleasantly distracted air, a low, easy laugh that stops just short of raucous, and a way of making you feel she is letting you in on a delightful and slightly naughty plan. Which is why, when she said to me, with a flirtatious laugh and a little shake of my shoulder, "Now, you tell your mother that I'm going to give you a party. I'm claiming you right here and now!" I laughed right along with her, even though I had no idea what she was talking about.

"That sounds like Lainie." My mother sighed. "It's not your fault. You didn't know. Anyway, you probably don't remember this either, but Ruth Ann says she said something to you the same night. I'd already talked to Frances, and I just heard from a few more people today."

There were, to be exact, eight aunts who were planning to give me a bridal shower. We discussed a few options. ("Can't they just team up, Mom?" "Oh my God, no. Eight of them? They wouldn't get past arguing about the invitations.") And my mother promised to do her best.

And then, just before she got off the phone, she said, in an offhand way that suggested the matter was barely worth mentioning, "Oh, and I decided the perfume is okay."

"Really? Are you sure it's not too expensive?"

"We'll plan around it. I still don't know what you're going to do with all that perfume. But Frances remembered talking to you about perfume last Christmas, and she told me I had to listen to you. So . . ." I could practically hear her shrugging.

"I can't believe she remembered. That's so nice of her."

"Yes. It's very nice."

"Oh, Mom, I think it's going to be great. I already have some ideas about how we could do it so it isn't just about everyone watching me open presents."

"Uh-huh. Well, just remember the ladies have very short attention spans. And thank Frances. You owe her one."

Stubborn, soft-spoken, as thoughtfully introspective as my mother was determinedly extroverted, Frances was one of the very few of my mother's friends who could directly overrule her. Something about her clothes, her opinions, the books she read, made her stand out in my mother's crowd. Once, when I was still in high school, I saw her walking across a downtown plaza with her friend Jeanne, the owner of Boise's only import shop, a traveler who was forever returning from China, India, Africa. The two women were walking away from me, arm in arm, heads bent toward each other, deep in conversation. Jeanne was tall and strong, Frances short and soft, but they were dressed alike, in long, dark, straight skirts, simple white blouses, and richly patterned shawls wrapped around their shoulders. They moved slowly through a crowd of people in jeans and T-shirts—an apparition from an older, more gracious world. They made me want to be grown up—and to grow up to be just like them.

I remembered telling Frances about my perfume, standing in line for dinner at yet another holiday party. I remembered the moments before that party, too, when I stood staring at the packet of sample vials I'd brought along with me, wanting, but not quite daring, to put one on. With a slight sense of betrayal, I set aside the more complex perfumes and picked the simplest, most innocent thing in my little bag.

More a smell than a perfume, it was a perfumer's sketch of picking apples from his grandfather's orchard as a boy. There was nothing ripe or juicy about it. It wasn't the memory of biting into an apple—crisp, tart, cold. It was the memory of standing in a room—an outdoor room, like a barn or a shed, with rough wood floors and a wide door open to the evening sky—full of baskets upon baskets of just-picked red apples, whole and still untasted, their sweet, wild scent of wine and frost and dying leaves filling the air.

Maybe because I wanted to make up for my cautious choice, but probably because it was Frances and I knew she would listen, I found myself telling a little more of the truth than usual about what I was doing with perfume. I talked about my growing collection of tiny vials and about what I was learning online. I talked about the bloggers and their personalities. And I even talked, just before we reached the buffet line, about how out of character all of this was for me. And Frances nodded, and laughed and said, "Well, why not? Why wouldn't you do something that wonderful, if you could?"

Though Lainie and Liz were also hosting the shower (my mother had managed to split the eight potential hostesses up into three teams and three parties), Frances was the one who responded to my e-mails. We settled the details—the shower would be in June, when V. and I had already planned to visit Boise for a week to see my parents and meet the DJ, the caterer, and the rest of the small army of people my mother had assembled for us. I cobbled together something resembling a perfume registry and ran a few ideas by her: *I was thinking we should let people smell the perfumes they give me,* I wrote to her. *What do you think about my writing up descriptions of the perfumes on my wish list for the invitation? What if we asked people to tell stories about the scents and perfumes they remember? The perfume they wore for their own wedding, the scent of the hair spray they wore in high school, the flowers that grew in the gardens they remember from childhood.* And Frances said, *Yes, yes, that sounds like a fine idea,* stepping in to slow me down only when I suggested that I give away samples of some of the perfumes: *I think a good whiff will be enough.*

Which was how I ended up writing the invitations to my own bridal shower. It was almost May when I sat down to write—five perfume-soaked months since my mother's first phone call about the shower. I thought about the trip to New York, the monthly meetings at the Curator's house, the countless hours reading about and testing perfume, my slow but steady series of confessions to my friends. My perfume life was no longer a secret, but it was one thing to sit alone with a friend, listening to her stories and tempting her with samples, and another to state, clearly and unapologetically, to the women who had watched me grow up, what I wanted for myself.

I looked at my wish list. I remembered how I'd felt when I found that first golden honey scent, the one that still made V. follow me around the house. I thought of a soliflore that I loved but hadn't really understood until the early-spring day in Austin when, walking my dog along the creek by our house, I was caught in the wave of living perfume rising up from the honeysuckle vines growing rampant along its banks and recognized it as the exact thing I'd been dabbing on my wrists: the scent of flowers mixed with green and growing things—simple, cheerful, but also tender, crystalline, new. I remembered browsing through the shelves at Sephora with Rubi and Erica, and my JAR experience, and all the little packets that came to me in the mail. I thought of the white flowers that had saved me. I thought about the aunts, and my mother, and how to invite them into that charmed circle. *Perfume tells a story, right there on your wrist,* I began.

I sent the invitation off to Frances with a note apologizing for how long it was and saying she could use as much or as little of it as she liked. *This looks great,* she wrote back, and I didn't hear another word. Two weeks later, my mother called again.

"You're famous," she announced.

"What do you mean?"

"You're the talk of the town."

"Mom, what are you talking about?"

"Well, I don't know what's in those invitations, but I just saw Liz in the supermarket and she went on about how much she enjoyed reading what you wrote, and then she started telling me about the perfume she wore in high school."

"So what was it?"

"I don't remember. I was just trying to get my shopping done. Anyway, then when I got home there was a phone message from Ada saying how excited she was about the shower. She said she'd been talking to Shirley about it. And then Mary-Lou called."

"Really?"

"I told you, you're the talk of the town. I got an e-mail from Judy Friedman, and Nancy, too. They're all excited. Oops—" I heard her nails clicking on the computer keyboard. "Just got another one. You're in for it now."

"But you haven't seen the invitations yet?"

"No. You know, I think they forgot to send me one."

"I haven't gotten one, either. Now I'm really curious."

My invitation arrived a few days later, in a slim envelope of dark, richly marbled paper. I pulled it out and squirmed in embarrassment. They'd printed every word I'd written, in tiny italic script, on four separate parchment-paper enclosures. Surely, I thought, squinting at my own words, no one was reading all of this.

But it seemed they were. My mother's report was just the beginning. There were more phone calls, more encounters around town, more e-mails. And for the first time in my life, I began to hear directly from the aunts themselves. First from Frances: "I just spent forty-five minutes reading perfume descriptions on LuckyScent instead of re-searching my stocks. You are a very bad influence." Then from Shirley: "Yesterday I got a massage, and I stopped and smelled the different oils before I picked one because I was thinking about you. You have me thinking about all the smells I like. I love all the smells around springtime . . . the flowering trees, and, like this evening, that quick little surprise shower. I love the lavender-scented lotion my daughter Kate uses on her little ones. I hope others are discovering what they love." Linda wrote about perfumes she had saved from her mother's collection—could I tell her about them? How could she open them without breaking the glass? Ruth Ann asked if I could help her find a perfume she had loved and lost. And I wrote back—with information, recommendations, and further temptations.

Then my mother forwarded the e-mails from Judy. Small, athletic, with a bare-scrubbed face and cropped hair, she had always seemed a little nervous around the more elegant aunts. "I have never worn any-thing that smells—even my deodorant is scentless," she wrote. "But, after reading that invitation this former tomboy is intrigued. I do like the scent of roses and lilacs and cinnamon." And then again later: "I wanted to tell you I bought Alyssa something on her wish list because it sounded like something I might like. I got a sample for me! I think I'm hooked. What a world this has opened up for me."

"I gotta tell you," my mother said later that week, in the middle of a conversation about something else, "I really thought this perfume thing wasn't going to work. But I think maybe I was wrong."

A few weeks later, V. and I left for Boise. We arrived on a gorgeous, clear June day. The weather held for our meetings with the caterer, the DJ, the videographer, and the florist, but the day of the shower was cold and gray. By late afternoon it was sleeting.

"This is really too bad." My mother sighed. "Lainie is going to be so disappointed. She's been working on her garden for weeks to get it in shape for the party. And her house is tiny. I don't know how we're all going to fit in."

I said goodbye to V.—he and my father, it had been decided, would be allowed to come to the end of the shower—and left with my mother. She drove us down one of Boise's grand old oak-shadowed boulevards to Lainie's white colonial, a tidy box with proper green shutters and a border of sheared hedges. Walking up the straight-edged path to the front door, I prepared myself for crystal and silver, tea and white linen, a quiet formality.

I was right about the crystal and silver. I was wrong about the quiet. Though we'd arrived only fifteen minutes after the starting time, the door opened on a party already in full swing, the series of small rooms packed with women all talking at once. And they weren't drinking tea.

"Well, hello there! You're here at last!" It was Lainie, threading her way through the crowd to hug first me and then my mother. "Now, come with me," she said, taking my arm. "I'll get you a drink and show you *everything.*" We left my mother to her hellos at the door and made our way through a sea of hugs and exclamations to a table full of crystal champagne flutes on silver trays. Lainie put one in my hand. It was filled to the brim with something pink and sparkling, and garnished with a red rose, the stem cut just long enough to let the flower rest above the rim of the glass.

"Try it, try it," she urged. Holding the rose gingerly to one side, I took a sip. Champagne bubbles ran over my tongue, followed by a wallop of pure alcohol so strong I nearly dropped the glass.

"Isn't it lovely?"

"Delicious," I spluttered. "What's in there?"

"Oh, let's see. Champagne. Vodka. And just a touch of raspberry liqueur."

"To make it pink?"

"Yes, yes! Now let me show you the flowers."

Scattered throughout the rooms were bouquets of fragrant flowers, each in its own low china bowl: Madonna lilies rested next to the drinks, there were freesias on an end table next to the couch in the living room and stephanotis on the coffee table. Lainie led me over to a bowl of pastel roses tucked into a nook under the stairs in the hallway. "Smell them!" she ordered. I bent over the flowers and breathed in their delicate scent of black tea, sun-warmed apricots, and rain. "They're very beautiful," I said. Lainie ran a fond hand over the soft, blowsy petals. "I picked them just before the party," she said with a contented sigh. "They're my favorite."

I turned to find Liz at my elbow. "Did Lainie tell you about the flowers? They're from our wedding bouquets. Mine are the lilies."

"And the roses?" I said, turning to Lainie. "Are they from your wedding?"

Lainie waved the question away. "Oh, who can remember," she said, her low, easy laughter rolling over us.

"The stephanotis are mine." Frances had made her way over to us. I was glad to see her calm face. "Have you seen what Donna Davies brought?" she asked. "You have to see it. Come on, it's in the back room."

Frances led me down the dark, narrow hallway to a quiet room filled with clear light from the tall French doors that looked out over Lainie's beloved garden and settled herself in one of the enormous over-stuffed armchairs crowded together in the corner. Next to her, on the end table, stood a small leather case set on one end. The side facing me was split down the middle, like a miniature wardrobe, with two tiny brass knobs. Frances gestured toward it. "It's a traveling vanity. Donna's mother took it with her on her honeymoon. Go on, open it."

I tugged gently on the knobs. The panels swung open to reveal four slim glass bottles tucked into individual leather sleeves. Below them were two drawers and a writing blotter that had folded down of its own accord when I opened the doors. A silver-backed hairbrush, comb, and mirror were tethered to the insides of the panels. They gleamed against the blue velvet lining.

"Can't you just imagine her on the train," said Frances, "brushing her hair and then sitting down to write a letter to the family she'd just left behind, maybe scenting the envelope before she mailed it? You can take the perfume out and open it. Donna was showing it to us before you came."

I eased the bottles out of their leather sleeves. They were labeled in gold filigree: AMBRE, CHYPRE, VIOLETTE, EAU DE COLOGNE. The glass stopper of Ambre gave way easily. I sniffed cautiously at the rim. It had the familiar, musty top notes I'd encountered in other vintage perfumes—they were always the first to degrade—but I could smell the still-true heart notes lurking underneath. I dabbed the stopper against the back of my hand and warmed the traces it left behind with my breath to encourage the heart and base to come forward.

"There's so much perfume left in the bottles," I noted. "Do you think she was saving them for special occasions?"

"Maybe." Frances grinned. "Maybe they were a shower present and she didn't like them."

I grinned back at her. "What was your bridal shower like? Do you remember?"

"I remember it very well. It was horrible. Just my mother-in-law, her awful friends, and me. I spent the whole time sitting in a chair, answering their questions."

I pictured a younger Frances, her thin blond hair long around the same serious round face and pale blue eyes, sitting in a straight-backed chair, facing down a circle of disapproving older women. "What kinds of questions?"

Frances leaned back in her armchair and blinked a few times behind her glasses, her mouth tightening to a thin line. "Oh, backhanded questions about who I was, what kind of wife I'd be. You know how women can be." She was silent for a moment. "So what does that perfume smell like?"

I let her half-told story hang in the air and sniffed at the back of my hand. Perfumes as old as the ones in the case took their cues from a slower, more formal world. They were meant to unfold in languorous waves through cocktails, multiple courses, dessert, coffee, and a brandy or two, or a night at the opera followed by a midnight supper and dancing. They were meant to linger until morning on the skin and the sheets of the women who wore them, a delicious reminder of the previous night's debaucheries. I wouldn't really know what this one was like for another hour or two, but I could already smell a hint of the dirty, leathery vanilla at its base—a mixture of smoke, burnt sugar, and hot skin that had nothing to do with today's perfumes. It was a scent from a time when stealing a dab of perfume from your mother's vanity table meant something, because sex was dangerous, and there were things that *une femme d'un certain age* could do that younger women knew nothing about. A time when the most popular perfumes said not *I am fresh and sweet* but something more along the lines of *I am a powerful female animal. Forget this at your peril.*

It was a limited power, I reminded myself, thinking of Frances and her circle of female judges. Still, it was hard not to admire such a fierce and unapologetic claim.

I was saying some of this to Frances when Shirley burst into the room. "There you are!" she cried. "Come see what I brought!"

A little reluctantly, I left the quiet parlor and plunged back into the thick of the party, moving along slowly from aunt to aunt until I reached the living room, where Shirley had lined the mantelpiece with antique perfume bottles. Gertrude arrived, looking bewildered but very chic in her Japanese coat and the fuchsia satin trousers she had sewn herself. She showed me a lacquered box with a few sticks of rare incense she had brought along to share. Someone introduced me to a new daughter-in-law who had come along at the last minute because she, too, was scent-obsessed, an archaeologist who had been digging up ancient perfume bottles and analyzing their contents. Somewhere on the other side of the room, I could hear my mother telling stories about our meeting with the caterer the day before. Someone brought me a beautiful plate of food—translucent coral slices of smoked salmon on perfect toast points, bright-green spears of asparagus, a few ripe red strawberries—that I scarcely touched because someone else had already given me a second, lethally pink cocktail. I answered the same three or four questions from seven or eight women, smiling until my face ached, partly because of the champagne but mostly because everyone was so tender and excited and encouraging and interested. And then it was time to open the presents.

The party gathered itself and flowed into the small living room. From an armchair against the wall, I watched as the women packed themselves in on the long couch and the love seats in front of the fireplace, filled up the extra chairs Lainie was dragging in, perched on ottomans and armrests, and found a place to lean against the backs of the couches or along the walls until, finally, all of them were settled and had turned, as one, to face me. I scanned the faces of the loving mob—so many people who had known me for so long—and felt an electric flicker of fear. The sheer number of beribboned boxes and bags piled on the coffee table in front of me seemed like a rebuke—clinical evidence of an unhealthy obsession. Beside me, watching everything, was my mother.

But then, at Frances's command, I began to unwrap the first box. And when I held the beautiful bottle I had seen only in photographs, I couldn't resist taking off the cap to sniff at the thrilling abundance of a perfume I'd been doling out to myself a drop at a time. Suddenly, everything went silent, the room receded, and I closed my eyes and disappeared into the private world conjured up by the beautiful scent. It was just a moment, but when I opened my eyes and the world rushed back to life, I was in love with perfume all over again and I wanted only what all lovers want: to talk about the charms of my beloved, in detail and at length, to anyone who would listen.

So that was what I did. Box after box, I introduced my gifts to the crowd, less like a docent at a museum than a devoted vaudeville promoter parading his favorite showgirls. *Now, this one, ladies, hails from the house of Annick Goutal, founded by a model and concert pianist turned perfumer. It's named after an oil extracted from the flowers of the bitter orange tree. It starts tart and green, like the leaves and fruit of the tree, and then it softens into this light, transparent floral, like the scent of the blossoms in the air. Did you know it's traditional for brides to wear orange blossoms in their hair?*

I described their various talents and attributes: *This one takes you on a walk by the sea through a cypress forest, and then suddenly you stumble on a grove of lemon trees and just one fig tree, covered in ripe figs. It's the perfect thing in hot, humid weather. Just one spritz and you can feel that salty breeze coming in off the ocean.*

I dropped the names of their famous relatives: *Have any of you ever worn Chanel No. 19? This is one of her granddaughters. It's got the same feeling of chilled white wine, with just a touch of rose, and a little growl down there in the base.*

I revealed their little quirks: *This one smells exactly like a creamsicle when you first put it on, but if you wait two minutes it turns into a rich, sophisticated amber. It's like you put on a bright orange corduroy jumper and then it suddenly morphs into a little black velvet dress with pearls.*

I even shared a few of the jokes they liked to tell: *Now, this is from a house called Parfum d'Empire. Their perfumes are inspired by fallen empires. They have one for the Ottoman Empire, one for Napoleon, one for Alexander the Great. This one is supposed to be a tribute to the Russian Empire, and it starts off with a big blast of vodka.*

The whole time, I was sending the bottles back out to the women who had given them to me, inviting them to take off the caps and sniff, to take a chance and spray a little and see what they would find on their own skin. Every now and then, I couldn't resist dabbing a bit of something very special onto my own wrist, and when this happened the women would clamor to smell it and I would make my way around the packed room, offering my outstretched arm to aunt after aunt, each of them bending to sniff and exclaim.

Half an hour into all this, I realized with a start that while there were a few skeptics in the room—women sitting up very straight, with their mouths closed and their hands in their laps—no one was bored. The cake sat forgotten in the kitchen. And I wasn't the only one talking: The women were chiming in with bits of description they remembered from the invitation. "That's the one that makes him follow her around the house!" shouted the team of women who had gotten together to buy my honey perfume when I pulled the gorgeous bottle—a blown-glass globe etched with a cluster of grapes—out of its little copper-colored satin bag. "The great lady of the eighties!" called out the group packed onto the love seat as I unwrapped my beloved Coco from Chanel.

The renegades who had ignored my wish list made their own introductions. "Oh, you'll love this one—it's a classic. Every woman should have some," assured one of the women who had teamed up to give me the rich, *extrait* version of Chanel No. 5. "That is a pure oil from Egypt," Donna Davies informed me when I pulled out the fragile spindle of a bottle. "A little goes a very long way, and it will last forever. Perfume is very important in Egypt, you know." "Those come from a monastery in Italy," said Frances as I pulled a series of small, dark-brown bottles of essential oil out of the bag she'd given me. "I picked them up on my trip. The monks make them from the flowers and plants that grow on their land."

Joan Drake, the mother of a girl I'd played with in fourth grade, handed me a small box. Tall and patrician, I had noticed her among the skeptics. But the box held something priceless: a vintage bottle of pure *parfum* still in its sealed box, the original version of a masterpiece long since ruined by cheap reformulations. I gasped and thanked her profusely. Did she know what she had here? "Yes, of course. It used to be my signature scent," she said, her face still unsmiling, "but I stopped wearing perfume years ago when my allergies started acting up." She shrugged slightly. "It's just been sitting in my drawer."

Shy, freckled Tina Smith, who had been my junior high school librarian, stepped forward with a tall bag. Inside was a beautiful narrow-necked bottle of painted china. "It belonged to my aunt," she said. "She ran a fancy boutique in Portland that sold gifts—fine china, stationery, that kind of thing. I used to love visiting her there when I was a little girl—it seemed so glamorous. They sold their own signature perfumes from big glass urns behind the counter. You chose which one you wanted, and then they put it in a bottle from the store. I've been saving this bottle for thirty years. The perfume has evaporated, but you can still smell it." I began to demur—surely this was too special to give away—but she silenced me. "It is special," she said firmly. "That's why I've been waiting so long. I wanted to make sure I gave it to someone who would understand what it was."

I barely noticed when V. and my father arrived and gingerly made space for themselves on the edge of the circle. But V., in his quiet way, saw everything, as he always does. That night when we were lying in bed making sense of the day and I was telling him all about the shower and the perfume and the women, he said, "But did you see your mother's face?" When I tried, and failed, to remember what my mother had looked like at the shower—she was sitting next to me, I explained, so I couldn't really see her—he said, "You should have seen her face." But when I asked him what she looked like, all he said was "Surprised. And very proud. But mostly surprised. Like you were someone she'd never seen before." And then he added, "She really loves you, you know. All those women do." I said nothing, but I lay in the dark thinking of my mother and what she might have seen, what I might have looked like, praising my gifts to those who had given them to me.

The laughter that had filled that packed room was still ringing in my ears. It was the laughter that made me sure the aunts understood not just my vaudeville patter, or the beauty and the art of the scents, but the thing running and humming along underneath all that, the thing that had made me bold enough to ask for the perfume in the first place. The laughter gave the tail end of the party, when everyone was finally eating cake and then milling around to find their coats, the feel of an after-show gathering, as though we were a crowd streaming out of a great movie, exhilarated and chatty, the glamour and emotion of those hours in the dark still with us. It explained why, just before I went out the door with my mother, Judy Friedman came up to me with a glowing face and made me blush all the way home by standing on tiptoe to throw her arms around my neck and whisper, "Thank you. Truly."

It started when I launched into my first description—just a few nervous, smothered giggles. Then I began sending the perfume out into the crowd and it got louder and less polite. The first few aunts who dared to spray their wrists did so furtively, as though someone would rush over at any minute to scold them. When no one did, their faces bloomed into pleased little smiles and they leaned into their neighbors, tittering behind their hands at their own bravado. Then, as the perfume warmed on their skin and rose up in the air around them, they remembered why they had sprayed it in the first place and bent their heads to their wrists. Some jerked away, laughing at the strength of their reaction. But others closed their eyes for a moment, the room falling away for them as it had for me, and breathed out a sharp "Ha!" of delight as they came back to the world. Then, one by one, they offered up their wrists to the women sitting around them. All over the room I could see the women bending their heads together over each other's arms. Even Joan leaned toward her neighbor for a tentative sniff, smiling a little as the scent reached her. The sighs and exclamations swelled and subsided in waves as the women grew bolder, reaching out their hands for the bottles as they traveled around the room. Every now and then, there were cries of recognition: "Oh!" gasped Judy. "It really, truly smells like roses! I never thought I'd find something that smells like that!" By the time I was describing one of the final bottles and the gifter called out, "Yes, that's it exactly!"—and then, blushing bright red, "I only sprayed it once!"—the room was full of perfume and laughter: big guffaws and naughty little hand-over-the-mouth snickers, raucous belly laughs, and clear peals of sheer glee.

And though I hadn't seen her face, I'd heard my mother laughing, too.

8: A KISS AND A DREAM OF
WHITE FLOWERS

When at last the day arrived, our wedding was not very different from most weddings. The out-of-town guests poured in, with their stories of delayed flights and long drives. There were tearful reunions and awkward first meetings. There were snatched chances to catch up, an argument or two, and a lot of well-meaning small talk—*Do you know the bride or the groom?* There were small disasters and modest acts of heroism. There was a great deal of eating and drinking, and a few people did too much of both. There were hugs and handshakes. There was dancing. There were flowers. And V. and I were in the middle of it—the reason for it all, hailed and congratulated everywhere we went but also, somehow, unnecessary. The party went on—and it did go on, for a full three days, the seamless ribbon of celebration rolling out over the solid, invisible structure of my mother's endless work—whether or not we were in the room.

But the details, the small variations on the theme, were important. Erica had made our invitations out of deep-brown, ocher, and bright poppy-red papers printed with an old botanical drawing of a sunflower so lively it looked like it might bite. Folding them into their envelopes, I'd felt sure that as soon as the guests opened them they would know about the golden foothills and what the flowers would look like and how my mother and I had decided that nothing, not even the plates, would be white.

Though I hadn't seen some of them in a long time, and one was newly pregnant, all the friends I had asked to stand with me had said yes. The aunts held a party for V.'s parents, and one of them slipped me a sample of perfume when she said hello. At the bridal brunch—the final aunt-hosted party—we sat at round tables in a backyard garden and ate quiche while a high-school string quartet played Bach. At the rehearsal dinner, V. and I crowned our mothers with tiaras.

In the hour just before the ceremony, my friends and I climbed the stairs to my old bedroom and helped one another get dressed. Kat had come over one night after the Curator's salon to show me how to put on my makeup, and I remembered all her directions. Julia lent me bobby pins so I could put flowers in my hair. In the end, even after last-minute help from another tailor, my dress still looked homemade. But a friend from graduate school zipped up the back, and a friend from high school helped adjust a generous silk wrap I loved—deep russet lined with coral pink—around my shoulders, and my golden shoes slipped easily onto my feet, and at the last moment I gave everyone who wanted one a dusting of shimmery powder so we would be ready for the cameras.

We were standing around admiring one another, feeling relieved to be ready and a little nervous for what was next, when I realized, with a start, that I'd nearly forgotten to put on my perfume. Laughing, I fumbled through the little bag that held my makeup, looking for the two tiny vials I'd brought along, one a clear gold and the other a deep rose pink. I put on the pink first. It was the perfume I'd found the day I bought my shoes—Songes, it was called, the French word for *dream*. And then, because it was the first one that swept me off my feet, and because it was a day for extra sweetness, I added a tiny dab of the golden honey scent that V. so loved.

I was still struggling to replace the caps on the vials when someone came to the foot of the stairs and called up to us. We hurried out onto the landing and came tumbling down, giggling and hushing one another because the ceremony was already in progress—when we got to the back door I could hear Julia and her co-officiant, Patrick, at the bottom of the sloping yard, cheering on the guests, teaching them the lines we'd written for them. And I could see V. and his friends lined up just outside the door, on the other side of the yard. The day was warm and clear, and though a haze of smoke from distant wildfires hung over the horizon, the sky was blue.

We waited. The guests applauded themselves. And then the music began.

I did not walk down the aisle. There was no aisle. But there were two paths, curving around the yard to the bottom of the hill, where our friends waited for us. My parents and I walked down one of them while V. and his parents walked down the other. There was no chuppah, and no altar, but the arbor my father had put up was just big enough for the two of us to stand underneath, and our friends stood by us on either side. There was no rabbi and no priest, but Julia was just Jewish enough to invite me to seder every year, and later that evening Patrick would talk over the finer points of Vatican II with V.'s father. There was no Latin, and no Hebrew, but our parents stood up, one pair at a time, put their hands on our shoulders, and gave us their blessing. There was no glass to crush, no cup of wine to pass back and forth, but there was poetry, and there was Andrew, who had introduced us all those years ago under the magnolia tree, reading part of an essay titled "On the New Use of Old Forms." There were no old vows to love and obey, but there were new ones, spoken in the same ancient rhythms. There was no *By the authority vested in me*—we had given away the authority to all the guests, and when the time came they gave us their blessing with one united voice, and then they pronounced us married with so much enthusiasm that if V. had not been holding my hand, that solid wave of joy and love would have knocked me over.

Then, of course, there was a kiss. How could there not be a kiss? And the wave of joy rose up again and swamped us both.

Later, much later, after the toasts had been made and dinner had been served, after everyone had let their food get cold so they could walk out from under the tent and admire the smoky sunset lighting up the sky in great washes of russet, coral, pink, and gold, after the cake had been cut and the ceremonial dances had been danced, but before the real dancing began, for the first time in days I found myself alone. By the dessert table.

I helped myself to a piece of cake—my ceremonial slice had disappeared somewhere, no doubt to the same place my dinner had gone. I took a bite. It was delicious.

My head swam with champagne and the stories I'd been hearing all night about other weddings and other vows. Floating from guest to guest on a tide of laughter and earnest good wishes, I'd felt myself dissolving, the edges of things growing soft and blurred. The brief moments of the ceremony seemed to ripple outward in ever-expanding circles that took in all the months that had led up to them—every phone call, every mistake, even the mismatched seams on my golden dress, which, the photographs would confirm, was still the wrong color for me. I had been thinking about alterations and the new use of old forms and all the other brides before me, going back and back and back.

But when the small swarm of servers appeared to clear the table, I was mostly thinking about buttercream frosting. How superior it is to ganache. And how, now that all the photos were done and the guests were starting to leave, I could go upstairs in a minute and take off my dress and the various binding things underneath and put on the more comfortable clothes I'd brought along for the end-of-night dancing.

Maybe I would leave the flowers in my hair. And I would still have on my perfume—that beautiful dream of white flowers, that touch of honey. It had hovered around me all through the ceremony and everything that followed, an extra measure of comfort and grace. My private story. My perfect, invisible dress.

A young woman with a swinging ponytail apologized as she leaned in front of me and began piling the remaining slices of cake onto a large serving tray. I smiled at her and took another bite. She smiled back, then paused a moment and leaned toward me.

"I hope you don't mind my saying this, but you smell amazing."

Before I could respond, she turned away, hoisted up her tray, and hurried off toward the house.

I took one more bite of cake, and then I followed her.

PART III

COMING TO MY SENSES

9: SUNFLOWERS AND CITY LIGHT

V. had been away from work for six months on his writing fellowship, so a few days after the wedding we went home, and life continued on more or less as before. It surprised me, the continuing on. I was unmoored, not quite myself. I wandered into rooms and stood there trying to remember what I'd wanted. I thought about decompression chambers and understood, for the first time, the wisdom of honeymoons. I recalled all the books I'd read and all the movies I'd seen and all the ancient stories I knew that ended with a wedding.

There was a pile of work waiting for me—two sets of test questions, some copy for a Web site about training triathletes, an article on the biology department for the alumni magazine of a local college. I tried to settle down to it, but my restlessness got the better of me and soon enough I'd wandered off to catch up on the blogs. Which was how I came to be sitting in front of my computer, feeling the blood rush to my face: Marina was welcoming a new writer to Perfume-Smellin' Things. She'd put out a call two days before we'd left for the wedding. I'd sighed and let it go, sure it would be too late to apply once we got back. But if this was the first new writer—I clicked through the posts I'd missed while we were gone and saw no other new names—maybe I'd been wrong.

For nearly a year, I'd woken up knowing that perfume would be a part of my day. I had a vocabulary now, a collection of private rituals and memories. I knew I liked a cheering burst of citrus on a cold, cloudy morning, a spritz of smoky tea to clear my head, a dab of thick, resinous sweetness and spice to perfume my dreams. I had cravings—for an urgent hour, or a few days at a time, I would long for the sharp green chill of galbanum, or the sunny leather-and-ripe-apricots smell of osmanthus, or the peculiar, buttery narcotic of tuberose, thinking about the scent until it took on color and texture in my mind and I could almost reach out to stroke it. And sometimes, in the lull of an afternoon or the middle of an errand, I would find myself haunted by some unidentifiable olfactory phrase—a hallucinatory fragment of a perfume hovering just out of reach, like a snatch of a melody playing in my head, or a forgotten name on the tip of my tongue.

The bottles I'd brought home from my bridal shower had provided me with plenty of perfume to share and trade. Now my perfume closet was full of gifts—fancy packages from the aunts, and rows of decants in neatly labeled generic atomizers from my fellow perfumistas. My sample collection had grown so large I'd had to add another box—or two. I had a feeling of plenitude, of heaped-up treasure that I could spend and spend or just give away.

It was a feeling that went far beyond perfume. Sampling, reading the blogs, my evenings at the Curator's salon—all of it had given me the habit of paying attention, of noticing, naming, and describing. Smells I'd always loved leapt toward me, vivid and three-dimensional: the wet, loamy richness of overturned earth, the scratchy lemon green of tomato leaves, and the rich, tangy caramel of sautéing onions. But so did all the smells I had cherished without knowing it: the mossy, cold-stone scent of the spring-fed pool where I swam on summer mornings, the damp-cement-and-coffee scent of the little café where I liked to work, the musty stale-corn-chip smell of my dog.

It didn't stop with smells. Flavors had a new clarity and complexity.

I invented new recipes with familiar ingredients and sought out spices and fruits I'd never tasted. I paused to enjoy the silky cool of the flour between my fingers, the heft of the knife in my hand, the satisfying *thwack* of the blade against the cutting board. The world had more color and more contrast. I paid more attention to the way strangers walked, and I looked longer at my friends' faces. There was more noisy birdsong and more—much more—of that subtle hum I can sometimes hear when I'm concentrating on a difficult but satisfying task or sitting around a dinner table late at night, laughing and talking with people I love.

It was something like the way I remembered feeling at the swoony beginning of a love affair, when my heart swelled full at the slightest breeze and everything and everyone looked beautiful. And it was something like the way I used to feel in graduate school at the end of a very long, very good day of writing when I was deep into a project—an intoxicating sense of connection, as though the sentences on the page were slender threads cast out toward something much larger, something beyond my imagining. (V. called it my "rapture of the deep," as in "When you recover from your rapture of the deep, would you mind emptying the dishwasher?")

But my new way of paying attention was a far calmer, simpler, more solid kind of pleasure. I wasn't stretching out toward some idealized person or idea. It wasn't about losing my heart or my head—it was about coming to my senses. And every sight, sound, smell, taste, and texture was a link to my place in the splendid world at hand.

You might think, given all this, that I would have pages and pages I could send to Marina—notes on my latest samples, rapturous descriptions of my favorites, maybe even a story or two about my adventures as a perfumed bride. But like most real changes, this one had snuck up on me gradually. To tell the truth, for a long time it didn't feel like much of a change at all, just a series of enjoyable moments—and what could there be to say about that?

So I carried on, in my usual stubborn, earnest way, with the kind of writing I'd done in graduate school—the writing I thought of as real work, serious work. Now, as I read through my various outlines and half-written essays (I never could seem to finish anything) looking for something for Marina, I saw them as if for the first time—abstract, opaque, odorless. Far away from the new world I'd discovered. I had told almost everyone I knew about my perfume life, but I was still keeping it a secret from the gimlet-eyed tribunal of literary critics who lived in my head.

There was one thing, just a scrap of a scene. A memory of a graduation party for a friend, just after I'd finished my own degree. Late on a summer night, sitting in an unlit garden, we were drinking and giggling, confessing to things we were embarrassed to like. We traded a few bad pop songs. My friend waved a despairing hand at the smoke from his cigarette. Then I mentioned perfume. And he turned to me and said, in that sharp, contemptuous way we had all learned to use in class, "Perfume? Really?"

I read the scene over again, feeling very puzzled. I could remember that night clearly. I remembered the velvet feel of the humidity, the cicadas, my burning face, the way I'd brushed off the question—*no, of course I don't really mean perfume.* How I sipped my drink in the dark and waited for the subject to change. But I couldn't, for the life of me, remember being interested in perfume in graduate school. Had I even owned any perfume? I searched my memory and came up blank. Then I thought again, got up from my desk, and walked to the bathroom.

I knew there was a jumbled basket of old stuff in the back of the cabinet above the toilet. I'd shoved it there three years ago, right after we moved in, and I'd been meaning to throw it away ever since. I re-membered it every time I put away the folded towels, because it took up just enough room to make my task difficult, and then I forgot again. Now I stood with my foot braced against the toilet for balance, reached up, grabbed the edge of the basket, and pulled it out, just to see.

And there they were, mixed in with a half dozen other bottles of shampoo and lotion. The dusty, half-empty bottle of Elizabeth Arden's Sunflowers smelled, when I sniffed at the neck, somewhere between bright fruit and expensive shampoo, and just a touch of what I remem-bered smelling when I first wore it: sunflower honey. It was a cast-off, I remembered when I sniffed again, from a friend who offered it when she saw me cooing over it in her room. The two squat glass bottles with the apothecary-style labels had come from the soap aisle at a fancy gro-cery store: a thin, pink tea rose that I could never bring myself to throw away, though it had disappointed me right from the beginning, and a dark, sweet fig, ripened with cassis, that I had truly loved. All three were missing their spray nozzles. I'd removed them so I could dribble tiny, controlled amounts of perfume onto my skin. I sniffed at the fig, again remembering how nervous I had been about wearing too much.

Three bottles—honey, fig, rose. Three of my favorite notes. And sunflowers: the flowers on our wedding invitation, and on every guest's table . . . the flowers, burnished brown and gold, in my bridal bouquet. I'd forgotten. But I'd remembered, too.

A few days later, I sent my writing sample off to Marina with my fingers crossed. I waited a week for a response. Then I waited a second week. At the end of the third, another new writer appeared on the site and my heart sank. *Too late after all.*

If I had written a straightforward perfume review, that would have been the end of it. I'd have chalked it up to my lack of expertise and gone back to being a fan. But I'd told my small story about forgetting perfume and what I'd remembered since I'd discovered it again. I'd written it thinking of all the bloggers and the commenters whose voices had become as much a part of my daily pleasure as perfume itself. It was a confession—and a thank-you note. My skin had prickled with embarrassment and hope when I sent it.

So I moped. For a full afternoon I walked around grumpy and distracted, prickling with the realization of how much I had been hoping for a different answer. Or any answer, really. *Wait a minute.*

"Dear Marina," I wrote, "did you receive a writing sample from me a couple weeks ago?" The answer came instantly: "No, so sorry!!" Had I, by chance, sent it as an attachment? Forty-five minutes, a flurry of e-mails, and one yelp of surprised delight later, I was an official member of the Perfume-Smellin' Things team.

A week later, my post went up. It is the custom on PST to answer every comment on a post. I spent the day hovering over my computer, refreshing my screen every ten minutes—it might have been five—to see if there were any new responses. One by one, the comments appeared. Patty, from the Perfume Posse, said she got asked the "Perfume? Really?" question all the time, and March wondered why no one ever felt harassed for stocking up on wine. I had to call V. when Andy Tauer, a Swiss perfumer whose work I greatly admired, wrote to say that when he told people what he did for a living, either they were completely baffled or wanted to tell him about their sex lives. Angela, whose post on Now Smell This had been on my mind as I wrote, said she agreed with every word. And Victoria, from Bois de Jasmin, whose writing I'd been thinking about, too, made me feel like I'd just gotten a gold star from my favorite professor by thanking me for my honesty. *We know exactly how you feel. Welcome.*

In hindsight, that first article was almost as opaque as the rest of the unfinished things in my files. But it was a beginning, and I kept going, slowly but steadily. Remembering how I'd felt when I was new and unsure of myself and my taste, I wrote about perfume cool. Still a scholar, I wrote about what "oriental" meant in perfume. Still just a fan, I tracked down the perfume godmother, Chayaruchama, and interviewed her.

I became fascinated by the small handful of artists and designers working with scent, re-creating everything from the smell of fear and the Cold War to the imagined scent of the sun. I talked my friend Anna into including one of the best—the globe-trotting Norwegian provocateur Sissel Tolaas—as a speaker at the annual symposium she organized for Parsons the New School for Design. Because I'd put the two of them in touch with each other, when I went to the symposium, people knew who I was and treated me like I knew something about scent. My friends began introducing me as someone who wrote about perfume.

And each time a new post went up, I was amazed all over again by the evidence that people were reading and enjoying what I had written. The evidence, solid and irrefutable, that I was part of the circle.

I even made a real-life perfume friend. The night my first post went up, I stumbled across a beautiful blog pairing poetry and perfume, written by a woman who lived an hour away from Austin. Still giddy and grateful from the responses I'd gotten to my own writing, and excited to find a fellow perfume fanatic in Texas, I wrote the author an e-mail saying how much I liked her work. She responded with compliments about my post. Soon we were writing back and forth so often that when I told V. about her, I called her the Correspondent.

Like me, the Correspondent had been a poet as an undergraduate— a far more promising one, from the hints she gave. Unlike me, she had never stopped writing, and she'd read widely over the years in several different languages. Her letters were full of lines and stanzas and references that sent me scrambling to look up unfamiliar names. It had been years since I'd read poetry. I'd held on to my passion for it for the first few years of graduate school, but my advisers had ignored it, and eventually I did, too.

Once the conversation was rolling, though, I was surprised to find how much poetry had survived, singing softly to itself, in some unused corner of my brain. I would be out on my morning walk, feeling my thighs and calves stretch and loosen, sniffing as the latest sample of rare perfume the Correspondent had sent me unfurled on my warming skin from a spiky bud of fiery black pepper and cloves into one of the richest carnations I've ever smelled, and a line would drift into my head—*I knew a woman, lovely in her bones*—and stay there, haunting me until I went home, pulled a once-familiar book from the shelf, blew the dust off the top edge, and flipped through the pages to find the rest of it.

How, I kept asking myself, did that one go? That one that begins: *Body my house my horse my hound.* That one where the river merchant's wife is remembering, something about plums, oh yes: *You walked about my seat, playing with blue plums.* That one where the grieving poet feels his heart lift as he watches a whale find its way out of the harbor, the enormous body slipping through the dark water to the sea: *What did you think, that joy/was some slight thing?*

I remembered how I'd learned to read, sitting next to my mother on the front steps, nestled into her, repeating the rhyming nonsense syllables of the book she held open in front of us—first her voice, then mine, until I had them by heart and my brain made the vital leap that connected up the slip and tickle of the words in my mouth and the sound of my mother's voice with the warmth of her body and the crisp, flat black and white of the letters underlined by her moving finger. *One fish, two fish, red fish, blue fish.*

And somewhere in the middle of all the perfume posts, and the letters and the poems and the perfume, I remembered what it was like to stretch and swim in language for the giddy pleasure of it, what it felt like to nestle down into that place where a single intuitive leap could be enough to connect up a world. I remembered, though I hadn't known I'd forgotten, why I had wanted to write in the first place.

A few months after my first perfume post went up, I went to meet Parker for lunch. Not long after the wedding, he'd sublet his apartment and moved to San Francisco to test out the possibility of moving there permanently. He'd just come back to town. We hadn't seen each other since before his surgery. Stepping out of the stuffy house into the cool air, I paused to take a deep breath and realized I was nervous.

We hadn't just been living in separate cities, I thought as I got in the car, we'd been living in separate worlds. My own suddenly seemed very small—a silky, froufrou little dog of a world. The critics in my head had been quiet lately, but as I drove to the restaurant to meet my old friend—my old colleague, my comrade-in-arms—they had plenty to say about how else I might have been spending my time.

I parked and got out of the car. When I turned to walk to the restaurant, I saw Parker, ten paces ahead of me. I called out, and he stopped, turned, and came back to meet me. We hugged hello, then drew back to look at each other.

"Want to see?"

He stood in front of me with a mischievous grin, hands gripping the bottom hem of his T-shirt, eyes darting from side to side to see if he could get away with lifting it up. I glanced back and forth at the empty lot, then nodded, leaning in with a giggle, my hand over my mouth.

Under the black shirt, his chest was smooth and white and ordinary, the two flat brown nipples as simple and familiar as any others I'd seen. "No scar . . ." I murmured, looking in vain for evidence of the knife, some hint that things hadn't always been this way. I'd been talking to myself, but he heard me.

"No. I healed up really well. The surgeon did a great job, didn't he?" He glanced down, grinned again, then dropped his shirt, smoothing it down over his chest and hips.

I looked at my friend, so fit and stylish in his city clothes, with a hint of stubble along his new square jawline, and he looked back at me.

"I like your new haircut," I said, reaching up toward the feathery spikes.

"It's my fauxhawk!" He preened, running a hand through his hair with a mocking flourish, and then bowed his head so I could run my hand along the ticklish edges of the soft black fringe.

While I'd been trying to write for Marina, Parker had been quietly posting a series of videos online documenting his thoughts and his changes, physical and otherwise—the visual version of a blog. Watching them was like peering through a peephole into a world I wasn't sure I was meant to see. But I was grateful for the glimpse of what his work meant to the people talking back in the comments, offering their own stories and links and an endless chorus of *thank you, this is so brave, thank you for helping me understand, thank you for saying this out loud.* I could see he was important—known, respected, desired, beloved.

And I liked looking at him, that part of him the camera caught and held. Something—the distancing effect of the screen, a trick of the light—resolved the blurry doubleness I always saw when I looked at him in person, my memories hanging like a veil between us. In the videos, he was sharply handsome, a still-recognizable but distinctly different person. The person, maybe, he'd meant to become.

What I couldn't see, what I will never be able to see, is what strangers see when they walk by him on a city street. What the college kid in the baseball cap saw the afternoon he bullied and threatened my friend in front of a dozen people lined up to buy tacos. What the waiter saw when he looked at us, twisted his mouth in surprise or disgust or both, and then turned away for a moment to make his face smooth and pleasant before steering us to our seats. I tried to imagine how it would feel to be looked at like that. Whether the stare would be hot or cold on my skin. Whether I would flinch and shiver, or set my jaw and ball up my fists. I wondered if it was something you could smell, the way you can smell the rank, metallic sweat of fear and anger.

But I knew I was just guessing—that guessing was all I could do. So when, after we'd talked for a while about how much he loved being in San Francisco, how much easier things were there, the conversation faltered and came to an awkward halt, I felt afraid that the silence might go on forever.

My friend looked down at his plate. He glanced back up at me, blushed slightly, then looked down again. He slid his water glass a little closer, a little farther away. He cleared his throat.

"You know," he said, "I've been hanging out with a lot of artists in San Francisco. I think that's been the best part about being there."

There was another pause. His blush deepened. I sat up a little straighter—there was something familiar about that embarrassed hesitation.

"I've been taking a lot of photographs," Parker said, still fidgeting with his glass.

He looked up, his eyes bright.

"It's just an amazingly beautiful city. I mean, the people are amazing. But the city is just—the light, and the buildings—everywhere I look. The view from my apartment. I just can't . . ."

He trailed off, took a deep breath, and tried again.

"So I've been taking all these photographs. A lot. Hundreds. I have my camera with me all the time. Videos, too. And some friends of mine asked me to be in a film they're making."

He leaned back in his chair and sighed deeply, but he still looked happy. "I have no idea where it's all going. I feel completely ridiculous. I haven't told very many people about it. Just a few of the artists. My thesis adviser is still sending me job announcements. She wants me to work on an article with her."

"But I was thinking," he smiled shyly at me from across the table. "It reminded me. Of the way you were about your perfume. In the beginning."

"Did I tell you?" he continued. "I bought a whole bottle of that stuff after what you gave me ran out. God, it's great." He reached his arms out in a luxurious stretch and then leaned back toward me, elbows on the table. "So. Your turn. Tell me what you've been up to."

I took my own deep breath. And then I leaned forward and told him as much as I could about all the ways I knew exactly how he felt.

10: BREAKFAST AT BERGDORF'S

The quiet, tree-lined street was dappled with late-afternoon spring light, and every other brownstone had a small flower garden just coming into bloom. I stopped at the corner, intending to cross, then turned and walked toward the sunlight instead, simply because I could. There was no one waiting for me anywhere. My destination was more of an excuse than a goal. The shop would be open for hours yet, and if I was still wandering by then, well, it would be there tomorrow.

After our frigid February trip to New York the year before, I had promised myself I would look for reasons to visit the city as often as I could. This time I had come for another wedding—a wedding and perfume.

Ten days earlier, my brother had gotten married in a cavernous rented space in lower Manhattan that looked, when V. and I arrived early to change into our formal finery for photographs, like an empty stage set. Only a half-dozen rows of white chairs and a small army of busy workers suggested that a wedding would take place in a few hours. The photographer pointed me behind a temporary wall into a narrow, cluttered dressing area. I struggled into my Serious Underwear behind a flimsy curtain strung up for the occasion and zipped up my long dress—a flattering deep-brown satin this time—in front of a mirror propped up against a long table littered with proof sheets. When I peered at the thumbnail images, I saw they were from a fashion shoot.

I was still getting to know the bride. Jenny was slender and fair-haired, and she had the kind of quiet composure that tends to make me feel I'm talking too loudly even when my mouth is shut. But, I soon learned, she also had a healthy appetite, a dry wit tempered by kindness, and a way of quietly taking in everything about a room and the people in it that reminded me of V.

I'd met her for the first time over the Christmas holidays at my parents' house. We spent a few slow, careful days finding out about each other. Then my brother teased me about my perfume. "But I love perfume!" she exclaimed, too loudly for mere politeness. So I brought my box of samples out from their hiding place and went through them with her just as I had with Parker, asking questions and handing her things to sniff, looking for something she could wear on her wedding day. Basil or cinnamon? Leather or lemons? What was she wearing now? What did she remember, from high school, on friends in college? And how did she want to feel? Happy, romantic, elegant . . . ?

"Elegant," she had said firmly, before I could give her any more choices. And she was, I saw, when I stepped back out into the open room, very elegant. Her dress, a narrow column of white silk, had a modest train that draped gracefully onto the floor, but it left her pale arms and shoulders bare. Her hair was coiled into a loose chignon at the nape of her long white neck, and she held a bouquet of white flowers—orchids and lilies and trailing sprays of tiny, starlike blossoms I couldn't name. She stood very still and straight against the dark drapery that had been hung to mark the altar, lit up from every angle by the photographer's bright lights, moving only to pose—once, twice, and a third time, while the rest of us watched and blinked at the flash, caught in a spell that was only partly broken when the photographer lowered his camera and ordered the rest of us to join her.

I took my place next to V. and my parents, and when I turned around I saw that the room had been transformed. Chandeliers hung from the metal girding of the high ceiling now, and the drapes had been pulled back from the old factory windows to let in the last of the evening light. Soon there would be music and champagne and trays of food, and the guests would arrive in their evening clothes to fill up the space with talk and laughter and exclamations over the beauty of the bride.

She was beautiful, I thought as the photographer put his camera away and we all began to disperse. Walking toward me in her white dress, bouquet still in hand, she looked, for a moment, like no one I knew or could have imagined knowing. But when she stood in front of me, she leaned in close, smiled, turned her head away slightly, and pointed to her neck.

"Smell!" she said.

I did as I was commanded, sniffing gently at the perfume I'd sent her. It smelled of new green leaves and the cool, ineffable scent of iris— neither root nor flower, but a touch of each dusted smooth with powder, a scent as soft as the thinnest kidskin gloves.

"It's perfect," I said, and gave her cheek a kiss. "It smells like you."

"I know," she said. "Thank you." And she gave me a kiss in return.

The night of the wedding had been chilly enough to require a winter coat, but by the middle of the week spring had truly arrived, and Central Park smelled of damp earth and growing things. After V. and my parents went home, I'd decamped from the wedding hotel to a friend's Upper West Side apartment to begin the perfume portion of my trip. Most of the boutiques I wanted to visit were on the East Side, so I'd been walking across the park almost every day. Each time, there was something new to see. Yesterday, a cluster of purple crocuses had appeared at the west entrance. Today, small white flowers were beginning to unfurl on the black branches of the trees that arched over my head just before I reached the street on the other side.

A few blocks away, I found the boutique I was looking for, pulled open the glass door, walked into the middle of the empty store, and stood there, looking left and right.

A thin, pretty woman with a sunburst of blond corkscrew curls stepped out from a back room. *"Bonjour, madame.* May I help you?"

"Hello," I said, and smiled. "I was hoping to see Marina. Is she here?"

"Ah, no, I am sorry," she said, shaking her curls. "She has just stepped out for a moment. May I show you a few things while you wait for her?"

The niche line was one of my favorites, and I had already sniffed my way through most of the collection, but I nodded and followed behind as she clicked over to the shelves on her heels, taking short, quick steps in her long black pencil skirt.

I asked to smell a couple I'd skipped: a delicious, not-too-sweet amber and a scratchy wool sweater of a scent redolent of hazelnuts and tobacco. I revisited a stony incense-and-lilies perfume that I have always wanted to like more than I really do. We talked about the perfumes, trading descriptions. And then she sprayed a strip without waiting for me to ask.

"This is one of my favorites," she said, handing it to me. "It is quiet, but it smells different on each woman's skin."

I took the strip from her politely, but I was not enthusiastic. I had sampled it before, and found it to be one of those pale, pretty perfumes that speak in a register I can't quite hear. But when I brought the strip to my nose, my eyes widened in surprise. Maybe it was the memory of Jenny's soft perfume. Maybe it was the walk I'd just taken under those barely blossoming trees. Maybe it was me. But now I could smell the tiny, golden, powdery-almond mimosa blooms—very light, but warm as skin—that were supposed to be there. I sniffed, and sniffed again.

"Oh." I sighed. "It's so tender."

"*Oui,*" she agreed, "that's it exactly. It is tender." She narrowed her blue eyes at me. "Are you one of those bloggers?"

"Yes," I admitted, "but I only write for Perfume-Smellin' Things, Marina's blog. And I don't write very often."

She waved away my caveat. "I knew it! From the moment you started to talk about the perfumes, I knew it! Ah," she said, turning as the door jingled open, "here is Marina."

The woman at the door was, like her colleague, thin, blond, and very chic in her tall, high-heeled leather boots and narrow black skirt. But her hair floated in a wispy bob just below her high cheekbones, and her accent, when she greeted me, was not French but Russian.

"Hello, hello! I am so glad you are here!" she said, giving me a hug. She looked at the sales assistant with a raised eyebrow and got a nod of approval. "Come!" she ordered. "We will go next door."

A moment later we were ensconced at a corner table in a tiny deli with paper cups of takeout coffee in front of us. Marina sniffed at hers and grimaced at the burnt dregs—the odor permeated the whole shop. "We don't have to drink them," she explained, "but I must buy them or they will kick us out. They hate us here, because we are always coming over to hang out on our breaks."

Settled in her plastic chair under the fluorescent lights, she looked exotically out of place. The lavender silk scarf draped around her shoulders was very nearly the same color as her eyes, and her curving mouth twitched up at the corner as though she were trying, and failing, to keep a secret. She looked as though she should be reclining on a divan while someone in a tuxedo brought her a drink. She looked, in fact, almost exactly as I had imagined she should look from reading her blog, and for a moment I was nothing more than a nervous fangirl. But then she put her elbows on the linoleum tabletop and leaned forward.

"Tell me," she began, and we spent the next twenty minutes gossiping about all the perfume people we had in common.

"Do you know what Robin looks like?" I asked when we paused for breath.

"I haven't seen her," Marina said. "But March told me she looks like a little doll. A porcelain doll. *Perfect* skin." She rolled her eyes at the impossibility of it, though her own skin glowed. "And you met Victoria. She is so lovely, isn't she?"

"Very," I agreed. "And so gracious. But she's so—I almost feel . . ." I paused, remembering, trying to think of a way to put it.

Victoria and I had met for dinner at a Korean teahouse the previous evening. I had expected her to be well traveled, intelligent—brilliant, even. But I was not prepared for the intensity of the enormous hazel eyes that dominated her small, pale face. And I had not expected her to be so exquisitely petite. I am not tall, but I towered over her when we exchanged kisses—left cheek, right cheek, left again.

She had recently quit her PhD program in international economics to begin training as a perfumer, and we'd scheduled our meeting around her full-time job, her dance practice, her Arabic language training, and the seminar in French literature she was taking—"just for fun," she said, "to keep up with my reading." At home on the weekends, there were always "projects, projects, projects," she explained, her accent drawing out the word itself into something long and onerous. She wrote her blog on the train, during her one-hour commute. If she had not attacked her enormous bowl of noodle soup with such relish, or smiled quite so broadly at my nervous joking, the evening might have passed in silence. As it was, I chattered so much trying to make her smile again that I forgot to eat.

I tried to say some of this to Marina, who held a hand up to interrupt me.

"I know," she said. "Believe me, I know. When I first met her, she made me feel like a peasant." She leaned back in her chair, crossed one very long, unpeasantlike leg over the other, and adjusted her scarf. "You get used to it."

I smiled and nodded, but I wasn't entirely sure I would get used to it. Not to Victoria's glamour, or Marina's, or the simple fact that I knew them. Not to going in and out of fancy stores as though I belonged there. I wasn't even sure, I thought, as we chatted about how Marina liked her new job at the boutique, that I wanted to get used to it. I liked being a little dazzled. I wanted to keep being surprised. Even if it sometimes meant feeling out of place or—our conversation slowed and came to a pause—at a loss for what to say next.

But Marina knew what she wanted to hear. "Now," she said, pushing our cold coffees to the side, "enough about perfume and me. I want to hear about your wedding. Tell me!" she demanded. "Tell me *everything*."

A few days later I crossed the park again, this time very early in the morning, walking as fast as I could go without breaking into a run. I was due for breakfast at Bergdorf's, and I needed to arrive well before eight o'clock. I couldn't rely on last year's luck.

Not long after we returned home from Anna and David's wedding, when I was longing for a reason to go back to the city, I stumbled across a ridiculously tempting one: Sniffapalooza. The name conjured up a festival full of drunken, dreadlocked Frisbee players confused to find themselves at a perfume counter, but the schedule listed on the Web site was high-luxury overload. The uptown day began at Bergdorf Goodman (with breakfast, if you reserved in time), went on to Henri Bendel, paused for lunch at a French restaurant (natch), continued on to the now-late, lamented Japanese department store Takashimaya for tea and cupcakes, and finished up at Saks Fifth Avenue. Then it happened all over again the next day downtown, beginning with brunch at one of the niche boutiques and going on through half a dozen more until the final stop for perfume and Bellinis. There would be presentations, gift bags, special sale prices, a chance to meet a long list of perfumers. "Serious perfume lovers by invitation only," the information page warned. The organizers, Karen Dubin and Karen Adams, signed their open letter in the plural: "Viva La Sniffa, Baby! Love, the Karens."

Lacking an invitation, and not yet realizing that I didn't really need one, I picked a Karen at random and wrote an e-mail vouching for my seriousness. Her reply came immediately: "You sound like one of us!" Before I could tell myself all the reasons why it was a ridiculous expense, I bought a plane ticket and confirmed that I could stay with Lois. Two months later I was back in the city.

But on the morning of that first day, I arrived at Bergdorf's a bare five minutes after the appointed time to find every door locked tight and no sign of life within the store. I knocked on the doors. I paced the length of the building. What to do? The store, I was dismayed to realize, wouldn't open officially for another hour and a half.

I was standing on the corner, pondering my options, when a stylish young man walked toward me, then turned, opened a nondescript metal door in the side of the building, and disappeared inside. A minute later, an equally stylish young woman did the same. Without stopping to think, I walked up to the door and tugged. It opened easily, and I stepped inside.

Walking briskly, I followed the young woman into the building, nodding slightly at the security guard who gave me a wave from his booth as we passed. Down the long dark hallway we went, she striding ahead of me in her stilettos, ponytail swinging slightly, me with my fingers crossed, wondering what I had just done. A few moments later we emerged, by some small perfume miracle, onto the beauty floor. I kept walking, making my way through a forest of black-clad sales assistants toward the joyful noise I could hear coming from the basement café.

"My God, it's like a Greek wedding in there!" exclaimed one of the assistants as I passed her. And it was. A Greek wedding, a daytime slumber party, a sniffing bacchanal, a bonanza of free samples, a highly entertaining weekend-long sales pitch, a wild rumpus of a reunion—the Sniffa is all of these things and a few more besides, but most of all it is, like a wedding, a rare moment when all the varied members of a widespread and fractious community come together in one place and time.

That first time, alone, familiar with only a few of the more flamboyant participants (that had to be Chayaruchama, singing snatches of an aria to her neighbor three tables over), I was like a guest who knew only the bride. Half the time I floated, temporarily adopted by one welcoming group of strangers or another. Half the time I peered in from the outside, taking notes. I was thrilled to meet the perfumers, taken aback by the sales presentations, and completely dizzied by the number of perfumes on offer and the speed of everyone else's sniffing. By the end of the day, one of the women who had befriended me was wearing a different perfume on each wrist, each crook of her elbow, the backs of her hands, her forearms, her upper arms, her ankles, and, when all that failed, the littlest finger on each hand. It was a far cry from my JAR experience—I couldn't keep up.

This year, I knew better than to try. This year, I knew the sales presentations were performances to be rated and applauded. This year, I could reel off the names of the perfumers participating as though they were my aunts and uncles and second cousins. This year, the Correspondent would be joining me for the day after breakfast. This year, I had come less for the perfume than for the rare privilege of spending a long day with a large group of very happy people doing exactly what they wanted to do.

This year I could already see, from half a block away, a crowd of women, and a few brave and discerning men, waiting on the sidewalk in front of Bergdorf's side entrance. A small woman with dark hair buzzed from circle to circle like a delighted hostess at a lively party. It had to be March. She had posted photos of herself on the Perfume Posse now and then, but it was how she moved that gave her away, chatting with this person and that and occasionally stepping out and away from the crowd to welcome a newcomer—as she welcomed me when at last I arrived and came to a breathless stop.

"Well, hello! Are you a Posse person? Oh, you *are*. It's so good to finally meet you! Do you know Patty?" I said hello to the handsome, comfortable-looking blond woman standing just to March's right. "And I want to make sure you meet Louise," March continued, introducing me to a tall, slim woman with a striking short haircut whose name I recognized from many of March's anecdotes. "And this is Kristen; I believe you know her from the comments section as the fabulous Divalano. There are so many of us here today. I'm sure you'll all be able to find each other once we sit down."

"Oh, I know you!" said Kristen after March had left us to greet the next group of arrivals. "You wrote that post on Perfume-Smellin' Things. The one about feeling embarrassed at the party. I loved that post." Just as I caught my breath enough to thank her, March brought another Posse person over to us, and then another, and another, until I couldn't keep track anymore and just stood there, pleasantly bewildered, knowing something, but not everything, about how the day would go, whom I would meet, and what I would smell. I just stood there, glad to be part of the circle, until the doors opened and they welcomed us all in.

Perfume and a wedding, a wedding and perfume. I had known it would be a long, delirious week, so I had planned a few days at the end of my trip with nothing in them—a pause, a little honeymoon of sorts. Time to wander alone through the city I now loved.

Which is exactly what I was doing, down in that part of Manhattan where the streets turn crooked and small and repeat themselves and it's easy to get a little lost and stumble over things you weren't looking for but are glad to find. I had gotten there slowly, walking through a few other neighborhoods along the way, chasing the slant of the late-afternoon light down that particularly pretty street, crossing back and forth to look in a shop window or stand under a tree dripping with blossoms. Now, as the light began to fade and the air turned cool, I was a little footsore and ready to rest awhile. I dug my map out of my bag and checked it just to be sure, then set out again, left and right and forward, and then back again, because I had walked right past the place I was looking for.

It's easy to do. Aedes de Venustas is a small shop at the far end of a long street crowded with small shops. The gilt lettering on the window is thin and delicate, and the window itself is tinted to protect the perfumes inside, so the artfully arranged bottles and candles and the splendid stuffed peacock presiding over them are rendered in shadowy sepia tones. The door is always closed. In fact, it's locked— you have to press the buzzer to be let in. Every time I hear the answering buzz and pull the door open, I feel like I've managed to guess the secret password, and I felt the same way that afternoon.

Stepping inside, I paused a moment to lean on the comfortable leopard-print chair near the entrance and let my eyes adjust to the light. The dusky purple walls were lined with dark wooden cabinets and shelves. Another peacock, a white one, looked over the lines of bottles glinting in the light of the enormous crystal chandelier hanging over an equally enormous bouquet of flowers. Both looked just right against the backdrop of plush shadows, in spite of the fact that the entire room was roughly the size of a large jewelry box.

It didn't need to be any bigger. Perfume doesn't take up much space. As those of us with perfume closets know, it's amazing how many bottles you can fit onto a shelf. The perfume I was looking for was very small, so small—and so precious—that it was displayed on its own table, under a heavy glass dome. It felt wrong to lift up the glass, and I gave a guilty start when a sales assistant looked my way. But he only smiled and nodded his encouragement, so I set the dome down carefully on the table next to the tiny bottle, then picked up the bottle itself and carefully applied a single drop of the thick amber liquid it contained to my wrist.

It was an attar, one of the highly concentrated perfume oils that are the East's answer to alcohol-based Western perfumes. This one had been created by a French perfumer in homage to classical Middle Eastern perfumery for a house founded by the Sultan of Oman. The Oman region has been the center of the world's frankincense trade since the days when perfumes and incense were more valuable than gold. It is still a place where fragrance is woven through all the rituals of everyday and sacred life. Next to the complex, ancient story of perfume in the East, all of Western perfumery is nothing but a recent plot twist.

There was still so much more to learn. I should, I thought—as I sank down into the leopard-skin chair and a silvery cloud of frankincense began to rise up all around me—learn Arabic, like Victoria, and

follow the ancient incense trail. I should go to India and see what remained of the Mysore sandalwood forests, and learn what was coming
next. I should find a way to walk in the fields of Afghanistan where they
were trying, after many years of growing opium poppies, to once again
grow flowers for perfume. Then the hallucinatory richness of oud and
roses joined the frankincense, and the chorus resounded in my head
and heart in a way that made it impossible to think about anything for
a while except—once I could breathe again—the way that beauty can
stop time.

"Are you doing all right?" asked the sales assistant who had nodded
at me earlier. He stood by my chair, looking down at me. "Anything I
can help you with?"

I blinked up at him from behind my perfume haze. One of the
store's two small dogs ran up behind him. I leaned down to give it a pet,
then smiled back up at the assistant.

"Thank you," I said, "maybe in a little while. I have everything I
need for now."

11: MY MOTHER'S FEMME

What should a woman smell like?

Should she smell of lipstick and powder, of silk and fur? Of cookies, clean laundry, and homemade chicken soup? Should she smell of apples? Should she smell of soap and hot water, of toothpaste and shampoo? Of milk, of blood, of her own warm skin? Should she smell of earth? Of forests? Should she smell of the sea?

My mother swears she can't choose a perfume by testing it on her own skin. "I have to smell it on someone else," she explains, waving away the samples I've proffered. That's how she found Femme, the perfume that haunted her, the one she knew she just had to have. It wafted past her from the white neck, round arms, and no doubt ample cleavage of that Texas heiress when my mother stepped aside to let her pass. Stepped aside (though not without speaking up to compliment her perfume) because my mother was a waitress and the heiress was one of the people she served.

It would have been summer in the mountains of upstate New York, cooler than a Texas summer, but still sunny and warm enough for swimming and tennis, the way it's supposed to be at a resort. If my mother smelled of anything at that moment, it was probably sweat and hard work—the specific, peculiar smells of kitchen work that I remember lingering in my own hair and clothes, a mélange of rotting vegetable scraps, stale fry oil, clouds of steam from scalding, grimy dishwater, and the sour metallic smell, pale but insistent, of a steam table when the pans of food are pulled out at the end of service.

But those smells were not her whole world. She was young, strong, beautiful, and very much in love with my father, who was working at the same resort. She was sharp-tongued, persistent, and resourceful. It was a good job, one that she had finagled for herself against the rules—all the other servers were men. She survived endless practical jokes: Once, at the beginning of a formal service, all the waiters lined up to enter the dining room at the same time, making sure my mother was at the front of the line. With a wink for the men, the head waiter gave the signal and my mother sailed out into the big room alone, heavy tray held high. It was only when she arrived in front of the podium, and the speaker paused in the middle of his talk to peer down at her, that she realized what they'd done. Flustered, she dropped her tray with a huge crash, right in front of a dashing young Bobby Kennedy. She must have, somehow, smelled of all these things, too.

And the heiress: What did she smell of? Money, certainly. Luxury. Leisure. The good life. And a few other things.

Should a woman have a smell at all? In the Victorian era, smelling strongly of anything—food, sweat, sex, perfume—marked a woman as a worker, an actress, a prostitute, or all three. "A woman should smell of nothing but flowers, and that faintly," admonished one arbiter of taste and good manners. Women were to be seen, not heard or smelled, and that only under strict conditions of chaperoning and dress. No woman of means and taste would have walked, like the heiress did, with a trail of perfume behind her.

Fashions come and fashions go, in perfume as in everything else. Hot on the heels of women's liberation, the 1980s was the decade of big shoulders, big hair, and great big perfume, lavishly applied from the first stroke of dawn onward. Woe betide the unperfumed office work-ers riding in an early-morning elevator with their newly promoted boss or her even more ambitious younger colleague, at least one of whom was probably smoking.

Now everyone has allergies, and there are lawsuits. The entire city of Halifax has banned the public use of perfume. And though our yearning for scent continues unabated—consider the market for can-dles, soaps, lotions, the endless varieties of laundry detergent—many women are once again afraid to smell very strongly of anything in par-ticular. If my mother were still waiting for the right scent to waft by her, she would be waiting a very long time.

I have no desire to go back to riding in that 1980s elevator. But a little bit of *sillage,* the beautiful French word for the trail a perfume leaves—it means *wake*, as in the wake of a boat in the water—can be a wonderful thing.

I can remember only one professor from my graduate-school days who wore perfume, a tall, long-limbed woman with glowing brown skin, swinging braids, and an easy smile. She was one of a bare handful of tenured African American women at the university, a feat that surely took strength and struggle. But what made her truly rare was that she seemed happy. While the rest of us scurried through the hallways, eyes down and shoulders hunched, she walked with her head held high and her perfume trailed behind her like a blessing.

It was a full-bodied, balsamic scent, warm and resonant. I can't list the notes for you, but I remember its presence. And I remember, clearly, the day when the room where my oral exams were to be held was changed at the last minute. She was one of my examiners, and after a frantic fifteen minutes searching for the right place, I realized I was following her scent through the hallway. It got stronger and stronger, until at last I sat down with a sigh and a smile to wait outside the door I knew was the right one.

Years later—a lifetime later—I was walking down a street in New York when a fierce young woman brushed past me, moving fast on her clacking heels in the way that only a city woman can. I never saw her face, only the back of her tailored coat, her vivid shawl, and her wild head of springy, copper-colored curls. They had almost, but not quite, as much presence as her perfume. It had announced her like a sudden gust of wind, and I could still smell it as I watched her retreating back— a cool, sharp scent of just-split wood, the sap still fresh and sticky on the pale, newly revealed grain.

It was a perfume I thought I knew—or maybe I had just read about it. I was sniffing and thinking when a man appeared at my side, walking along with me. He had the rough-hewn looks of an artist, or a carpenter. If, say, that carpenter were played by a movie star.

"Is that you walking along smelling so great?" he asked.

"No, it's not me," I said, a little regretfully. "I'm pretty sure it's Curlyhead up there." I tilted my chin in the direction he might want to go.

He looked up at the woman's retreating back, nodded, and then continued to walk with me, chatting amiably, flirting a little, both of us coasting along in her brilliant wake for three, then four blocks, until I began to wonder just how far we were all going to go, and I turned the corner and continued on my way.

Strange though it may sound, I am still shy about my own *sillage*. The word is pronounced *see-yazh*, but for a long time, having only read and never heard it, I rhymed it in my inner ear with *spillage*. That's how I felt when someone complimented me on my perfume, as though I had spilled something that should have remained contained, internal.

Though I don't mind a compliment now, most days I still want my perfume to be an intimate thing, something only those who are close to me can smell. Perfume plays such a vital role in my dream life that it feels strange to flaunt it, to let it define and announce me.

But every now and then I give it a try. How else are those dreams supposed to become a reality? And though I might not know what a woman should smell like, I think she should have the right, on occasion, to move in extravagant clouds of her own making. The right to sail forth with all flags flying while the rest of us tumble about in her wake. The right, when she wants it, to take up some space.

"But Mom," I said, after my mother told me how she found her Femme, "I thought you wore Halston."

I had only the vaguest memories of how my mother's perfume smelled, but I remembered the organic curves of that heavy-hipped, vaguely anthropomorphic Halston bottle, the amber perfume in the round bottom, the white cap that began where the shoulders should have been and rounded into an abstract neck and head. I had coveted that bottle.

"No," my mother said, "that was a gift from Irma"—my father's mother, the same grandmother who had furnished me with my own perfume samples. "I liked it. But Femme was my signature scent. I only wore Halston because we couldn't find any Femme. Don't you remember that whole saga?"

"What do you mean?"

"It disappeared. Dad looked everywhere for it. He even called around in New York, but no one had it. Every time he traveled, he kept looking. Finally, a few years later—I don't even remember how many—he brought back a bottle for me from Europe."

"Wow. But I don't remember ever seeing it."

"Well," she said, lowering her voice slightly, confessing, "it didn't smell the same. Dad was so proud of himself for finding it, I didn't have the heart to tell him that it was different. I thought maybe it was just me—maybe I didn't remember it after not wearing it for so long, or maybe my sense of smell had changed. So I tried to wear it for a while. But eventually I gave up."

She sighed. "Even if it was me, it just wasn't the same."

Surely it doesn't matter very much what a woman smells like. A perfume is not a painting or a sculpture. There are hundreds of thousands of bottles of it—until the day when there are none. Or the day when the bottle remains, but the scent inside seems different somehow.

My mother's story had all the earmarks of reformulation: The perfume disappears for a while as the producer lets the old stock run out and then it reappears, smelling not quite like itself. There are many reasons for reformulation—companies are bought and sold, raw materials disappear or become too costly, the producer wants to sell the perfume to a younger consumer with different tastes—but in each case the producer wants to keep the expensive investment it's made in the perfume's name. Though some in the industry will go to their graves denying it, it's a very common practice.

The older and grander the perfume, the more faithful its following, the more likely it is to have been tweaked over the years, if not remade completely. Lately, this process has sped up dramatically. In what appears to be an attempt at self-regulation spurred primarily by anticipated litigation, the perfume industry has banned or severely limited the use of a long list of raw materials, some of which have been used for centuries, including citrus oils, jasmine, and very nearly—until many in the industry rebelled and the regulatory committee backed down—vanilla. (The official reasons vary, but in many cases the materials are cited as potential "sensitizers," i.e., allergens.) The European Commission has followed the industry's lead. Any perfume that depends on large amounts of these materials—and there are many, including some of the greatest icons of all—must be, probably already has been, reformulated. It is possible that they will still be beautiful, but they will not be the same.

All of this is just business. It is only a cruel coincidence that the generations of women who grew up with the idea of a signature scent—a single, carefully chosen, dearly beloved perfume, worn year in and year out until death do us part or at least for the better part of a life—are the same women most likely to have worn those grand perfumes. Women like my mother.

The idea of a signature perfume, as the industry created and promoted the notion (it was a marketing strategy, but such a lovely one), was to leave your mark, to be recognized and remembered. Your Wind Song, as the old ad went, stayed on his mind. But anyone who has worn the same scent for more than a day or two knows how quickly it gathers memories to itself, how it marks your days. When we lose a fragrance, we miss its particular beauty, but we miss the bit of our lives it takes along with it even more. For better or worse, we miss the person we were when we wore it—even when we think we could not bear to smell it again.

When the heiress left her full bottle of Femme on the dresser as a tip for the lively young waitress who had admired it, my mother was in her early twenties. When my father began his fruitless search, she was in her forties, on the opposite side of the country, with two nearly grown children. I will probably never know all the stories that vanished along with that perfume.

* * *

As soon as I got off the phone with my mother, I looked up Femme. It took me all of five minutes to find a post on Bois de Jasmin confirming that it had been launched in a new formulation a few years after the time when my mother noticed it was gone. Victoria sounded genuinely moved by the perfume the great Edmond Roudnitska had created in the rubble of wartime Paris, the year before my mother was born. It was clear she thought it belonged in the circle of the great classics. Even the reformulation, a respectful modern tribute, came in for its small share of praise.

I felt proud—what fantastic taste my mother had!—and just a little more tasteful myself, by association. More important, I thought that what I'd been hoping to do would be possible. I e-mailed the post to my mother, who was deeply relieved to find out that she wasn't losing her sense of smell, her memory, or her mind. And then, armed with all the necessary information from Victoria about the ever-so-slight changes in the bottle, the cap, the box, and the placement of the name, I headed off into the wilds of the Internet to hunt down a genuine vintage bottle of my mother's perfume.

Because it's not so easy to get rid of the past. Those hundreds of thousands of bottles make their way all over the world. Retailers send what they don't sell to the discounters, discounters dump them onto the gray market, and a fair number are diverted by nefarious means. Even when it reaches its intended owners, perfume has a way of a hiding out in the backs of closets and the bottoms of drawers and all the other places people put the special gifts they think are too good for daily use. There it waits, for years, even decades, shielded from light and heat and humidity, until a well-meaning someone who believes the marketing hype that perfume turns bad after a year sells it at a garage sale or dumps it at a thrift store or, just maybe, puts it up for sale on a certain well-known online auction site that has been the ruin of many a poor perfume collector. Especially after eleven at night, when there has been wine with dinner.

The auction site was the first place I headed. I admit I had been there before. (It's where I got my supply of Scandal.) In the first flush of my perfume romance, overwhelmed by all the gorgeousness I was discovering, I found it easy to resist the lure of vintage perfume. I was irritated by all the ravishing descriptions of perfumes that had been discontinued or had become pale shadows of themselves. I chalked them up to the human lust for the unattainable, and the belief, common to all passionate underground fans of anything, that things were really so much better last year, or ten years ago, or anytime before *you* arrived. But after a while, listening to the same names spoken again and again with reverence, awe, and regret, my curiosity got the better of me. Could anything really be that great?

Not always. Not every time. But to my everlasting delight and misfortune, my first winning bid was. A few drops from a tiny bottle of vintage Mitsouko *parfum*, no bigger than the hollow in the center of my hand, warmed on my skin into a stunning, larger-than-life presence, a living, breathing being with demands and ideas of her own. *Oh,* I thought as the dry, delicate spices in the opening came to life—just as the reviews promised they would, with a breath of peach, like sun glowing through an autumn leaf—*oh, oh, oh,* as the oakmoss in the base turned that golden autumnal scent into something warm and utterly human, but undeniably regal, a queen sure of her power. *Oh . . . this. This is what they're talking about.*

I was not always so lucky. Sometimes I was baffled. Occasionally I was repulsed. Smelling vintage perfume requires a certain fortitude and patience. The delicate materials in the top notes have often degraded, and even when all their notes are in perfect order, they can be difficult for our modern noses to decipher. But there are rewards. My first spray of vintage Joy went on like opening night at the opera, all haughty aldehydes and bergamot, formal, unapproachable, and decidedly old-fashioned. But a few moments later the opening faded and the flowers tumbled out, an endless cascade of jasmine and roses so pure and alive and abundant they brought tears to my eyes. *Oh. This.*

There were a few others like that. Enough to make me understand the absolute necessity of the Osmothèque, a sort of living perfume museum in France, dedicated to preserving the original formulas of the great classics—a place where you can go to smell the past.

I'm grateful for that work, and I want very much to visit, but I don't think the Osmothèque will do much to assuage the undertow of nostalgia in my perfume world. Because it's not just the perfume we mourn. It's another kind of loss, more difficult to describe but keenly felt, that has to do with our mothers and our grandmothers and what a woman is supposed to smell like today.

The French classics were as structured as couture gowns, and they required a similar presence and bearing from those who wore them. But their base notes were utterly human. They smelled, like Mitsouko, of oakmoss, a scent somewhere between moss, old wood, hay, fur, and hot skin. They were rich and heavy with true sandalwood oil. And they pulsed and growled with animalics—the dark raunch of civet, the oily, supple leather of castoreum, the frank fleshiness of musk, the salty glowing veil of ambergris.

These were not perfumes for little girls. They were a sign of carnal knowledge, and a fully embodied form of it. They spoke of power as much as they did of seduction. They made growing up look like a desirable thing, and they offered a way to do it. Even perfumes created specifically for young women gave them a taste of the future—their proper, ladylike florals and powder were nearly always balanced with a bit of feral shadow. As recently as the 1980s, Chanel's Cristalle, a popular success with teens and young women, was grounded with an oakmoss note that gave its sparkling green citrus an underbelly of sex and ashtray, as though that fresh-faced girl with the ribbon in her hair had just returned from a slightly unsavory rendezvous in the woods behind the tennis court.

Fashions come and fashions go. Now, in perfume as in everything else, the most desirable customer—and the thing it seems everyone most desires to be—is young. Very young. And what young girl wants to smell like her mother? Or, worse, her grandmother? So with only a few exceptions, all that formal structure and simmering darkness has been banished to the far edges of the market, and everything in the center has been systematically sweetened and lightened. Our grandmothers had Bandit and Narcisse Noir. We have Clean and Pink Sugar.

There's nothing wrong with a little sweetness. I have no wish to return to a time of gloves and hats and Serious Underwear worn every single day. I love my spare, legible, casual perfumes the same way I love the easy breathing space of my modern clothes and my modern life. But oh, how I long for a little of that regal bearing, that carnal power, and the assurance that age has its advantages. I may not want to smell like my mother or my grandmother—not exactly, not every day—but I would like to know a little of what they knew. When we are all trying to stay young, who will be left to show us how to grow up?

It didn't take long for me to find a vintage bottle of Femme. There were dozens of them, in their boxes and out of them, half full and half empty. There were tall columns of eau de cologne and tiny bottles with frayed bows that might have been the coveted concentrated extrait but could just as well have been samples. And there were many ever-so-slightly different variations of that famous bottle, the one whose curved shoulders were supposedly modeled on the precise dimensions of Mae West's voluptuous hips. I picked a likely-looking candidate with golden script that read PARFUM DE TOILETTE, a concentration that rarely shows up in the United States these days. I pressed a few buttons, typed in some numbers, and a week later it was at my door.

It was only after I'd unwrapped the box—promisingly yellowed and imprinted with the old Rochas pattern of black Chantilly lace—and had taken out the nearly full bottle that it occurred to me I had no way of knowing whether I'd gotten the version of the perfume my mother was missing. I had Victoria's description, and a few other reviews, but no memory of my own. That was true for the other vintage perfumes I'd tried, but I'd often had a modern version to guide me. And it hadn't mattered then, as it did now, if I was wrong.

There was nothing for it but to try it on and hope I would be able to tell somehow. It was an unsealed splash bottle with a screw-top cap instead of a sprayer—less promising, because empty unsealed splash bottles are so easy to refill with another perfume, or colored water—but the original price tag was still pasted on the bottom of the box, and when I sniffed at the neck, it had the thin, sharp smell of slightly spoiled top notes. I spilled a little on the back of my hand and waited.

It warmed quickly into something sweeter, but still relatively thin. An hour later it was warm and smooth and much rounder, but it was no Mae West. The reviews had described a big perfume worthy of those ample hips. I tried again the next day, with a bolder application, but the results were no better.

Back I went to stalk and capture another bottle, this time a spray bottle of the eau de toilette. It was smaller than the first one, its curves were slightly less voluptuous, and it had no box, but when I sprayed it on, the top notes were gloriously intact. The thin sharpness I had smelled in the first bottle revealed itself in this one to be bergamot, a smattering of aldehydes, and a lemony wood-polish note—rosewood maybe—that I recognized from my sniffing at the Curator's salon. Within twenty minutes the warm sweetness had arrived, but this time it was lush and thick with flowers. I thought I could smell the slightly funky, just-this-side-of-cloying sweetness of ylang-ylang and, a few minutes later, a bright, luscious peach, much rounder and juicier than the haunting touch in Mitsouko. The resulting scent, now floating all around me, was neither fruit nor flower, but decidedly human, very female, and almost embarrassingly sensual. I could even smell a touch of unwashed warmth, like the traces of sweat on a lover's once-damp skin.

Sweat. Oh, no. I came out of my reverie with a curse. I had smelled that sweaty warmth before in other perfumes. It was the modern perfumer's answer to the more intimate smells once provided by those old base notes, and it came from a cumin note. The *modern* perfumer: There was cumin in the reformulation—a good dose of it, according to the comments I'd read on the blogs—but none in the original. I had the wrong one.

I bent my head toward my arm and inhaled deeply. I was finding it difficult to feel sorry about my mistake. But, my God, if this was the pale imitation, what was the original like? The thought startled me awake, and I headed back to the computer.

Clearly I needed another strategy. So far I'd been gambling—bidding on likely-looking bottles and hoping for the best. My mother's daughter after all, I'd been thinking like a bargain hunter. But three mistakes do not a bargain make. I needed to think like a collector. I'd heard about another source for vintage perfumes, a legendary purveyor who had inherited an enormous amount of old stock from a relative's perfume shop and had been slowly selling it off over the years. He'd started out on the auction sites, but then he'd disappeared. I looked up the thread on one of the forums and began chasing down dead ends and connections. An hour later I was browsing through his online store.

And there it was. A 100-percent-guaranteed authentic bottle of vintage Femme. And not just any bottle, but the precious, hard-to-find *extrait de parfum* in its original presentation box—an elaborate affair designed to look like a hatbox and covered with actual black Chantilly lace. It wasn't cheap, especially compared with the bottles on the auction site, but the price was fair, and it was less expensive than many modern luxury perfumes. The seller was trustworthy. It wouldn't be a fake. It's always a strange question anyway, the price of a vintage perfume. (How much are you willing to pay for something that doesn't officially exist anymore and will soon disappear entirely? How much for a piece of the past? Of your own past?)

I hesitated. Without smelling it first, I wouldn't know the true condition of the perfume. For the length of a day, I went back and forth between the desire to buy a gift for my mother and the knowledge that she probably wouldn't approve of my gambling on a luxury. I bought it—of course I did—but with my heart pounding like it had the first time I smelled that Paloma.

It arrived two weeks later, packed in old newspapers, the round presentation box safely snuggled in its original rigid outer box. The lace was rough under my fingers when I pulled it out, and it had the same vague scent of powder, perfume, and old paper that I remembered from my grandmother's dusty blue velvet jewelry box. And like the jewelry box, it did not yield up its contents easily. When I finally pried open the lid and lifted out the bottle inside, I found its top was stuck fast. It took me two weeks and every trick in the book to get it open.

When at last I dabbed a little on the back of my hand, it went on sharp and dry as a bone. And stayed that way. I shrugged and went about my business, trying hard not to be disappointed. Maybe, I thought, while I walked the dog, shivering a little in the chilly evening, I could post on the boards and see if anyone would sell me a sample from their collection, just a token reminder. I sniffed again as I came up the walk to the front door and reached to unhook the dog's leash—it was a little warmer, a little closer to leather, but not much. Maybe, I thought a little later, bending to take the still-warm sheets out of the dryer, it hadn't been such a good idea after all. Maybe, I thought, as I began to fold the sheets, holding them out at arm's length, doubling them, bringing the corners in under my chin along with a gust of warm air—and then I stopped thinking and just stood there, sniffing.

In her review on Bois de Jasmin, Victoria had marveled at Femme's balance—dryness softened with fruit, flowers wrapped in sandalwood and oakmoss. She had written about the heaviness and the longing she smelled in it, about what it meant to her to think of Roudnitska creating such beauty while the war continued on around him. Such sensual beauty: "a perfume that smells of a woman's skin and ripe summer plums."

I am wearing Femme as I write this, and I can smell some of what Victoria described. I can smell the human warmth of oakmoss and creamy sandalwood balanced against the dry, leathery sharpness in the opening. I can feel the beauty and the gentle gravitas of the classic structure that sets the old version apart from the brighter, sweeter, looser, louder reformulation. And, yes, especially after the fragrance has settled and warmed, I can smell dark, dark plums and the scent of a woman's skin—a woman loved, and remembered, and longed for.

But when I stood there with the sheets in my hand, not moving, I smelled none of these things. What I smelled was my mother.

Not my mother dressed up to go out, her newly applied perfume wafting all around her, hanging in the air after she goes out the door.

Not even my mother in the dark of my childhood bedroom, saying good night after coming home from the party. Just my mother. My mother the way she smelled, still warm from sleep, after I woke her up from a nap on the couch when I came home from school. The scent of her coat when I borrowed it for a quick trip into the garage. The smell that had worked its way deep into the wool of the afghan she used to ward off the chill on winter evenings. A smell I didn't even know I knew. Her smell.

I cannot explain this, and I am not sure I want to try. My mother wore perfume only for special occasions. She was not the kind of person whose fragrance clung to everything around her. But every time I smell Femme, she is there.

My mother prefers to spray her perfume lightly onto her clothes rather than wear it on her skin, a preference I thought I understood a little better now, in spite of my own prejudices. (When your perfume already smells of skin, of your skin, why not just spray it on your clothes?) So I made three spray-bottle decants for her, one of each Femme I had found. I labeled them and packaged them up as I had learned to do for my swaps, with electrical tape to keep them from leaking, and bubble wrap. I wrote a note explaining which one was most likely to be closest to the one she had worn and offering to send more of whatever she preferred, and then I put them in the mail, hoping they would get there for Mother's Day. They arrived on time, and I got a happy e-mail saying that yes, the *extrait* was the closest to what she remembered, and that what I had sent would last her for years. We talked about it on the phone. And that was that.

Except that it wasn't, quite. Because I couldn't seem to stop looking for Femme. Every time I walked through an antique store, I checked for bottles. Every few weeks or so, I ran another search on the auction site.

Sometimes I bid, though I wasn't very serious about it and I almost always lost. Almost. I told myself I was looking for a better version, a more perfect vintage bottle, one that would let me see into the past clearly instead of through the cracked glass of those slightly spoiled top notes. I told myself I just needed a little more, to make sure that later, when what I had given my mother was gone and the old stock had become absurdly expensive (or vanished altogether), there would be enough. Sometimes I just couldn't bear the thought of a bottle going for cheap. Going unvalued. Unloved. I felt myself traveling along the far edge of dangerous compulsion, trying to hold on to something that had already slipped away.

A signature scent's promise—the promise that you will be remembered—offers a kind of immortality. After you are gone, your scent remains: on a scarf, on a dress, or on a stranger, swirling by someone you know, catching them up, catching them off guard. I have heard many stories from people haunted or comforted by the lingering scent of someone they loved. But we are moved by these traces because they are fragile and ephemeral. They touch us lightly, and then they let us go.

A perfume is a living thing, and it lives by disappearing. In the bottle it is meaningless, some liquid in a pretty chunk of glass. It is only when you put it on and it rises into the air that it can tell its story. It says what it has to say, and then it's gone.

I tell myself all this, and sometimes I believe it. But the itch is still there. While I was writing this, looking up old reviews and remembering, I stumbled across a link to an ongoing auction for Femme and I couldn't resist going to look. I bid. And then, to my disappointment and to my relief, I lost.

Fashions come and fashions go. And then they come around again, in a slightly different form. A few weeks ago I went back to the university where I did my graduate work—not to the English department, but to the school of architecture. I was there in my new guise as writer and perfume obsessive to talk about perfume and design.

There were ten students in the seminar, all young women around nineteen or twenty years old. I began by introducing them to the basic structure of perfume, and I passed around some strips to demonstrate my points. I assumed their taste in perfume, if they had any, would be mainstream, so I kept my examples on the sweet, light side. Even so, there were a few wrinkled noses. The room was small and poorly ventilated, and there was far too much perfume in the air. But everyone listened and everyone talked, and everyone sniffed. At the end of the session, by way of connecting the smells to visual design, I showed the students a few of my favorite bottles.

I'm not much of a bottle collector. I'd rather have small amounts of many different perfumes in plain-labeled vials than a single expensive showpiece. But every now and then I fall for one, and I fell for Kingdom's so hard that when I ran across someone selling hers for cheap, I bought it without caring much what was inside. "Hope you have better luck with this than I did!" she wrote in her note. And then (it was summer): "Definitely don't recommend trying it in the heat. Whoa."

Kingdom is, or rather was—it's been discontinued—the women's perfume from the late designer Alexander McQueen's line. On one side, the bottle is a perfectly smooth silver egg that tapers to a point at the bottom, a shape reminiscent of a movie alien's head. The spray mechanism is tucked so neatly out of sight that the box features a small diagram showing you how it works. On the other side, the silver skin of the egg has been cut away in two facets, like a slice of fruit, to reveal the heavy, ruby-red glass within. If you turn the bottle just right, the facets come together to make a heart. Not a hearts-and-flowers sort of heart. A gothic, bleeding heart. A deliriously tempting poisonous apple of a heart. By way of a spaceship.

And the perfume? There's a reason it didn't stay on the market very long. It is brilliantly constructed along classic lines—spices, flowers, and woods—and startlingly beautiful on the right person on the right day. But its allegiance to the classics doesn't stop at the structure—the jasmine in its floral heart is ripe and heady, almost rotting, and running through the whole composition is a huge cumin note, that touch of sweaty warmth I smelled in the new Femme turned up all the way to eleven.

I held that poisonous apple up in front of the students and we talked about McQueen and design. "But what does it smell like?" asked one young woman, a little more adventurous than the others. So I told her most of the above, trailing off when I got to the part about the cumin. "It's dirty," I concluded. "Very, very dirty."

There was a pause, some smothered giggles, looks traded back and forth. "Well, now I want to smell it!" burst out the same student, laughing, and all around the table there were blushes and nodding heads and hands reaching out for the bottle. I passed it along to them, very happy to be wrong yet again.

How many smells should a woman have? What on earth, everyone wants to know—so maybe you do, too—am I going to do with all that perfume?

I admit, when I open my perfume closet (or the drawers—did I tell you about the drawers?), I sometimes wonder myself. But then I turn around and look at all the books on my shelves. I think of all the hundreds of songs stored on my laptop, and all the art I've looked at and still hope to see. I consider the countless good meals I've eaten. And I remember again what I will do with all that perfume.

I will wear it. I will talk about it. I will give it away. I will dream about some bottles and forget that others exist. I will get very excited about new additions, and I will come back to old favorites. I will think about it, and I will let it convince me to stop thinking. I will depend on it for comfort, and turn to it when I want to celebrate. I will treat it, in short, the way I do all the other pleasures in my life. All those things that exist because someone besides me thinks that life, no matter how difficult it becomes, should be about more than the bare necessities.

A woman, I think we can all agree, should smell like herself. But which self? I will smell of honey and roses and saffron, of cloves and vanilla and sandalwood, of vetiver and leather and big white flowers, of summer plums and my own warm skin. I will smell of forests and of earth and of the sea and many, many other things. Because I am no longer so sure of who I am and what I have to do, and because I don't know what's coming next.

ACKNOWLEDGMENTS

I am deeply indebted to all the people in these pages who allowed me to tell their stories so that I could tell my own. My first thanks goes to them.

This book began its life as my obssessed fangirl attempt to publish a collection of writing from my favorite perfume blogs. Thanks to all who responded to my queries for that project: I remain your devoted reader.

A gigantic thank-you wrapped up in glittery polka-dot tissue paper with a passel of hard-to-find extras to all my fellow swappers, decanters, and commenters. Your intelligence, generosity, and kindness continue to astound me. Special thanks—and an apology for the short shrift they got in this book—to all the men in my perfume world.

Many bloggers not featured in this book taught me about perfume and gave me something delightful to read on a regular basis. I look forward to adding your names to the roll. Special thanks to Maria Browning of Bittergrace Notes, for her graceful example, and to Caitlin Shortell of Legerdenez for her Alaskan surrealism and all the sweet cheerleading.

*   *   *

Robin Krug became my editor at Now Smell This when I was halfway through writing this book and I thank her for her flexibility and support while I buckled down to finish it. March Moore sent me e-mails that were unfailingly funny and gracious. Victoria Frolova found time to answer my questions, connect me to her colleagues, and best of all, to meet me for lunch more than once. Marina Geigert gave me my first yes and then went on saying yes. The world is a better place for her wit and glamour.

I owe much to Heather Ettlinger whose friendship and writing came to me at a crucial time.

Lois Weinthal, Lenore Gale, and Jerry Waisman welcomed me into their lives, their city, and their New York apartments over a span of three years. This book and many of the events in it would not have happened without their friendship and generosity. Thanks also to Matt Harad and Annie Stone, who let me know I'd always have a place to stay on the Upper East Side, and to Carla Trujillo and Leslie Larson for letting me sit by their lemon tree in Berkeley.

Sylvia Gale, Chris Strickling, Julie Sievers, and "Parker," talked me through all my ups and downs from graduate school to the present moment, and didn't laugh when I wondered out loud whether perfume might be a worthwhile subject for a book. Peggy Whilde egged me on, gossiped to me about the book business, and let me regale her with the minutiae of my writing process. I was bolstered throughout the writing process by Sunday dinners with Erin Mayes and Steve Wilson. Erin predicted this book would happen, and her advice and help have been invaluable. James McDermott provided invaluable enthusiasm in the scary final stretch and gave me a talking to about the importance of beauty and pleasure that I will not soon forget.

Carole DeSanti's incisive editing gave this book much-needed shape and taught me a great deal about writing and how to tell a story. Every first-time author should be so lucky. Thanks as well to the whole team at Viking, including Beena Kamlani, whose line-edits provided crucial nuance; Christopher Russell, who kept everything moving along smoothly; Kathryn Court, who made me feel welcome at the very beginning; and Francesca Belanger, who proved that perfumistas are everywhere.

I have gained so much from Stuart Bernstein's intelligence and kindness that I cannot adequately thank him. His unfailing insight, humor, and boundless enthusiasm are woven into the heart of this book, and I would write it all over again just to have the pleasure of his company.

Many thanks to all the Boise Aunties—Sally Briggs, Susi Cagen, Leslie Drake, Frances Ellsworth, Sydney Fidler, Randa Giles, Diane Graves, Mimi Hayes, Ramona Higer, Lois Lenzi, Carol MacGregor, Susan Meuleman, Betsy Pursley, Surel Mitchel, Esther Oppenheimer, Trudy Littman, Karyl Hayden, Kay Hardy, Pam Lemley, Mary Peterman, Sally Richards, Susan Smith, Linda Swanson, Mary Jane Hill, Jacquie Wilson, Bonnie Thorpe, Mikel Ward, Stephanie White, Layle Wood, Ann Wieck, Liz Wolf—and Driek Zirinsky, for everything I've written about here and much, much more.

My parents, Bev and George Harad, have given me unstinting help and support all my life. This project was no exception. Thank you for your stories, and for putting up with weeks of silence and a deadline that made me miss the holidays entirely. I love you both.

Two years before I started writing this book, my husband, Vicente Lozano, sat me down and told me sternly that I was a writer and that the sooner I stopped trying to be something else the happier we would be. For that, for being so much more than V., and for a world's worth of other things, I thank him and give him my love.

APPENDIX: MORE TO READ AND SMELL

Note: Blogs, artisan lines, and specialty boutiques are often run as a labor of love. The information below is subject to change. For updated information or to learn more, please visit me at www.alyssaharad.com.

Blogs and Web Sites

The number of perfume blogs has increased exponentially since I began reading. The best way to find a few you like is to start with one and then begin clicking through the links on the blogroll. Now Smell This (www.nstperfume.com) keeps a regularly updated page solely for this purpose. If you are interested primarily in natural perfumery, I recommend beginning with Scent Hive (www.scenthive.com).

Now Smell This, Bois de Jasmin (www.boisdejasmin.com), Perfume Smellin' Things (www.perfumesmellinthings.blogspot.com), and Perfume Posse (www. perfumeposse.com) are all still up and running as of this writing. To read the posts and comments I describe in this book, look in the archives between August 2006 and April 2008.

Some perfume fans prefer discussion sites such as Perfume of Life (www.perfumeoflife.org), Basenotes (www.basenotes.net), and, of course, the fragrance board at Makeupalley (wwww.makeupalley.com). There are also several sites that combine official information with discussion, including Osmoz.com and Fragantica.com.

Books

Perfumes: The A-Z Guide, by Luca Turin and Tania Sanchez
Turin and Sanchez have sniffed it all and lived to tell the tale. Pithy reviews of hundreds of perfumes ranging from mass-market to obscure. Sharp, beautifully written, and so funny that I only wince a little when they savage one of my favorites.

The Emperor of Scent, by Chandler Burr
Tells the story of the perfume-obsessed biophysicist Luca Turin's efforts to promote a new theory of smell. A great character study with many in-depth asides on perfume.

The Perfect Scent, by Chandler Burr
Follows perfumer Jean-Claude Ellena and actress Sarah Jessica Parker on their separate adventures in bringing new perfumes to market. An entertaining look at the industry and a good primer on how mass-market perfume is created.

A Natural History of the Senses, by Diane Ackerman
Ackerman blends science, bits of personal memoir, and lyrical description in this gorgeous celebration of our senses. First published in 1991, her chapter on smell is still regularly cited.

Essence and Alchemy: A Natural History of Perfume, by Mandy Aftel
    As described in this book. Worth reading for the beautiful descriptions and literary quotes about smell alone.

The Foul and the Fragrant: Odor and the French Social Imagination, by Alain Corbin
    A fascinating social history that traces the role of smells in everything from city planning to courtship.

Perfume Legends: French Feminine Fragrances, by Michael Edwards
    A de facto history of French perfume told through profiles of selected classics. Edwards's research is excellent, and his personal interviews with designers and perfumers provide many wonderful anecdotes. Hard to find, but worth pursuing.

Perfume Boutiques

The world of specialty perfume boutiques is worthy of a book unto itself—a nice glossy one with plenty of photos. Because the owners are often collectors trying to make a profit on their obsession, they sometimes turn up in unexpected places. Try sniffing around for one in your own hometown. The following have excellent Web sites and sample programs. The staff at Aedes de Venustas and the Perfume Shoppe are particularly good at making recommendations over the phone.

    Aedes de Venustas, New York; www.aedes.com
    Beautyhabit, Los Angeles; www.beautyhabit.com
    The Scent Bar (the brick-and-mortar counterpart of LuckyScent),
        Los Angeles; www.luckyscent.com
    The Perfume Shoppe, Vancouver, British Columbia;
        www.theperfumeshoppe.com

Artisan and Natural Perfumers

Many perfumers who bottle and distribute their own lines sell their wares primarily through their Web sites. Below are a few perfumista favorites whose work I have enjoyed. Several offer bespoke (custom-made) perfumes. Asterisks indicate natural perfumers.

Mandy Aftel,* Aftelier Perfumes; www.aftelier.com
Laurie Erickson, Sonoma Scent Studio;
     www.sonomascentstudio.com
Dawn Spencer Hurwitz,* DSH Perfumes;
     www.dshperfumes.com (natural and traditional perfumes)
Vero Kern, Vero Profumo; www.veroprofumo.com
Ayala Moriel,* Ayala Moriel Parfums; www.ayalamoriel.com
Anya McCoy*, Anya's Garden, anyasgarden.com
Neil Morris, Neil Morris Fragrances;
     www.neilmorrisfragrances.com
Andy Tauer, Tauer Perfumes; www.tauerperfumes.com
Roxana Villa,* Roxana Illuminated Perfumes;
     www.illuminatedperfume.com
Liz Zorn,* Liz Zorn Perfumes; www.lizzornperfumes.com
     (natural and traditional perfumes)

Places to Purchase Raw Materials

Enfleurage, New York; www.enfleurage.com
     The extraordinary collection of botanical essences in this tiny shop are all sourced—and in some cases commissioned—directly from artisan producers by owner Trygve Harris. They're not cheap, but they're the real, often rare, thing. Unlike other reputable suppliers such as White

Lotus Aromatics, Enfleurage has no minimum-order requirement. Bonus: The descriptions on the Web site and the newsletter make for highly entertaining reading.

The Perfumer's Apprentice, Felton, California;
www.perfumersapprentice.com

Sells raw materials and reasonably priced "Perfumery Education Kits" featuring a collection of common natural and synthetic raw materials employed in perfumery. A fantastic way to wake up your nose and begin understanding the notes in your favorite perfumes.